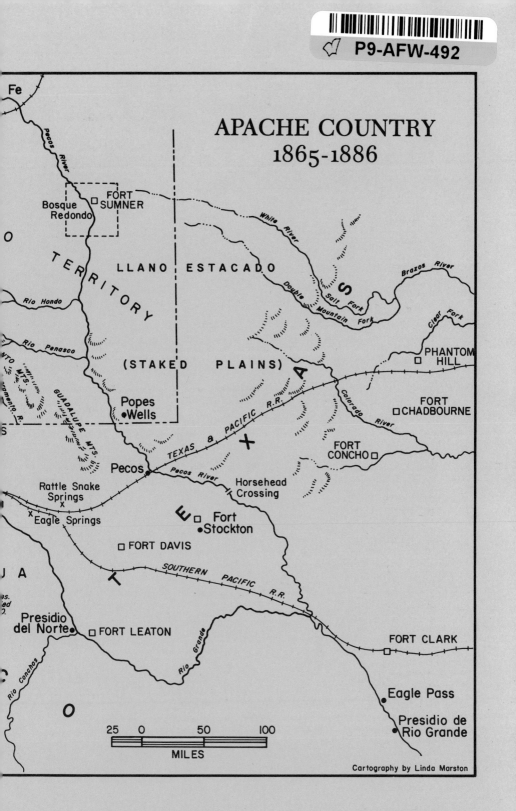

APACHE COUNTRY
1865-1886

Fe

Pecos River

FORT
SUMNER

Bosque
Redondo

O

TERRITORY

LLANO ESTACADO

White River

Brazos River

Double Mountain Fork

Salt Fork

S

Clear Fork

Rio Hondo

Rio Penasco

(STAKED PLAINS)

PHANTOM
HILL

FORT
CHADBOURNE

Colorado River

A

MTS.

GUADALUPE MTS.

Popes
•Wells

TEXAS & PACIFIC R.R.

X

FORT
CONCHO

Pecos

Pecos River

Horsehead
Crossing

Rattle Snake
Springs
X

E

Fort
•Stockton

X Eagle Springs

□ FORT DAVIS

JA

T

SOUTHERN PACIFIC R.R.

Presidio
del Norte•

□ FORT LEATON

Rio Grande

FORT CLARK

C

Rio Conchos

O

•Eagle Pass

Presidio de
•Rio Grande

25   0   50   100

MILES

Cartography by Linda Marston

WILL HENRY'S WEST

WILL HENRY'S WEST

Edited and with an Introduction
by Dale L. Walker

TEXAS WESTERN PRESS

The University of Texas at El Paso
1984

COPYRIGHT 1984

HENRY WILSON ALLEN

Published by Texas Western Press

The University of Texas at El Paso

Library of Congress Catalog Card No. 83-051163

ISBN 0-87404-077-9

"The Trap," "Sundown Smith," and "Isley's Stranger" reprinted from *The Oldest Maiden Lady in New Mexico* (New York: Macmillan & Co., 1962) by Clay Fisher.

"The Tallest Indian in Toltepec" and "Lapwai Winter" reprinted from *Sons of the Western Frontier* (Philadelphia: Chilton Books, 1966) by Will Henry.

"Will Henry and the Indians," "Once Upon a Western Story," "The Horse Puckey Hucksters," and "Sex in the Sagebrush" appeared in *The Roundup* (Western Writers of America, Inc.) but have been revised and retitled for this book.

All other material in *Will Henry's West* is published here for the first time.

*To the Old American West, its writers and its readers
and to all of us who never wanted to be dragged into
the Twentieth Century in the first place.*

CONTENTS

I am but a solitary horseman of the plains,
born a century too late and far away. When I
was fair of years I rode the endless combers of
tall bluestem, the fabled prairie tides of short-
curled buffalo grama, akin to timber wolf, shy
coyote and the race and wheel of wild mustang
band along the line of cotton-clouded skies
most distant to the eye. I ride them yet, these
lonely outlands of the past, but only now in
poignant callings-back of my imagination, a
creature at once imprisoned and set free, a cap-
tive helpless to the years, entrapped thereby as
everyman who is the son of mortal gods.

— Will Henry

Introduction

SHADOW WRITER:

In Appreciation of Will Henry

I

What we call the West was so full of humor in reality that I do not believe that the Great American Western can ever be written by an author essentially lacking in humor.

"Will," said I, "what are 'the fantods'?"

I had been reading *The Summer of the Gun* (1979), Will Henry's last published novel, where Bubba McAlister was being described as having not only the sharpest eye in the family, but what his brother Junior called the "cutest" ear — meaning the keenest — and "a nose better than a blue-tick hound."

"Yep," Junior said, "gives a body the fantods, don't he?"

"The fantods," Will wrote me, "is an expression I first consciously encountered in the works of my lesser-known Missouri colleague, Samuel Langhorne Clemens. If it were not in *Huck Finn*, then it ought to have been.

"I have the ingredients for anyone who wants to make up a mess of the fantods. Here it is:

THE FANTODS

(Will serve any number)

1/2 cup Spunk-water (sucked from a dead stump in the graveyard at midnight.)

1 Tablespoon ea.
   a. The Shakes
   b. The Willies
   c. The Creeps

Dash of Jitters (AnGHOSTura Brand)

Pinch of lo-cal Hants (also available in saltfree and sugarless)

Mix well and inhale the fumeries ten times, or until you commence to hear the hootie owl and the Werewolf singing in the swamp.

Leave off the sniffing and don't go home from the graveyard the way you came. What will get you, if you do,

will be the Fantods."

My link with Will Henry, and this book, grew out of my editorship of *The Roundup*, monthly magazine of Western Writers of America, Inc., which is published at The University of Texas at El Paso. As *Roundup* editor, I have been Will Henry's supernumerary "editor," and what began as somewhat routine contacts over his contributions to the magazine, evolved into a long and to me priceless correspondence, dozens of telephone hours, a friendly get-together at his home in Encino, California — a friendship.

Call it rapport. Will Henry is easy to have rapport with, despite his reputation as a loner, "a skulker about the edges of the main herd," a Tom Horn-like "shadow rider." He is, in fact, a preternaturally "generous to a fault" man, helpful beyond the bounds of ordinary courtesy to writer friends, to the literary investigators whose work is a source, variously, of mystery, awe, and grievous indignation to him, and to his fans. He is a shy man, famous for his self-effacing manner, who would like you to believe that in any group of more than three, he will be the one peering at the carpet behind the potted palm. He is a Jack London style "writer's writer" who has time for young writers and would-be writers and never-will-be writers, without drawing much distinction between them.

He has the quickest, most devastating sense of sardonic humor I have ever encountered, especially keen when he is honing in on Will Henry in his various guises and lamenting his self-styled role as "the Snail Darter of the Western Writing World, gone with the Dodo, the Passenger Pigeon, the Woolley Kotzebue Polled Moose, the Bifurcated Red-Scrotumed Lesser Antilles Cave Bat, and, most likely, North European Man."

Over the years, I have had great fun as straight-man in the game of Bucking Will Up.

I remind him that Bantam Books has sold 15 million Will Henry and Clay Fisher novels and he reminds me that in the latest Bantam edition of his *Pillars of the Sky* there is a tear-out coupon where you can order a leather-bound set of the works of Louis L'Amour.

Yes, I say, but the Twayne U.S. Author Series will soon publish a full-length critical study of Henry Wilson Allen, a/k/a Will Henry and Clay Fisher. This is true, he counters, but Prof. Robert L. Gale's book has been scheduled as Number 400-and-umpteen in the series, lined up *after* works on such celestial literary lights as Adelaide Crapsey, Princess Troubetzkoy, Ruth Suckow and Albion Tourgee.

Well, that may be true, I aver, but the TUSAS book will be the *second* critical study of you; don't forget the monograph Prof. Gale published in the Boise State University "Western Writers Series." Correct, Will says, although mine was #52 in the series, following hagiographies of such sainted figures as Mary Hallock Foote, Joaquin Miller (the California "Poet of the Sierras" who once rhymed Goethe with "teeth"), and a whole separate study on Scandinavian Immigrant Literature.

True enough, I admit, but please don't overlook the strengthy write-ups Jon Tuska did on you in *Twentieth Century Western Writers* and the *Encyclopedia of Frontier and Western Fiction*. I'll grant you that, Will rejoins, but the editors of that out-sized *50 Western Writers* didn't even *include* me in their crowd of half-a-hundred.

Don't forget the loyalty you have, I insist. Will Henry and Clay Fisher fans are loyal. And 15 million books is nothing paltry, now admit it. He opines this is true, but points to another Western writer for comparison:

> His readers are legion, mine are hermits and outlaws and rascals and scofflaws. His readers clamor for his works and order them direct from the publisher. Mine encounter me, discarded

copy by discarded copy, on the dank cement floor of men's rooms in blighted areas. His readers reach him in six zero numbers. Mine reach me via ruled notebook paper and stub lead pencil with plenty of spit and sweat marks joining the otherwise nonexistent punctuation. His are in the main *hidalgos*, while it is to my certain knowledge that *mis coyotes* come under the international wire each night...

These funny lamentative "bleats," as he calls them, are private, inside jokes, but Will Henry is genuinely troubled and puzzled over the obliviousness of scholars and critics toward the American Western novel. In several essays in this book — "Once Upon a Western Story," "The Real Western Novel," "Captive to the Clanging Gates," — he writes on the entire Western genre as an object of benign, or perhaps even malignant, neglect, misunderstanding and bald ignorance.

He does not understand why the only unique American form of fiction is just now being "discovered" by academic literary scholars.

Will Henry doesn't understand that.

And he is not alone.

No matter how often he withdraws, privately and mischievously, into his Snail Darter shell and exclaims he is becoming extinct in his own lifetime, Will Henry knows who he is and what he has done and, on balance, takes rightful pride in both. He may pretend to furrow his brow in comparing his sales to those of the "Big Two" of Bantam Book Westerns, Louis L'Amour (whom he admires as a veritable "force of nature") and Luke Short (Frederick D. Glidden, 1908-1975), but Will Henry is virtually alone, even among the biggest-named Western writers, in having 46 of his 53 books published in hardcover by America's most prestigious houses — Random, Lippincott, Simon & Schuster, Julian Messner, Houghton Mifflin, Macmillan, Morrow.

He also has the uncommon distinction of having written 54 books, of which 53 were published.*

---

*The single unpublished novel, variously titled *The Manchu Dragon, The World on Another Wednesday, The Big Cold, The Day the Sun Died*, and *Mongol Raiders*, was apparently too weird-before-its-time. The late John W. Campbell, then editor of *Analog*, wrote in 1964 that he was rejecting it as even "too wildly improbable for a science fiction story." It was seen by 27 publishers between 1964-71 when Will retired it once and for all. It *was* sold to Hanna Barbara Productions for filming, but was never produced. I read the manuscript of the novel and loved it — a story set in a nuclear future and having to do with survival in the Alaska-Alcan Highway-Idaho region, an invasion by Mongol soldiers with high-tech weaponry; in all, very much in the vein of "Raiders of the Lost Ark."

He has experimented outside the Western field, publishing a modern-day treasure search novel (*Tayopa!*), a science fiction novel set in the 21st century (*Genesis Five*), a realistic contemporary novel (*See How They Run*), and several excellent children's books (*Valley of the Bear, In the Land of the Mandans, Wolf-Eye, The Texas Rangers, Orphan of the North.*)

He has earned five Golden Spur awards from Western Writers of America: for his novels *From Where the Sun Now Stands* (1960), *Gates of the Mountains* (1963), and *Chiricahua* (1972), and the short stories, "Isley's Stranger" (1962) and "The Tallest Indian in Toltepec" (1965). He was the first recipient (1961) of the Levi Strauss "Saddleman" award for overall contributions to the American West, was awarded the 1972 Western Heritage Wrangler Award, and an Outstanding Service Award in 1970 from the National Cowboy Hall of Fame.

His *From Where the Sun Now Stands* has been judged by his peers as one of the 25 best Western novels of all time, and his *I, Tom Horn* was one of five runners-up.

Then there are the film adaptations of his books. And Robert L. Gale's book-length studies of his work. And the 15 million Will Henry and Clay Fisher titles sold by Bantam Books alone. And the awe in which he is held by his Western writer colleagues.

I wouldn't want him to abandon his feigned delusion of vanishment ("I have never learned how to be graceful under kind treatment," he says), but the truth is that Will Henry is pretty much living legend rather than dead dodo.

II

I wrote my first Western in entire ignorance of the fact it was a Western.

If there ever was a case of a writer who hit the ground running, it was Will Henry and *No Survivors* in 1950. I read it in the early 60s, knowing nothing about the author, least of all that this was his first novel. To me, it remains the finest fictional evocation ever written of the Custer battle at the Little Big Horn in 1876 and its hero, Colonel John Buell Clayton, C.S.A. (known among the Oglala Sioux as Cetan Mani, Walking Hawk, protegé and adopted son of Tashunka Witko, Crazy Horse), is among the most memorable creations in all Western fiction.

Even today, 33 years and 53 books later, the magic of *No Survivors* survives. Loren Estleman, a fine young Western novelist, in an essay titled "The Wister Trace: A Century of Western Classics,"* selected *No Survivors* as Will Henry's enduring "classic," saying that its author "has erected a Parthenon of Western lore and scraped the dust of decades from its icons."

And so, I knew Will Henry 20 years ago, long before I knew anything about him, and I knew Clay Fisher too: *Red Blizzard*, published a year after *No Survivors*, was one of my favorite Western novels long before I knew that its author, Clay Fisher, and Will Henry, were one and the same man. I knew them both in the way most of us get to know authors — by reading their books.

In baseball, it is said there are only five elements separating the truly gifted players from the ones with the ordinary talent required to make it to the Big Leagues: the abilities to hit, hit with power, field, throw and run.

Willie Mays comes to mind as that rare player with all the gifts.

In Western historical fiction, the elements of greatness would surely include the ability to create memorable characters, to tell a good story, to evoke time and place, to be judicious and true in the use of history, to have a sense of humor, to make the reader feel something besides the mere forward march of the narrative — emotions of some kind — and to employ the English language to its fullest potential.

"Willie" Henry comes to mind as that rare writer with all the gifts.

In my view, to take the first of these elements, Will Henry has created more memorable *horses* in his fiction than most writers have created memorable humans.

I think of Luther Sage Kelly's Appaloosa, Spotted Eagle, in *Yellowstone Kelly*, Pawnee Perez's Kentucky Boy, in *Red Blizzard*, and Sheriff Charley Skiles's Kickapoo, "sired by a mesquite-bean wild stud out of a Percheron plow mare," in *Summer of the Gun*.

Or Charlie Shonto's linebacked buckskin dun, Butterball, in "The Tallest Indian in Toltepec."

Or Button Starbuck's Gavilanito, Little Hawk, in *The Blue Mustang*, a slatey-blue *grullo*, "the sorriest-looking horse ever foaled

---

The Roundup (Western Writers of America), June, 1983.

[*xiv*]

north of Ciudad Juarez . . . barrel-bellied, straightheaded, wide between the eyes, spindly boned, ewe-necked, rattailed, knee-sprung, spur-scarred and cowhocked behind. Ribby and saddle-galled with a stiff hock and a hip knocked down on one side. Just about everything you could hope for in a Mexican raised and rode mustang."

Or, greatest of them all, John Clayton's stallion Hussein in *No Survivors*. One of the saddest moments in Western fiction occurs at the end of the novel when Clayton, before disappearing northward toward the Great Slave Lake, heads for the Wolf Mountains above the Tongue:

> In a grassy valley, two days' journey north of the line, Hussein and I parted trails for the last time. His feet were split and broken to the frog; cannon and hock so splintered he could hobble but a few steps at a time. His eyes, never right since I broke him down on the long run after Star, were gone.
>
> I fed him hand-picked meadow grasses all the while crooning and clucking to him, gently rubbing his scarred back and rusty flanks with a handful of tough wire-grass. When he had fed, I lead him to the stream. He nuzzled the cold water but would take none of it. I put my left arm around his neck, my cheek hard-pressed into the tattered mane. The ugly head swung around, eyes staring dimly, soft muzzle reaching for me.
>
> He didn't feel the barrel of the Colt sliding in under his flopped ear. The shot echoed strangely flat and dull in the silent valley.

That kind of chilling moment is almost a hallmark of Will Henry's books, handled with consummate skill, moving the reader with a gentle, melancholy magic. I think too of a scene in *Journey to Shiloh* that reminds me greatly of one of Wilfred Owen's poems from the trenches of World War I. Here, Tobin Earl Luckett, called "Little Bit," dies in Buck Burnet's arms at Shiloh:

> He tipped the candle to make sure he wasn't imagining things. He was not. Little Bit's eyes were wide open and they had a strange, glassy light in them. There was a froth of blood at his mouth corners. His lips moved but made no sound. Buck felt a fear grow in him which was the coldest thing he had ever felt. He could not bring himself to touch Little Bit after that.

He could not move to clean off his face, raise his head, or help him in any way. He was afraid of him, deathly afraid.

"Easy now, easy," was all he could think to say.

"Buck!" The whisper was so thin it barely escaped the stilling lips, yet it was high and sharp with a nameless fear. "The candle has gone out. . ."

Buck looked at the candle. Its flame burned steadily. When he looked back at Little Bit, the ticking in his friend's throat had stopped.

He put the candle down and drew the scant rag of soiled blanket over Little Bit's face. He picked the candle up again, blew it out, set it back down.

"You are right, Tobin Earl," he said. "The candle has gone out."

Similar moments are to be found in *Maheo's Children* as the reader stands witness to the Sand Creek Massacre in Colorado in 1864, and the same event is told in *The Last Warpath*, with searing visions of the rifle pits — human slaughtering pens — at Sand Creek, ringed by 400 of Colonel J.M. Chivington's pitiless Third Colorado Volunteers; and in *The Bear Paw Horses*, in the account of the death of Crazy Horse, war chief of the Oglala Bad Face band, with Touch-the-Clouds giving his epitaph: "It is good. He has looked at death, and it has come to him." And in *The Feleen Brand*, with the death in Palo Duro Canyon of Hush Feleen, "a man whose mind had failed, or had never been normal to begin with."

Even apart from the deaths of Hussein, Tobin Earl Luckett, Black Kettle's Cheyenne at Sand Creek, Crazy Horse, or Hush Feleen, there is yet another variety of sadness in Will Henry's books, a wistful yearning for times and places irretrievably lost. This yearning for "Out There" is one of the loveliest pervasive elements in his work.

In *I, Tom Horn* (another Will Henry masterpiece, as is *No Survivors*, *From Where the Sun Now Stands* and *Gates of the Mountains*), this longing for vanished times and places is the very foundation of the novel. "Lord God," Tom Horn says,

> . . .but those were times few white men then living knew, and no white man now living can ever know again. The times are gone, and the wild Apache vanished forever. I wish I had died

in those grand years when Tom Horn rode knee-and-knee with names like Mangas, Loco, Del Shay, Nana, Kaytennae, Alchise and Eskiminzin. And when he was the true *chi-kis-in*, "full brother," to the Four Families of the Chiricahua people, the children of Cochise, Juh, Victorio and Geronimo.

Ay de mí, as the Mexicans say.

Those were the hours of our lives.

And, ah! how swiftly flown.

In *From Where the Sun Now Stands*, Heyets, the same Nez Perce lad you will find in "Lapwai Winter," expresses the longing in this memorable passage:

> It was a grand time. Every sunbeam which smote the dew dazzled my eye. Every stir of pine smell coming from the hills hurried my blood. Every bird song struck my heart like a sweet arrow. And why should it not? Was I not astride my good blue pony, Tea Kettle? Was I not leading the magnificent Sun Eagle? Was I not the proudest of all Nez Perce boys from Oregon to Idaho? Ah, those times, those times.

And there are echoes of this yearning in the description of the Upper Gallatin Valley, Montana's virgin grasslands, in *The Big Pasture*, "before the bite of the timber cruiser's ax or the slash of the settler's plow," and in the description of Baylor's teeming cantonment on the Salado in *The Crossing*, and of El Paso in *The Seven Men at Mimbres Springs*.

Out There.

We all yearn for it.

III

So I write my little songs, and my little circle of readers-romantics cheer me on, and I guess that's about the way it is going to end.

There is little doubt that Will Henry is a romantic, especially if it means "appealing to the emotions by its imaginative or heroic or picturesque quality," as one dictionary defines it, and without question under the guidance of the *Oxford Companion to English Literature* which sensibly says: "Romantic: a word for which, in connexion with literature, there is no generally accepted definition."

Who, his readers might ask, but a romantic could have written of the love of John Clayton for Star of the North in *No Survivors* and have told of her death this way:

> "Cetan — my love!" That haunting half-smile was on her curving lips. I covered them with mine. And when I brought my lips away, hers still held their graceful, taunting arc. Would hold it forever.

Personally, I have always admired Will's tender Victorian touch in the love affairs of his novels: the love of Yellowstone Kelly for the young Absaroka woman, Crow Girl; or in Jesse Callahan's love for Lacey O'Mara in *Warbonnet*; or of Judah Reeves for Estrellita Cavanaugh in *The Crossing*; or of Hush Feleen for Graywing Teal, the outcast Kwahadi squaw in *The Feleen Brand*, or of Francois Rivet for Sacajawea in *Gates of the Mountains:*

> She was no more than a girl when we first saw her, sixteen summers Charbonneau said, and she was swollen big with the seventh month of her pregnancy. Yet when she came up the bank of the river to stand before Clark and myself at the construction site, and to murmur in her low voice, "I am Sacajawea, my chiefs, the younger wife of Charbonneau," I loved her. When she raised her eyes and looked at me, my heart stopped beating. For other women, it never beat again. I loved Sacajawea beyond time, beyond place, beyond reason. It was that way in the beginning, that way in the end; it was the *all*, the final thing.

Or of Heyets for Meyui, Light of Morning, in *From Where the Sun Now Stands:*

> We let the snowflakes whirl and hiss above the smoke hole. We let the prowling wind tug and whine at the tight-laced flaps. We let the feeding horses stomp and whicker in the sheltered comfort of their picket place just beyond the lodgeskins at our head. We let the fire pop and smolder low, and we lay and talked soft and caressed one another in the furry warmth of our winter bed.

Small wonder he detests the modern "adult Western" with its emphasis on steamy slam-bam sex. His is forever the romantic approach to love — tender, often tragic, always *suggested*, and light years distant from both the self-conscious "Aw, shucks, ma'am" treatment of a Zane Grey and the "straight-out pander shot" of the Western pornographer.

While dwelling on the subject of romanticism, ill-defined as it is, mention must be prominently made of Will Henry's treatment of Indians in his works. Nothing has been more important to him than this, and he states it with conviction: "The entire idea, first to last, 1950 to 1983," he says, "has been to recreate the Indian in a superior way that would, at the same time, be true to history and true to Indian belief, not violating any of the Indian trust but to work within it, honoring it as the whole reason for my books. This is not a heavy or pretentious approach. My Indian story has been first, last and finally, *a love story*. It's that simple."

Well, maybe not quite that simple, although one may read "Will Henry and the Indians" in this book for a fuller account of his attitude toward the Amerind. Although he calls it a "love story," it ought not be assumed that he is a party to the *au courant* notion of the ineffable purity and perfection of the Indian and the pervasive evil of the white-eye. "There is simply this love of the Indian in the breast of this old white man," he writes, "and I will defy any student of the subject to point out anything I have ever written that is anti-Indian. Yet I have never resorted to the drawing of the red man as some noble son of superhumanism far above the white race in all ways."

He takes, he says, the Gallic view, of *Le homme n'est ni ange ni bête:* man is neither an angel nor a beast.

Will Henry's awe of the great Indian chiefs is infectious — they *were* awesome — as seen in this passage on Dull Knife of the Cheyenne, from *Red Blizzard:*

> The figures of four mounted Indians loomed out of the blackness beyond the fire-glow. In their lead rode an old chief, very dark-skinned, ramrod-straight, long, braided hair as beautifully silver-gray as an old boar badger's roach. . . . From the high choker of five-inch bear claws which circled his neck to the extravagantly beaded moccasins of white elk which cased his feet, every lineament of the old man's body and bearing bespoke the savage patrician, the nomad commander, the hereditary chief.

[*xix*]

And on Sitting Bull's war chief, in *Yellowstone Kelly:*

> His name is as bitter for the white brother as his heart is black
> for him. Even in Hunkpapa it leaves an evil taste on the
> tongue. *Pizi!* The Sioux say it as though they were spitting it
> out. In English it has the same effect — an acid, caustic,
> scalding word . . . His name is Gall.

The encounter of Heyets, favorite nephew of Chief Joseph of the Nez
Perce, with Agent Monteith at the Christian School at Lapwai, Idaho,
in Will's "Lapwai Winter," is a reasonable standard of the author's
treatment of Indians in contact with whites.

In any such match-up, as he puts it in "Will Henry and the Indians,"
he "rides with the Red Brother."

IV

As a writer I have never needed any other beacon than to
get my facts right and keep them separate from my fiction,
then tell it the way that would seem fair all around, and let
the reviews fall whither they may.

Even when he is quietly revising what he considers warped historical
notions of people like Jesse James, Wyatt Earp, Butch Cassidy, Tom
Horn or George Armstrong Custer, Will Henry's treatment of historical
personages in his novels has always been a source of admiration among
his readers. One remembers his recreations of George Crook in *The
Brass Command*, Braxton Bragg in *Journey to Shiloh*, Chief Joseph,
Nelson "Bear Coat" Miles and O.O. "One Hand" Howard in *From
Where the Sun Now Stands*, Henry Plummer in *Reckoning at Yankee
Flat*, the James and Younger boys in *Death of a Legend*, Custer in
Yellow Hair and *No Survivors*, Chivington and Roman Nose in *Maheo's
Children*, Theodore Roosevelt in *San Juan Hill*, and Wyatt Earp, Doc
Holliday, the Clantons and McLowrys in *Who Rides With Wyatt*.

In some cases these are presented with daring but in all cases there is
historical fidelity.

"I expect the historical Western to entertain before it educates," Will
has stated. "But once the history is brought into the story, then that
history must not be violated. The writer may neither add to it, nor take
away from it. He may use it but must honor it. Building his fictional

tale around the real events never licenses the author to alter those events.

"There has been more historical revisionist nonsense practiced in the good name of The Western Story than in almost any other form of the American novel. History that is bent and shaped, reshaped actually, to fit any author's plotline, or political persuasion, or philosophical pitch, is the most tawdry of literary frauds. I detest it above all other wrongs in Western writing."

But for all these splendid characteristics of Will Henry's work — his ability to summon up lost times and places and people "Out There," his sense of tragedy, his romantic handling of man-woman relationships (especially white man and Indian woman), his ability to believably reconstruct in fiction actual historical personages, his genuine love for the horseback Indians of the plains and deserts of the West, his ability to evoke emotional responses from his readers — for all these extraordinary powers of the truly gifted writer, I admire that one quintessential ingredient, without which all else would fail: Will Henry's love for, command of, and unfailingly inventive use of, this *language*.

There is the poet in him, to be sure, as when in *Warbonnet* he writes: "The peepers in the fringe grass lowered their racking song to a drowsy hum. Somewhere down the slough, a plover raised his plaintive nightsong. Out-prairie, beyond the river, a sage hen muttered sleepily." Or when he gives us a trooper's cadence in this sentence from *No Survivors:* "Down the long valley of the Platte, guidons streaming, band playing, ammunition and field wagons rumbling, men shouting a lusty 'Hep! Hep!' as they swung along, came Carrington's command." Or when Tom Horn reminisces: "Buffalo grass! Wild horse manure! Cowboy saddle sweat! Longhorn dust! Tepee smoke! Grizzly sign! Gunpowder and rifle grease! Sagebrush in perfumery! Lord God but I could imagine it all brought a thousand and more prairie miles just for me to whiff and feel from far out there. Out there where the feathered redskins rode."

In simile, metaphor, a mixture of the two, in descriptive paragraphs, evocative sentences, is seen the genuine writer-craftsman at work; that the writing comes easy or difficult is not revealed but that it appears to have come easy is a tribute to a writer who *works,* and continues to work, at his craft.

How long did he linger over this line describing a morning in high Montana in *Reckoning at Yankee Flat?* "It was clear as rinsed crystal, still as the poised forefoot of a stalking coyote, fragrant as the breath of pine-filtered sunlight." Or this from *Warbonnet:* "The lumpy three-quarter moon, loppy and tired as a canteloupe that has lain too long on the vine, took a polite yawn and went sliding into the hills across the Black Fork."

His language can convey utter revulsion, and carry with it sight, sound, and stench. Here, in *Yellowstone Kelly,* Kelly works on the gangrenous leg of Crow Girl:

> It was a raging, festering, gray-green, bulbous mass of sloughing proud flesh, protruding bone snags of sick white fracture splinters and yellow, crustingly granulated serous scab . . . He carved away the curling layers of protuberent dead tissue in thick, ugly gray slices . . . The lancet sped on. Midway in the seventh cut, it rode searingly into living tissue. . .

But more often than not, he makes you grin:

> In late December in old Arizona it can freeze a man's nose-drips twixt nostril and mustache. Cold? You can break off your horse's breath and melt it in your mess-kit can for coffee water. . . . In Verde, I heard of a man up in Holbrook that froze his stream solid in a rainbow arch from his front-fly to the hole in the crapper seat. He couldn't bust himself loose, either, for fear of snapping off his pecker. So he set fire to the cob box on the wall next to the seat, figuring to free up his stream from the heat. But somebody had soaked the dry cobs in bear grease to soften the swipe of them against the winter chafe. The smoke from the oily cobs clotted up the outhouse air so thick and fast the poor feller strangled hisself and wasn't found till the spring melt thawed his body and let it fall out the door. (*I, Tom Horn*)

He writes so well, it gives a body the fantods.

V

Writers and academics and people who write about writers are all daft.

It is well known, Will Henry maintains, that fiction writers have no worthwhile real lives. If they had, he says, they wouldn't take up bookwriting.

Born Henry Wilson Allen and "somewhat" reared in Kansas City, Missouri, Will attended Southwest High School in that metropolis of the Way West. When Southwest published its Class of 1930 reunion booklet in 1980, the man who says he is still remembered there for failing freshman algebra four years in a row, was a contributor. Will wrote that his career as author came about as it would with anybody "having the basic gifts of indolence, cowardice, crass greed, sociopathic personality, the scruples of a mongoose, and a certain stray-dog survivability."

In a sketch provided the editor of *Twentieth Century Western Writers*, he listed some of the jobs he "survived" along the way to steady work in California; hardrock gold miner (mucker, hand-driller, powder man, mine blacksmith), house mover, sugar mill operator, tool and die shop swamper, veterinary hospital attendant, smalltown (Santa Monica, California, *Sunset Reporter*) newspaper columnist, dog magazine writer, General Motors (Van Nuys, California) assembly line worker. Then, in Hollywood, stable-hand (hot walker, stick-and-ball exercise rider, polo ponies) and 12 years as contract writer for the Metro-Goldwyn-Mayer short subjects department, with 50 screen credits; also sometime scripter for television ("Tales of Wells Fargo," "Zane Grey Theater").

Will once wrote of his early days in Hollywood, before and after landing the writing job at MGM:

> I lived in an operating $2 whorehouse in old Hollywood for some time after my 1934 return and permanent settlement in California. It was the absolute blind gut of the Great Depression and work was non-existent. Moreover, rents were high. I had to pay $3.50 a week for my suite in the hookshop. But I shouldn't complain. Everything was high. Wine was 15¢ a pint; port or muscatel, 20¢. But there were perks, mind you. My room had the big window on the street and I had my own bath! Certain conditions, obtained nonetheless. When the girls got busy in the back of the house, my lease called for me to "take a hike" so as not to be in restraint of trade.
>
> Since the "landlady" of this off-Sunset Boulevard seraglio weighed 365 pounds, had the disposition of a breast-caked she-grizzly and the voice of a herniated Irish banshee, when she said hike, you hiked.

In 1937, I was finally working for MGM making spectacular money. $75 a week. Every week. It was time to move up to off-Hollywood Boulevard, which I arrogantly managed with a swank $40 per month bachelor apartment on Gramercy Place, safely within the required "north of the Boulevard" neighborhood. There I met my fate. Her name was Amy Geneva Watson, a slim elf of a studio (Busby Berkley) dancer calling herself Dorothy Hope. We still see her in the old big Hollywood Musicals on the late-late shows on TV and I want to tell you, son, it makes the old eye glisten, and I know that she will always dance there for me. We were married Thanksgiving Day, that year, and moved into the San Fernando Valley where we lived happily ever after. I might add in eternal gratitude that no life can be called wasted or gypsied away that has brought an Amy Geneva Watson to a not-near-good-enough man's forever love and trust. And here come the glistens again.

In 1950, having been "let out" by MGM, ostensibly for writing a novel on company time, Will was working at the G-M Chevrolet plant in Van Nuys, packing spare parts up to the assembly line, when *No Survivors* was published. *Red Blizzard*, which appeared under the Clay Fisher byline, came a year later, as well as an award-winning children's book, *Wolf-Eye*, by Will Henry. (*Wolf-Eye*, a very special book to its author, was 20 years in hardcover print with Julian Messner Company, 1951-1971, a remarkable record for any book.)

"The two pennames blunder is the worst mistake any writer can make as a commercial novelist," Will told me in a 1981 interview. "It came about in my case because at the time, before the success of *No Survivors*, I had gone back to MGM on a one-year contract and among the terms was one that anything I wrote while frequenting the studio lots, front or rear, belonged to them. So I was forced to invent a penname for *No Survivors*. Then, still on MGM golden time, along came *Red Blizzard*. It was too soon on the heels of *No Survivors*, which was still at Random House. It had to have another name and another publisher, so Clay Fisher was born and *Red Blizzard* went to Simon & Schuster.

"Had I all 50 Will Henry and Clay Fisher books under one name — Will Henry — today, I would be incalculably better off professionally, commercially, historically, and in my worried mind. But a man does what he has to do. It is the Code of the West. I took the money and ran."

The Will Henry/Clay Fisher matter has even been the subject of some scholarly pursuit in which literary detectives have drawn distinctions between the novels under each name and have deduced that the Clay Fisher books are "more formulary" than the Will Henrys.

Since Will Henry has never written a "formulary" novel in his career, under any name, the deduction is specious. He does say the Will Henry titles "seem to have more substance and seriousness," but concludes there is ultimately "no definable difference" between the Henrys and Fishers.

Robert L. Gale, in his excellent study, *Will Henry/Clay Fisher* states: "Ever since 1950, Allen has been writing steadily. On a typical day, in spite of real and hypochrondriacal ills, he expertly touch-types at his battered Olympia from 7 a.m. until 6 p.m. at his home in Encino. . . . Although he deprecates himself as a man of 'nonexistent' energy, his productivity is astounding. And he has met with uncommon popular success. Sales figures are almost impossible to come by, but it is likely that Bantam Books' estimate of 15 million copies sold (9 million by Will Henry, 6 million by Clay Fisher) is quite accurate. Innumerable translations of his novels have sold phenomenally in Italy, France, and Germany — to name the countries in which Allen enjoys his greatest popularity abroad, along with Great Britain, Spain, Portugal, Sweden, Yugoslavia, Norway, Brazil. . ."

Fifteen of Will Henry's novels have been sold to the movies and eight films have actually been produced, about the industry average for initial sales to eventual production and theater release. Of the quality of the films based on his works, Will says, "I think the score is about 50-50, half bad, half worse." Actually, such Will Henry/Clay Fisher films as "Mackenna's Gold," "The Tall Men," "Yellowstone Kelly," "Pillars of the Sky," and "Journey to Shiloh," are enduring, if not classic, movies of their Western kind, and give no sign of diminishing their late or early show TV re-runs.

The film versions of his books, Will sums up, provided him "important development money," and, he continues: "What the studios bought of my work has financed the writing of my novels for 30 years. I find the return to have been consistently 60/40, books to movie sales."

VI

Unfortunately, the better the scholar-critics are, the harder they tend to throw the critical ball. And we writers do at times grow weary of the "high hard one, tight and inside."

As the essays in this book illustrate, Will Henry has some weighty, introspective attitudes about what he and other serious Western writers are doing, and what he and his colleagues are perceived as doing by academic scholars who, sniffing the trail of such pioneers in the study of Western fiction as C.L. Sonnichsen, have "discovered" the field anew. He is, one could say, emphatically ambivalent toward the attention being paid him by the scholar-critic but is determined to understand what "Serious Criticism" really is, so that, as he once wrote tongue-in-cheek, "I can direct a little of the pure stuff toward my own works," and find out why some of the practitioners of it seem determined to "obstruct justice by throwing themselves between whatever I write and any chance of it being accorded serious attention."

"I am willing to learn," he says. "It is always better to be on the cobblestones than in the tumbrel."

These essays also show a Will Henry annoyed by the notion that to be "significant," the Western writer must be a humanist (subscribe to what he calls "the sterile doctrine of the wonderfulness of humankind"), and be willing to "graft the political and social miasmas of our own moribund times upon the vital body of our frontier past."

Here also is a writer deeply offended at the maiming of the Western novel by such hackery as the so-called "adult Western" which has had an anything-for-a-buck vogue among paperback publishers in the past half-decade or so.

Ambivalence about *being* a "Western writer," or labeled as one, is a persistent thread in these essays, too. He wrote me recently, "Everybody suddenly wants to be the Boris Pasternak of the Purple Sage. Who is going to write the Westerns when all the Western writers are writing 'real' novels?" But, conversely, he asks: "Can you imagine the day when any Western writer will be honestly and honorably afforded the same respect and homage and acceptance as a writer in any other known discipline? I simply can't. All the Western writer can do — the serious one — is fight the good fight to the best of his gift, never giving up, never admitting publicly what I have just admitted here, going on to the end defending the myth and its magic from the spoilers. That's all any of us can do who love the West and want to preserve its past for our children and their children."

The six pieces of short fiction included in this book were selected as illustrative of the elbow-room Will Henry has made for himself within a relatively narrow field — the Western. "Isley's Stranger" and "The Tallest Indian in Toltepec" earned the Golden Spur Award from Western Writers of America as the best short Western stories of their year of publication. The former of these, together with "The Trap," depict the eldritch qualities often to be found in Will Henry fiction. "The Trap" can be seen as reminiscent of Ambrose Bierce's celebrated "An Occurrence at Owl Creek Bridge," and there is surely no more mysterious character in all Western fiction than Eben in "Isley's Stranger," nor any more fetching young hero than Chamaco Díaz in "The Tallest Indian in Toltepec."

"Sundown Smith" might be viewed as a more conventional Western hero story, but it can scarcely be called "formulary," and "Not Wanted Dead or Alive," never previously published, is Will Henry at his Bret-Hartish best, presenting a wonderfully outrageous glimpse of Jesse James quite in contrast to the chilling portrayal of "Dingus" in *Death of a Legend*.

"Lapwai Winter" is a poignant Indian story, directly related to Will's formidable classic, *From Where the Sun Now Stands*, and concerning the narrator of that novel, Heyets, a Nez Perce boy and nephew of the great Chief Joseph.

The stories range in place from Lapwai, Idaho, to the Chihuahuan border of the Rio Grande, from Clay County, Missouri, to the California Sierras — all the fabled Western outlands Will has roamed in the past half-century and which have been in the heart of all his books.

For this is the West that was — the spiritual sod shanty homestead of the American yearning for "out there." If its nobler times have vanished and its trails dimmed, it is not forgotten, nor will it ever be.

It is Will Henry's West.

— Dale L. Walker

El Paso, Texas
September, 1983

OUT THERE

M ost frequent of the observations I encounter as a writer of historical fiction is that I seem to have an emotional fixation with the mythic "out there," a yearning term for the Old West — an Old West that never really existed — an Old West that extended forever in the imagination — a concept not only of a wondrous land and time, but of a whole separate breed of hero people born larger than ordinary life, and needing to be that size "out there."

Well, let's square up to it.

I think it completely fair to say that the commonest thread in my historical storytelling, as in all my work, is the emotional longing for "out there."

The question, however, is not *is* this the case, so much as it is *why* is this the case.

Firstly, I was born with a real need to be someone other than who I was, or who I perceived myself to be. I was a very unsuccessful kid. I could not run fast, jump high, throw a ball straight, or catch one thrown straight by anyone else. I wore glasses. Was belligerent but couldn't fight a lick. Was totally attracted to little girls but could not find a single one of same who would walk home with me, smile back, say hello to me before I did so to her, or even after I had done so. When I was seven, a serious surgical procedure took me out of the company of my little peers for a good long spell. In the process of the protracted recovery, I discovered books. I got over the surgery but in the books had found that inner space where I would dwell all the rest of my life. And the essence of that inner world was that it harbored a hundred "out theres," a hundred routes out of and away from the real world, trails and pathways and byways by which the rejected and literally wounded child could protect himself with a surrounding of ideas and imaginations not even known about among his kid-worldly companions. While they were reading their third grade texts, I was consuming the *Britannica*, Omar Khayyám, Jack London, Kipling, Conan Doyle, H. Rider Haggard, H.G. Wells, the American Revolution, the Civil War, the Indian raids of the eastern forests, and then the Missouri River Valley settlements and, of course, inevitably, upon one blessed day in this direction, I had to discover the Trans-Mississippi "great Western" frontier opening outward toward the sun from the spout of its funnel which was, behold! our very own Westport Landing, since become Kansas City, Missouri, my hometown in the heart of storied Jackson County!

Hallelujah! Glory, glory!

Will Henry had discovered the Old West.

Right on his own front stoop.

And for *real!*

Although it was to be thirty years before I returned to the American West through my history-backgrounded novels of that wondrous time and place, there is no question but what the alone, but never again lonely spirit, set free by my discovery of the wonders of adventure and imagination in books, was what led me back to the far frontier of the Old West all those long years later.

What molds us in pliable youth imprisons us yet in adulthood.

I had a sense, long before I dreamed to write one line of any book about it, that the American West wasn't being painted as excitingly and as vividly as the simple truth of its very history would demand of honest picturing. My travels about the West, my working in its various heart-achingly beautiful places, all kept the spirit of dissatisfaction alive within me. When I then, at last, could abide it no more, and prepared to write *No Survivors* in justifiable protest, it was, I thought, simply mandatory to advance my fictional arguments from an accurate, clean, honestly heroic base of straight history.

I did so in *No Survivors*, my first book; I did so in *I, Tom Horn*, my last book based on real places and real people and real events.

To me, the use of real history as a requirement of honesty in my historical novels of the Old West, springs simply from a passion for equity drilled into me by a stern father. Dad hated liars and cheaters and traitors before most any other form of human wastrel. So does his son Will. Maybe that is why Will so loves the West.

"Out there" a man's word is his earnest money.

It always was.

It still is.

ONCE UPON A
WESTERN STORY

When one who has worked through thirty years and fifty books to protect and preserve it, then comes to that place wherein time bids him say godspeed to the Western Story, what is there for him to set down that will speak truly to the heart of the matter — the secret heart of it — as he has come to know and treasure it in his own life-time? What canvas can be painted in a properly few brushstrokes that will reveal, by half, his love affair — man, boy, and now old man — with the American West? What poetry can describe with adequate *amourette* the romantic dalliance ensuing with the American Western, that so uniquely salt-cured native literature of our vanished frontier past?

And what, really, is this unwanted child of our American storytelling heritage? What is there about the Western that, long-orphaned and roundly disdained by the world of letters, has survived to become our only original literature?

As well, who are we, the vintners of its thousand myths and legends? We who have toiled all lovingly amid its arid cacti vines to bottle the rawhide wines of the Old West against the day when minstrels may no longer stroll, and the voice of the storyteller fall silent upon the land? What wondrous alchemy of the sagebrush Magi did Ned Buntline bring to his *reductio ad impossibile* of the lore of the American frontier that it has since spread 'round the world to universal popularity? Indeed, that it has since become the glass of critical fashion, the very mold of academic form. Why are respected full professors of English Literature and staid Doctors of American History suddenly mad for what the ruder populace has been acclaiming, *vox clamantis in deserto*, since Edward Z.C. Judson personally created the Wild West — created it whole, out of the entire cloth of his posturing heroes, vacuous heroines, verdigreed villains and, beyond all, his mythic land and time of their being which itself never existed?

Writers of the Western and the West have "come a far piece" from Judson's dreadful/marvelous dime novels.

The literature of the West has become a serious literature.

College courses are taught upon it and, as recruits from these classes go forth upon the land, more courses will be taught and more serious scholarship imposed upon the storytellers' original wares. Just here, let the keepers of the Western's watchfires beware. This riskful *abrazo* returns the matter to its positing:

What is the Western and why has it survived these hundred-plus years as the people's choice, and now the brand-new pet of the tenured campus guardians of the Literary Word?

The West, friends. That is what the Western is all about.

In the beginning, the Western spelled hope. It held out the West to unnumbered emigrants as the American Hope for a new day and a better life. It is no different today. Through the medium of the American Western, in all its art forms, hope is held forth to any and all the earth around who *must* believe there is a better day to come and that, if only man be true to himself, there is nothing he cannot dream to conquer.

It is a message, pilgrims. To all men everywhere. Don't give up. Fight on. Live clean. Be True. Be square. Be fair. You will always win in the end. You must. It is the Code of the Old West.

But we all know there never was an Old West.

Never could have been, really.

Still, something remains. Something poignant with yesteryears. Redolent of mountain red cedar and yellow aspen. Splashing with snow-cold water. Grand of raw blue sky. Cotton cloud. Woodsmoke adrift in the valley. Afar the metaled ringing of an ax. The bell of a cow. The alerting whicker of a pony, nostrils to the wind. The lowing mutter of the herdbull up on the bench beyond the fork. A woman's voice calling through the evening hush. A child's laughter, far away as heaven, near as the heartbeat it celebrates. Sunset cry of loon on mountain meadow marsh. Soughing of the pines, red with the downing sun. Man at musical chant driving cattle from the higher areas. *Whoo dogie, whoo dogie,* easy across the slide, *coo-ee, coo-ee,* we're home. The night is coming in and so are we. Safe off the mountain, *coo-ee, dogie, coo-ee.*

No Old West you say?

Listen to the cowbell. Smell the cedar incense on the wind. Hear the axblade sing. Hark to the rider talking down his cattle.

The Old West lives in untold legions of human hearts and minds. Let it stay there.

Don't ever change it. Cherish its myth, remember its legend, write down its folklore. Guard it, defend it, keep it safe, that you may pass it on in your own time as something you want your child to have and to know as you have had and known it, unspoiled and as a true believer.

Keep the faith, friends; we all know the real truth.

There was an Old West.

There *had* to be.

THE REAL
WESTERN NOVEL

One is perversely interested to learn from the trades that historical Western fiction is now being looked upon favorably by the publishing business, this in the same time that the traditional, or formulary Western novel, has become less attractive. We trust these prophets of our profession know whereof they herald and depose. But trust in one hand and work hard with the other and see from which member derives the spendable income. Either the trades are not playing with fifty-two cards, or they have been misquoted. Let us borrow the old John Wayne phrase for the idea that the historical Western is more wanted than the formulary: "That'll be the day." And, thank you, Duke.

Anyone who would believe such hype has never been a Western writer.

What is going on here is a nifty bit of disinformation. We are given a piece of advance knowledge as God's truth, only to discover that it is the opposite of that truth, or of any truth, yet that it rings like bell silver, all the same. Ergo, we act on it in gray-eyed faith and heavy-up on the history in our works-in-progress, eschewing the old reliable formulary mode as literary belled leper. And, lo, we learn nothing whatever has changed. We cannot give away our historical Western novels, while the market for the gunsmokey old-fashioned "Western" gallops on without a solitary break in stride, keeping perfect time to the merry jingle of the cash register.

Which is precisely what the canny writers of the "regular Western" have set us dupes up for, who know that one day our prairie schooners will come in and that they will be loaded to the frontier gunwhales with both history and fat bales of royalty beaver.

Get one thing straight, comrade authors of the Western historical novel: you are never going to expire wealthy.

The publishers of Western fiction have "historically" made the traditional formulary novel their clear and constant choice.

The patent reason for this is that the reader of Western novels has made the identical choice before them, and never wavered from it.

The money goes where the mice are fat.

Even so, it is not just a simple matter of profitability. There is some sagebrush and waterhole emotion involved. The formulary loyalist not only loves his traditional "Westerns," he despises what he calls the "high falutin'" Western novels of the so-called "serious writers." By which he means, of course, the historical novelists.

The plain publishing business truth is that the stipulated prescription for either struggling survival or sudden demise in the Western market is to depart the traditional form and treat of the West with authentic historicity and some determined effort at literary quality.

This will do you in every time.

But consider what lies the other way, indeed, what might have been.

Louis L'Amour is the giant of our times in the genre. A man who is, or ought to be, a hero to all the rest of us. Anything said here of him is intended to his credit. He is cited here only as the ultimate specimen of the true Western writer.

We started in the same decade, the writer with *No Survivors*, in 1950, Louie, with the justly celebrated *Hondo*, in 1953. We are within four of five years of one another, agewise. We both started late, coming to hardcovers and some small respect by the long way around. Substantially then, we came to taw together. But, *Jesus Maria*, once the starter's gun went off!

Well, it's thirty or forty years later, now, and Louie is rich and this writer is not. There's a reason Louis Dearborn L'Amour broke the bank. It's called smart. He stayed with the old original Western novel, the real thing, while this writer sailed off into the wild blue prairie in search of peer approval and literary acknowledgement — written proof, that is, that the Western historical novel was the only way to go.

It could be, one supposes.

If broke is where one wanted to go.

Whatever the given reasons of the historical Western novelist for his choice of that category against the traditional novel, he lies to you unless he confesses that the real motive was ego-blinded ambition. Not just ego-blindness, alone. Nor ambition by itself. But the fatal combination of the two, producing, as with potentiating drugs, a reaction in megaform to the effects of either factor considered separately.

There is no more hazardous combinant in the pharmacopoeia of popular literature than this Western-writing vanity that heroic inclusions of "true history," blended lumpily with kitchen-tested dollops of shake-and-bake fiction, will be notably reviewed and critically acclaimed, not as a Western but as a "real novel," and its author henceforward and forever called and considered, by K-Mart lip-reader and campus brahmin oracle alike, "a serious writer."

This business of the serious vs. the traditional, sometimes called "real" or "regular" Western novel, is nowhere more hotly contested than among the Western writers themselves. Their parent organization, the WWA (Western Writers of America), has battled the idea of a separate Golden Spur Award for Best Historical Novel since Year One. The Historical Spur has been in and out of fashion with the membership like a literary striptease — now you see it, now you don't. But one element in its checkered career has been faithfully constant. It has never successfully challenged the Best Western Novel in popularity with the people who count, the writers who write, the members who turn out the books which become the entries in any year's Spur competition, from Santa Rosa One, to Amarillo 1983. Year after year after year, the entries in Best Western Novel have outranked those for Best Historical Novel by wipeout numbers. The awarding of the same-value Spur for a handful of entries, as for a gunnysack full, never has made any sense. It has, of course, been a great break for those of us who had to defeat four other books, say, on our way to the Best Historical Spur, as against the embattled victor in Best Western division who must count coup on several times that number in order to claim his Golden Spur. Which, as any sporting historical novelist will embarrassedly agree, must make that the *really* real Spur.

Conceding this honor to the traditional Western novel is not to be translated to mean that this old writer of historical Western novels has gone over to the enemy.

To the contrary, one still dreams of that vista opening before him wherein he shall find acceptance and respect as a serious writer — a serious writer even if incurably romantic — who so loved the Old American West he devoted a writing lifetime to the proper retelling of both its true history and its grand, undying myth.

On-and-off campus, in-and-out of the publisher's office, upon-and-under the writers' round tables, the identity crisis in American Western Literature continues; the tri-partite debate rails on:

What is serious Western fiction? Must it be historical? If so, why?

What is traditional or formulary Western fiction? Why is it perceived to be non-serious? Why held to be somehow inferior to historical fiction?

What, indeed, is Western fiction, per se? How is it to be defined apart from other fiction? Mystery, romance, action/adventure, science?

All one can do with this inquiry is to answer its demands in his own individual way, speak to how he sees the problem, what he imagines or insists are the proper solutions to its three-forked dilemma.

What serious Western fiction is:

Serious Western fiction is that work in which the author, by his or her very approach, brings to that work in clearly unusual force or pattern the standard literary qualities of discipline, beauty, language, subject, scholarship, knowledge of genre, human spirit, dignity, the elfin trace of poetry, the passion for right and wrong, the saving grace of frontier humor and, above all, the God-given talent to tell a Western Story in such high art terms, and still have it hold true, and grippingly, to the hard and dangerous times of those unsung meek who inherited the wild earth of the American West.

It is difficult to imagine what being historical, or not being historical, has to do with excellence, or seriousness, in Western fiction.

The present categories of WWA Spur Awards which list "Best Western Novel" and "Best Western Historical Novel" as two different items of literary endeavor, are foolish. The "Best Western Novel" category ought to include every adult form and fashion of Western novel, beginning with inclusion of the Western historical novel as first priority.

Juvenile or young adult Western fiction however, is patently a rightful candidate for its own Spur. In this category we are, in a very real sense, "writing kid books." It means nothing that the book is a Western, or an Eastern. We are not, in rewarding it, giving out separate Spurs for equal novels. The one Spur is for adult books, the other for kid books. The kid book writers will be heard from on this comment. But just remember, brothers and sisters, that when you erupt you will be bloodying a working comrade, the very father of such immortal children as *Valley of the Bear, In the Land of the Mandans, Wolf-Eye, Orphans of the North* and *The Texas Rangers*.

What traditional or formulary Western writing is:

Traditional or formulary Western writing is that work of original American Literary Art called "The Western." It takes place in the

1800s, from Lewis & Clark, to Teddy Roosevelt & the Rough Riders, anywhere in the American West between Durango and Moose Jaw, and between the Barbary Coast and Westport Landing. Marc Jaffe, Bantam's famed "finder" of Louis Dearborn L'Amour, used to define it a lot tighter than that. The "Continental Shrink" meant nothing to him. Marc wanted his Westerns taking place in a chronology of 1860, and the Civil War, to a maximum of the 1880s, and the last of the Indian/Cavalry/Buffalo Wars. He wasn't 100% for Indian Westerns. Wanted no part of "Mexican Westerns." Was hardly more partial to Canadian or Alaskan themes. He knew where the Old West was, and where the best Old Westerns were being written. He was a traditional man in a genre dominated forever by formulary and traditional authors. He did his blessed best to advise Will Henry on where the highgrade ore was in the Old West. He failed. He was talking to a stone wall, otherwise known as a "serious writer."

Still, circumstances determine.

Irwyn Applebaum, following Marc Jaffe as western editor at Bantam, marched to the same traditional bookbeat as had El Jefe before him. But only to the beat. Irwyn carried the melody upon his own private set of eaglebone flutes. He *was* different. An innocent born-again frontier romantic with the aficionado's unsullied passion for the Old West of song and fable, he assumed command with a learner's modesty but a most contagious excitation of the spirit. The wise men of the trade made the sign of the circling finger at the temple, but Irwyn came not from a family of slow children. Betting the farm, he quietly teamed with the legendary L'Amour, then with his greatest fame waiting just ahead. What the partners accomplished in publishing sequence is Western writing history. What they did in fictive paraphrase was to ride the Bantam entry so far into the lead in the Chaparral Sweepstakes that the second place horse hasn't come in yet, and the third is still standing in the starting gate trying to spit its bit and whinnying, "Where did everybody go?"

In the end, Irwyn (now Publishing Manager of Bantam Books) has remained as tradition oriented as his storied mentor. But in the process he and The Sacketts pushed back the pasture fences of category prejudice to make "justice room" for what literary historian Jon Tuska has academically defined as the "formulary Western Novel." Surely not the worst thing to happen to the American Western in these latter days of its embattled years.

The traditional Western novel may, or may not employ history in its mix of literary qualities. It never need do so and, by any judgement, the very best of the traditional novels — which means the best of the Western novels, period — do not depend upon the so-called "true history" factor. Think about it. *Shane. The Virginian. Hondo. Hanging Tree. Paso Por Aqui. The Searchers. True Grit. The Ox-Bow Incident. Bugles in the Afternoon. Bronco Apache. The Big Sky. Sea of Grass. Riders of the Purple Sage. Tall in the Saddle. Ride the Man Down. Rimrock.* Make your own list. You see the drift. In the traditional Western, action speaks the important words. Yet message bearers, character studies, mood pieces and outright poetry of theme and resolution are not barred by any higher law from appearing as traditional Western novels.

In the formulary novel one knows what is going to happen by what has happened before.

Non-formularies, including historical Western treatises, may artfully deal in *maybe* and *what if* and *you think they went thataway but they went thisaway.* In the honest, the regular, the real Western novel, you always get just what you pay for. No tricks. No substitutes. No baits and switches. The traditional Western novel is THE Western novel.

You do not need a program to tell it from the historical Western, or any of the other uppity dodges used to cloud the issues of honest morality and dire retribution.

You say son of a bitch in a historical or other "serious" Western novel, you don't need to do anything more about it.

You say son of a bitch in a REAL Western novel, you better be ready to smile.

What Western fiction is in and of itself:

Original American artforms are precious scant and scattered out. There's jazz and the blues, baseball and the hotdog, and then there's the Western. That's about it. What we have in the American Western, and in its hearty descendant spawn of Western writers and Western writing, is an original artform. If we take away the prehistoric Indian pictographs, and question jazz and the blues, and indeed bluegrass and gospel, on the grounds that music is universal in all its forms, the Western, and Western writing, may be the *only* genuine American artform.

This writer believes that it is.

What is therefore important about Western fiction is that it has been, and presently remains, the very backbone of our homeland's only provable native literature, *née* artform.

There was only one Old West, *our* Old West. It can be meted and
bounded as neatly and patently as any estate of the people. The
American West was real estate. It was there. It didn't happen. It existed. It still exists, as definable today, as yesterday, and the day
before. It has a mythology and a legendstore and a folklore to be happily certain. But in the beginning the Old West was there in fact. The
protecting and defending of the real property has created the Western,
and Western writing. And it was not the historians who did this, or
who assured the ongoing life and vitality to the priceless mythology; it
was the fiction writers, the legend spinners, the talltale vendors, the
keepers of the frontier and its folklore. So that is what Western fiction
is, in and of itself:

The guardian of everyman's dream to "go West," and to be free.

The trichotomy persists.

But only in the advocate minds of the keepers of the faith themselves.
While the Western writers will continue to tell one another what is and
what is not serious, traditional, or original artform Western writing,
the hundred million *aficionados verdaderos,* from the Alamo to the
hanging of Tom Horn, the vast true readership of the genre, will continue to call them all "Westerns" and will look "withinward" only to
seek to know that a new L'Amour is out, or a new edition of a Haycox
or a Luke Short classic is on the stands.

You cannot fool the *aficionado verdadero.* No historical novels, no
artform classics for him. He wants a real Western.

One is somehow made to feel that, in the end, he shall always be able
to find one. The Western is not going to wither. Not going to go away.
It will know some poor winters, as it always has, but will thrive
beneath the snows, spring up again with the new grass, be fat and sassy
by the autumn, full ready for another winter and a good one this time,
porsupuesto.

The while, it is time to put a final point to this paper.

We know we have not here decided anything. We have only tried to
put some form to the native art of Western writing.

Definitions and cataloguing and pigeon-holing of something as simple and straightforward as the Western story would seem frivolous
were it not for the fact that they are important to the effort to keep the
Western story true to its origins and its basic nature as indigenous
folklore; a pure form of any art is to be treasured for itself, *and* for its
influence on the growth and development of what descends from it.
Considering our native Western story in that light, its identification

and descriptions become something worth striving for. The Western is a hardy breed. It flowers in the desert, upon the mountain peak, beside the mighty rivers. But it needs care. Cultivation. Shelter and weeding-out. It needs to be loved.

That is the purpose of this paper.

To cherish the Western Story. To show the reader what it is. Where it grows best, and why. What makes it flourish above all other popular literatures, and why it will remain America's favorite love affair in the wonderful world of wild adventure "across the Wide Missouri!"

The dusty cowtown history books are filled with faded tintypes of lawless men laid out with all their ghastly gunshot craterings and rupturings. They are not a pretty sight. One wonders always what possible prize of mere monies could have been imagined to exist in robbing a bank, stagecoach or train, that would induce the wild ones to take the chance? To place their very souls in hell for the opportunity to make a few dubious dollars without menial toil. The minds of old Western outlaws have always fascinated the author. He has written more than one or three stories about how they thought, why they would ride again and again against certain death, knowing that sooner or later they, too, must fall. "The Trap" is a story of one such man. Its telling was designed to place in the reader's memory an unforgettable picture of this man cornered in his last hour by a hanging posse of outraged citizens. What did he think of in his final seconds? How desperate or afraid was he? What real chances remained to him — in his own mind — of gaining freedom, riding away one more time into God's wondrous sunshine, away and across the fragrant pastures of the outer prairie, leaving the angry guns and the strangling rope forever behind him. He could do it; he could *—!*

— W.H.

THE TRAP

C anady felt the horse beginning to go rough beneath him. He had been expecting it. On this rocky going no mount could make it for long when he was already ridden out in coming to it. "Easy, easy," he said to the laboring animal. "It's only a posse." The horse seemed to understand the tone of the words, for it slowed and went better and steadier for a ways. "We'll rest on the rise ahead," Canady said. "I can see back a few miles and you can catch some wind and we'll go on. We'll make it."

He knew they wouldn't. He knew it before they came to the rise and he got down and walked out on the overhanging spur of gray-black basalt that gave view down the canyon behind them for ten miles. It wasn't a canyon, really, but a narrowing valley. The canyon proper lay before them. Canady grinned and wiped his streaming face. It was hot, and going to get hotter. "Hoss," he said, "they're pushing. They mean to take us. They must know the country ahead. They don't ride like there's any hurry." The horse, now, did not respond with its ears and a turning of its soft eyes, as it had before. It stood, head-down, blowing out through its distended nostrils. Canady came back and squatted down and put his hand below the nose of the horse, where the moisture of its pained breathing would strike his palm. "Damn," he said softly. "Blood."

He got his field glasses from the saddle pocket and examined the pursuers through them. "Eight," he said aloud, "and six ropes. I wonder how come it is that they always fetch so many ropes? Never saw a posse yet didn't feel they'd each of them ought to have a rope."

His fingers went to his sunburned neck. They felt it tenderly, and he grinned again. "Son of a gun," he said, "it could happen."

Canady's grins were not the grimaces of a fool, or of an unfeeling man. They were the grins of a gambler. And of an outlaw. And a thief. Canady knew where he was and where he had been and, most apparently, where he was going. It did not frighten him. He would grin when they put the loop over his head. That was his kind. He wouldn't curse or revile, and he wouldn't pray. Not out loud, anyway.

"Hoss," he said, "what do you think?"

The animal, slightly recovered, moved its ears and whickered gruntingly. Canady nodded, turning his back to the approaching posse and glassing the country ahead. "Me too," he agreed. "A grunt and a whicker is all she's worth. We haven't got no place to go." He tensed, as he said it, the glasses freezing on an opening in the rearing base rock of the closing valley. It was to their right. A good horse, fresh and sound, could take a man up to that gap in the cliff. The spill of detritus and ages-old fan of boulders and stunted pine that lay below its lip would permit of perilous mounted passage. There was water up there, too, for Canady could see the small white ribbon of the stream splashing down a rainbow falls to mist up upon the lower rocks in a spume of red and yellow and turquoise green lights, splendid with beauty in the early sun. "I take it back," he said. "Maybe we do have a place to go. Pretty, too, and handy to town. You can't beat that."

Directly ahead was a level sunlit flat, dotted with tall pines and scrub juniper and house-sized boulders. The clear stream from the high hole in the right-side valley wall watered the flat, growing good mountain hay upon its sandy red loam and making a ride across it a thing to pleasure the heart of any Western man.

"Come on," said Canady to his horse. "You canter me across the flat and I'll climb the fan afoot leaving you to pack up nothing but the saddle and the grub sack. You game? Least we can do is make those birds scratch for their breakfast. And who knows? Our luck might change. We might get up there and into that hole-in-the-wall before they come up to the rise, here, and spot us. If we can do that, there's a chance they'll ride on by, up the valley, and we can double back tonight and make it free."

He was talking to Canady, now, not to the horse. It was the way of men much alone and when they needed to do some figuring. They would do it out loud, the way Canady was doing. It sounded better that way, more convincing, and more as though it might really come off. Canady even swung into the saddle believing his own advice, telling himself what he wanted to know, then accepting it as a very good chance indeed. Again, it was his way. A man didn't live by the gun and the good fast horse without acquiring a working philosophy with lots of elastic in it.

"Move out," he repeated to the horse. "It's your part to get us across that flat in time."

The little mustang humped its back and shook itself like a wet dog. Running sweat, and caked, as well, flew from its streaked hide. It's gathering of itself in response to the rider's words was a visible thing. The horse was like the man. It wouldn't quit short of the last second, or step, or shot. They were of a kind with the country around them. It was all the edge they had ever needed.

Canady panted. He wiped the perspiration from his eyes and started upward again. Behind him, the little horse came on, unled, the reins looped over the horn so as not to trail and be stepped on. He followed the man like a dog, panting with him, struggling where he struggled, sliding where he slid, and lunging on as he did, after each setback.

They had made nearly the top of the fan of fallen rock below and leading into the opening of the side canyon. In another four or five minutes they would be clear of the climb. They would be off the slide and safely into the notch in the high wall of the valley. They would be out of sight of the posse, and the posse still had not come into view of them on the rise back across the pine flat.

"Easy, hoss," gasped Canady. "We're going to make it."

But Canady was wrong. Thirty yards from the top, the mustang put its slender foreleg into a rock crevice and drew back quickly. The movement set the slide moving and caught the leg and crushed it like a matchstick below the knee. When the horse had freed itself and was standing hunched and trembling behind Canady, the shattered leg hung sickeningly a'swing and free of the ground, and Canady cursed with tears in his eyes. It was not the luck of it that brought his angry words, but the shame of it. It was his pity and his feeling for a gallant companion that had given its all and almost found it enough.

The hesitation, the wait there near the top of the slide, near the safety of the hole-in-the-wall, was the natural thing for a Western man. His horse was hurt. It was hopelessly hurt. He would have to leave it, but not like that. Not standing there on three legs hunched up in the middle with pain and fright. Not standing there watching him with those liquid brown eyes. No, he couldn't leave his horse like that.

But how else? He couldn't shoot the mustang, for the noise would key the posse to his location. Had he had a knife he could cut its throat. Or had he an ax he could have crushed its skull above the eye-socket and put the poor devil down painlessly. With a rock he might be able

to stun the brave little brute, but he could not be sure of killing it clean-
ly. The same held true for the butt of his Colt or the steel-shod heel of
his Winchester. He could stun the horse, likely put it to its knees, but
not, still, be able to go on knowing it would not recover and try to get
up again and go on, and so suffer as no horse-riding man could think to
let his mount suffer. But, damn it, this was *his* life he was arguing with
himself about. It wasn't the damned horse's life. If he didn't do
something and do it quick, the posse would be over the rise and he and
the horse could go to hell together. Well, he would use the Colt butt.
He knew he could hit the exhausted animal hard enough with it to put
it down for the necessary time for himself to get on into the hole-in-the-
wall and for the posse to ride by and on up the valley. That was all the
time he needed, or at least it was all he could ask for. He pulled the
Colt and started back to the horse sliding and stumbling in his hurry to
get to the trembling beast and knock it down. But when he got up to its
side, when he looked into those dark eyes, he couldn't do it. He had to
be sure. "The hell with the posse," he said to the little horse, and spun
the Colt in the air and caught it by the handle and put it behind the
ragged ear and pulled the trigger. The smoke from the shot was still
curling upward, and the little pony just going slowly down, when the
first of the pursuing riders came up over the rise across the flat and
yelled excitedly back to his comrades that the game was in sight, and
on foot.

Canady went up the little stream. Behind him, where it fed the rainbow falls leaping outward into the main valley, the possemen were just
topping the detritus fan and closing in on "the hole." Back there
Canady had made a decision. It was not to stay and fight from the entrance cleft of the hole, where the little rivulet went out of the side canyon. He did not know what lay on up the side canyon, and feared there
might be a way by which the possemen, familiar with this territory,
could ride a circle and come in behind him. He could not risk that, he
believed, and must go on up the creek as far as he could, hoping it
would be far enough to find a place where he could put his back to the
wall and fight without their being able to get behind him.

Now, going along, the way becoming steeper and narrower and the
creek bank little more than wide enough to to pass a good horse and
rider, he saw ahead of him a basalt dike, or cross dam of rock, which
cut across the narrowing floor of the side canyon. Here the stream took
another plunge, this of about thirty feet. Above the dike, Canady could
see the boles of pine trees and hence knew that the ground above the

dike lay fairly level. The cross-laying of rock apparently served as a barrier against which the winter erosions of snow, ice and thaw had worked with the spring flooding of the creek to bring down and build up a tiny flat.

Canady's gray eyes lit up. His brown face relaxed and he said aloud, "By God, maybe this is it," and went on with renewed strength and some hope of keeping his life a little longer. Up there, above the rock cross-bank, a man with a good carbine and plenty of shells could hold down most eight-man posses for several afternoons. Well, two or three, anyway. Or one. For certain, until nightfall. Twelve, fifteen hours, say. It was better than nothing.

His luck held. There was a good angling trail going up that thirty-foot vertical face of rock. It was a game trail, and somewhat of a cow trail, too. He made out the droppings of elk, blacktail deer, range steers and, then, suddenly and strangely, a fairly fresh piling of horse sign. This latter find sent a chill through him. He was on his knees in the instant of the sighting, but then he straightened, grinning. It was all right. The pony was unshod. Moreover, he suspected, from the hard round prints that it left, that it never had been shod and was one of a bunch of broomtails — wild mustangs — that came into this rocky depth for the water that flowed so green and cool in the stream.

Clearing the top of the stone dam, Canady's grin widened. The flat above lay precisely as he had imagined it did. He laughed softly, as a man will who is alone. Now, then, it would be a little different from the way those hungry lawmen had planned it. This was perfect. At the apex of the triangle of the flat he saw the thick stand of sycamore and cottonwood, aspen, laurel and willow, and he knew that the water headed there. A moment later, he made out the source of the stream, a large artesian spring gushing from the native rock under great pressure. The spring was set above the grove some few feet, its stream falling rapidly to plunge into the foliage. Likely it pooled up there under the trees and at the foot of the down-plunge. That's what lured in the wild horses and the other game and the cattle, too, what few of the latter were hardy enough to come this far into the mountains for feed. All a man would need to do, now, was hole up in those boulders that girded the spring, up there above the trees, and he could command with his Winchester the whole of the small, open flat between the spring grove and the stone cross-dam that Canady had just clambered up. Taking a deep breath, the fugitive started across the flat, toward the spring and its hole-up boulders. It was not until he had

climbed safely into this haven at the canyon head and laid down pant-
ingly to look back on his trail and get ready for the possemen, that he
saw where he had come.

Below him in the trees the spring pooled up exactly as he had expected it would. Also the rim of the pool showed the centuries of wear
of the hoofed animals coming to its banks for water. But there was
something else — two other things — that he had not expected to see
there, and his grin faded and his gray eyes grew taut and tired and
empty.

The first thing was the wild horse. It had not gone on up out of the
little side canyon as Canady had hoped, showing him the way to follow
its tracks and escape over the rim where no mounted men might
follow. It was still in the grove of trees that sheltered the spring-pool
waterhole, and it wasn't still there because of its thirst. Beyond the
trees, back where Canady had come from, and so skillfully blended
and built into the natural cover of the canyon that even his range-wise
eyes had missed them, were two woven brush and pole wings of the second thing Canady had not dreamed to find there. Canady had stumbled into a wild horse trap. And he was caught there, with this unfortunate lone mustang that now cowered in the trees and could not get
out of the trap any more than could he, and for the same reason — the
posse and the box canyon.

"Steady on," Canady called down softly to the terrified horse. "We'll
think of something."

Two hours after high noon the sun was gone from the canyon.
Canady could see its light splashing the far side of the main valley still,
but in the side canyon all was soft shade, and hot. Canady drank
enough water to keep himself from drying out, yet not enough to log
him. He noted that the wild mustang did the same thing. It knew, as
Canady knew, that to be ready to fight or fly called for an empty belly.
"Smart," said Canady, "smart as hell." The horse heard him and looked
up. "Coo-ee, coo-ee," Canady called to him reassuringly. "Don't fret;
I'll figure something for us." But it was a lie and he knew it was a lie.

He had gone down, right after he first lay up in the spring boulders
and saw the trap and the wild broomtail in it, and closed off the narrow gate of the funnel-winged corral with his lariat. He had done that
in a hurry, before the posse had worked up into the canyon and taken
its position along the top of the cross-dam. His one thought had been
that the broomtail was a horse, wild or not, and that so long as a man

had a horse he wasn't out of it in that country. And he had wanted to keep hidden from the posse the fact that he did have a horse up there in that headwaters timber. The mustang had played with him in that last part of it, lying up shy and quiet as a deer in the trees and brush, not wanting any more than Canady wanted for the men to know that it was there. "It" in this case was a scrubby little stallion, probably too small and old to hold a band of mares. The little horse had not only the fixtures but the temperament of the mongrel stud animal. Watching him lie still in the spring brush and keep his eyes following every move of the men below him, as well as of the single man above him, Canady knew that he and the trapped horse were friends. The only problem was proving it to the horse.

Sometimes these old scrub studs had been ridden long ago and would remember man's smell and voice. He tried a dozen times to talk the mustang up toward his end of the spring pool. But the animal gave no sign that the sight, scent or sound of mankind was familiar to him, or welcome. He bared is teeth silently and pinned his ears and squatted in the haunches ready to kick like a pack mule on a cold morning. He did this every time Canady said more than three or four words to him, or accompanied his talk with any movement that might mean he was coming down to see the horse, if the horse would not come up to see him.

What possible good the horse could do him, even if, by some miracle Canady might gentle him down and put his saddle and bridle on him, Canady didn't know. Then, even in thinking that far, he laughed and shrugged. His saddle and bridle were down there on that rock slide below the hole-in-the-wall. He'd had no time and no reason to take them off his dead mount. So if he went out of there astride that broomtail it would be bareback, and that was about as good a bet as that the crafty old stallion would sprout wings and fly up out of the canyon. A bridle, of sorts, he could rig from splitting and unraveling a short length of his lariat. It would be sort of a breaking hackamore arrangement and might do to give simple directions of right and left and whoa-up. But even if he rigged this Sioux headstall and got it on the shaggy little horse, then what? That was, even if the rascal wanted to be good, or had been ridden in the past, and remembered it of a sudden? Nothing. Not a damned thing. Canady couldn't ride out of that canyon if he had the best saddle mount in Montana waiting and eager to make the try with him. It was all crazy, thinking of that wild stud. But just finding any horse up there was bound to start a man's mind going.

Especially when he had just shot his own mount and was fixing to put his back to the best rock he could find and go down with lead flying. But it was crazy all the same. All Canady could do was what the old broomtail stud could do — fight the rope to the last breath he had in him, then kill himself, if he could, before the others did it for him.

The afternoon wore on. The heat in the deep-walled little canyon was enormous. The deerflies swarmed at the spring pool and bit like mad cats. They nearly drove Canady wild, but he fought them with hand and mind and swathed neckband and, when evening came, they lifted up out of the canyon on the first stir of the night wind. In the early part of the waiting there had been some desultory talk between the posse and Canady, talk of Canady coming out peacefully and getting a fair trial, but the fugitive had not bothered to take that offer seriously. He knew the trial he would get. The posse had its own witnesses with it. They would bring up these two or three men who had "seen" the shooting and say to them, "Is that him?" and the men would say, "Yes, that's him," and the trial would be over. Witnesses! thought Canady. God, how he hated them. It wasn't that he minded being identified if he was the man. In his business no feeling was held against the witness who *had* seen something. It was those devils, like the ones with the posse, who had *not* seen the job and yet who were always ready to raise their right hands and be sworn, who were the ones Canady hated. There had not been any witnesses to what passed between him and that teller. All the other bank people had been on the floor behind the cage, and there had been no customers in the bank, or out in front of it. The shooting had happened and Canady had made it to his horse in back of the bank, and made it away down the alley and into the sagebrush south of town before he had passed a living soul. Then, it was two farm wagons, both carrying kids and driven by women, that he had ridden by well out of Gray's Landing. How those good folks — and they were the only real witnesses, save the cashier and the other teller on the bank floor — how they could identify him as anything other than a horseman not of that area, Canady did not know. As for the three shots that had killed the teller, and they must have killed him or the posse would not have pushed so hard, those shots had been fired *after* both barrels of the .36 caliber derringer that the teller brought up out of the cash drawer had been triggered and put their slugs, one in Canady's chest, and one in the ceiling of the Second National Bank of Gray's Landing, Montana. But the only witness to that fact was dead. Canady had reacted as all men with guns in their hands react to other men with guns in their hands. He had fired by instinct, by pure conditioned reflex of long experience, when that first .36 bullet went into the pectoral muscles of his left chest.

Armed robbery? Certainly. Twenty years in the Territorial Prison? Of course. A man expected that. But to be run down like a mad dog and cornered and starved out and then strung up on a naked cotton-wood like a damned Indian drunk or a common horse thief was not right or fair. Murder? Could you call it murder when the other man was a professional in his business and he could see that you were a professional in yours? When you told him he would be killed if he tried anything funny? Then, when on top of the fair warning, you gave him the first shot? Could you call it murder, then, if you shot in answer to his try at killing you? Self-defense was the actual verdict, but of course an armed robber could not plead self-defense. But he was not guilty of murder, or even of assault with a deadly weapon, or even of intent to commit murder, or of a damned thing, really, but to sack that cash drawer and clear out of Gray's Landing just as fast and peaceably as he and the old horse might manage.

Canady grinned, even as he exonerated himself.

It was no good. He knew it was no good. A man had to be honest with himself. If he was in another business he wouldn't need a gun to conduct his trade. Needing and using a gun, he was always in the peril of being forced to use it. The teller was an honest man. Frank Canady was a crook. The teller was a dead honest man and Canady was a live dishonest man. Canady was a killer.

"No!" he yelled down to the posse. "I won't do it; I shot second; I didn't mean to harm that fellow. He pulled on me and shot first. But he's dead, ain't he? Sure he is. And you say to me to come on down peaceable and you'll see I get a fair trial? With a dead teller back there on the floor of the Second National. That's rich. Really rich."

The possemen were startled. It had been two hours since the fugitive had made a sound. Previously he had refused to come down and they had thought he meant it. Now, did they detect a change? Was it that he wanted to reconsider and was only protecting his ego by the defiant outburst.

"That's right, you heard us right," the leader of the posse called up to him. "You come down here and we'll guarantee to take you back to Gray's Landing and get you to either Cheyenne or Miles City, wherever the court is sitting, by train and under armed guard. You'll get the trial we promised, and the protection beforehand." He waited a significant moment, then demanded, "What do you say? There's no use any more people getting hurt."

Canady's gray eyes grew tired again.

"That's so," he called back. "It includes me, too. I don't want to see anybody else get it, either. 'Specially me. No thanks, Mr. Posseman. I'll stay up here. I don't fancy that you brung along all them ropes just to tie me up for the ride back to Gray's Landing."

There was a silence from below the cross-dam of rock in the upper throat of the canyon that lasted perhaps two, perhaps three stretching minutes. Then the posseman called back. "All right," he said, "you'll have it your way. When it's full dark we're going to come for you, and you know what that will mean. There are eight of us, all good shots, and you won't have the chance of a rat in an oatbin. We've got bulls-eye lanterns to light you out. We will set them up behind boulders where you can't snipe them, and yet where they will throw light up there around you like it was bright moonlight. We mean to stomp you out. There will be no trial and no talk of a trial. You're dead right now."

Canady sank back behind his breastwork of basalt and gray-green granite. He hawked the cottony spittle from his throat and spat grimacingly down toward the mustang stud. The animal had been crouching and listening to the exchange of voices intelligently like some big gaunt sandy-maned dog. Seeing him, and noting his apparent interest, Canady managed a trace of his quiet grin.

"What do *you* say, amigo?" he asked.

The horse looked up at him. It was the first time in all the long hours that Canady had tried gentle-talking to him that the animal had made a direct and not spooked response to the man's voice. Now he stomped a splayed and rock-split forehoof and whickered softly and gruntingly in his throat, precisely as Canady's old horse had done.

"All right," said Canady, for some reason feeling mightily warmed by the mustang's action, "so we've each got one friend in the world. That isn't too bad. As long as you have a friend you have a chance. Rest easy; let me think. We'll still make it, you and me. . . ."

It was dusk when the old steer came down the cliff trail. He was a ladino, one of those mossy-horned rascals that had successfully hidden out from the gathers of a dozen years. He was sly and crafty and cautious as any wild animal, but he had to have water and he was coming down to the spring pool to get it. He certainly saw the men of the posse, and winded their mounts, but they did not see him and he knew that they did not. His yellow buckskin hide with the dark "cruz" or cross-stripe on the shoulders, and the dark brown legs and feet, blended perfectly into the weathered face of the cliff, and he made no more sound coming down that hidden trail than a mountain doe might have made. But he had failed to see Canady or to separate his scent, or the scent of the mustang stud, from the other horse and man scents coming from below. He came on, carefully, silently, yet quickly down the wall of the canyon from the rim above and Canady, seeing him, was suddenly lifted in mine and heart. He had been right in the first place! There *was* a trail up out of that blind box of a side canyon. A track up that dizzy sheer cliff, up there, that would pass a desperate man, or a catlike wild mustang, but not a mounted man or a man going afoot leading his tamed and trained saddle mount. "Come on, come on," he heard himself whispering to the old outlaw steer. "Come on down here and let me see how you do it. Let me see how and where you get off that damned wall and down here where we are."

He grinned when he said that, when he said "we," meaning himself and the wild stud, without thinking about it. It was funny how a man took to anything for a friend when he had run out of the real McCoy and was in his last corner. He supposed that if a sidewinder crawled along at the final minute and that was all he had to talk to, a man would find some excuse to think kindly of the snake tribe. Well, anyway, he was thinking with deep kindness about the animal kingdom just then. Especially the horse and cow part of it. And extraspecially about the latter half. "Come on, keep coming on, don't skip, for God's sake," he said to the gaunt dun steer. "Easy, easy. Let me see you do it, just don't fall or spook or get a bad smell and change your mind. That's it, that's it. Easy, easy. . . ."

He talked the steer down that cliff as though his life depended on it, and it did. And the steer made it. He made it in a way that caused Canady to suck in his breath and shake his head in wonderment. He made it in a way that even caused Canady to think for a moment about there being something to the idea of a divine providence, for it was the sort of thing no man could have figured out by himself, the weird, crazy, wonderful kind of a last-second reprieve that no force but God Almighty could have sent to a man in Canady's place. It was a miracle.

The dun steer performed it with an easy quickness that defied belief, too. He came to that place on his side of the canyon where it seemed to Canady that the trail must end. The man could see the sheer face of the

rock dropping sixty feet to the creek bed. A giant outcropping of
granite hid the exact end of the rightside trail, but Canady could see,
and with absolute certainty, that the trail did not continue downward
past that outcrop that hid its actual terminus. But as he watched the
steer disappear behind the outcrop and as he wondered what would
happen next, he saw the lean yellow body launch itself in a graceful
leap from behind the outer edge of the outcrop, and sail outward
through the thin air of the canyon's dark throat. It appeared as though
the leap would smash the ribby brute into the rearing face of the opposite, left-hand canyon walls, which lay no more than fifteen or twenty feet from the right-side wall. But again the steer disappeared, this
time seemingly into the very face of the opposing cliff.

There was a tricky turn in the rock wall of the canyon's left side at
just that point, however, and while Canady could see the creek's rag-
gedly broken bottom, he could not see where the steer hit into the wall.
All he was sure of for the moment was that the animal had made his
landing somewhere other than in the creek bottom. Difficult as it might
be to accept, that old outlaw steer had somehow made it from one side
of the wall to the other. But, even so, then what? Where was he now?
The questions were soon answered when the missing steer appeared to
walk right out of the waterfall that came down from Canady's elevated
vantage to strike into and begin following the brief section of creek bed
into the pool grove. While Canady gaped, the animal stole swiftly to
the pool, drank sparingly, returned and disappeared again behind the
curtain of misty water cascading down from the spring above.

So that was it. As simple and as remarkable as that. A trail ran from
behind the waterfall up the left-hand wall. At a point opposite the
right-side trail's end, it, too, terminated. But it was obvious that there
was room enough for a running jump and opposite safe landing, to and
from either wall, with both takeoff and landing spots completely
masked from the lower canyon.

Gaging the distance of the jump, Canady knew that he could make
it. With his boots off and laced about his neck, or better, thrown over
with his Colt and the saddlebags with the bank money, the Winchester
being slung on his back, alone, he could make that distance through
the air. But, then, what of that? He made the jump safely and went on
up the right-side cliff trail behind the ladino steer and gained the rim;
then what? He would still be afoot in a hostile land in midsummer's
blazing heat without food, water, or a mount. That was the rub. Even
if he made that jump and the cliff climb beyond it and got to the rim,

he would have to have a horse. Otherwise, the possemen, within an hour or two of dark, having come for him and found him gone, would go back out and climb out of the main valley and cut for his sign on both rims of the side canyon, and they would still get him. They would get him, easy, with them mounted and he afoot.

No, he had to take that broomy studhorse with him.

Somehow, he had to get that mustang to go with him up the cliff. If he could do that, could get the little horse to make the jump with him on its back — it would have to be that way for he could never trust the brute to follow him or to wait for him if he allowed it to jump first — if he could make that gap in the canyon on the back of that little wild horse, then stay with him hand-leading him up the cliff trail, then, oh then, by the dear good Lord, he would make it. He and the horse would make it together. Just as he had promised the raunchy little devil. Up on the rim, he would remount the tough wiry mustang and together they would race away and Canady would have his life and the broomtail stud would have his freedom and the Gray's Landing posse would have their ropes unstretched and their vengeance unadministered and left to God where it belonged.

The thought of the Almighty came very strong to Canady in that moment of desperate hope. He turned his face upward to peer out of the narrow slit of late twilight far above him where the walls of the canyon seemed almost to touch at the top and where, far, far up there, he could see the yellow steer climbing the last few steps of the steep trail and humping himself over the rim and losing himself to canyon's view. Canady nodded and said to the dusk-hushed stillness about him: "If you'll let me make it, too, Lord, me and that little hoss down yonder, I will try to set things as right as I can. I'll take this money, Lord, the bank don't need it and I won't want it any more after this night, and I will give this money to the widow of that poor teller. I will figure some way to do it, Lord, that she don't know where it came from. And I'll turn loose this little wild hoss, if you will let me gentle him enough to get on him and push him to that jump, up yonder. I'm going to try it, Lord. I'm going down there to the pool and try putting my loop on him right now. You reckon you could help me? I surely hope so, as I think you wouldn't send that ladino steer down here to show a man the way out, and then not help him to make it. Nor likewise do I think you would put that little old mustang studhorse down there in that trap by the pool unless you wanted him used. It looks to me, Lord, as if you truly wanted to pull me out of this here trap, and if that's the way it is, why thank you and I'll do my best. . ."

In the little light remaining, Canady went down from his rocks by the spring to try for the trapped wild horse. He took his rope from the trap gate and closed the gate, instead, with brush and poles, hoping it would turn the stud should he break past him when he came at him with the lariat.

The actual catching went, as such things perversely will, with a strange easiness. Oh, the little horse fought the loop when he felt it settle on him, but he did not do so viciously. The very fact that he permitted Canady to come close enough to dab the loop on him to begin with was peculiarly simple. It made the matter suspicious to Canady and he thought the little stud was merely stalling on him, was trying to tempt him in close where he could use his teeth and hooves on him. He knew the small mustangs would do this. They would fight like panthers in close, using their teeth like carnivorous animals, and their feet with all the savagery of elk or moose fighting off wolves. But this was not the case with the tattered broomtail in the mustang trap. When Canady got up near enough to him, he saw the reason why, or thought that he did. The telltale white marks of the cinch and saddle, the places where white hair had grown in to replace the original claybank sorrel hairs, showed clearly in the darkening twilight. Canady's first thought that this horse had been handled before was now assured. And it certainly explained the change in the animal the moment the man snugged the loop high up on his neck, under the jaw, in a way that showed the horse he meant to hold him hard and fast, and to handle him again as he had been handled years before. Memory is a strong force. The stud made Canady throw him on the ground, using the loose end of the rope to make a figure-8 snake and roll it around the front legs to bring the little pony down, but once he had been thrown and permitted to stand up again, it was all over. This man had gentled many horses. He had spent his life with them. Their smell had become his smell. The very sound of his voice had a horse sound in it. The mustang had heard it the first word of the day. He had sensed his kinship with this particular man, then, and he sensed his mastery of the horsekind, now. He submitted to Canady and stood quietly, if still trembling, while the man stroked him and sweet-whispered to him and got him to ease and to stand without shaking, and without dread or apprehension.

Then Canady cut and wove the makeshift breaking halter, the Plains Indian's simple rope rein and bridle arrangement, continuing to talk all the while to the small mustang. When, in half an hour more, it was full dark and the split-ear hackamore-bridle and its short reining rope were finished and put upon the horse, the animal was to all practical purposes reduced to a usable saddle horse. It was a piece of the greatest luck, Canady knew, that he had been able to catch and work the little brute. But it was not so entirely luck that it had no sense or possibility to it, and his success only made the fugitive believe that his hunch of higher help was a true one, and this thought, in turn, strengthened him and made his spirits rise.

"Come on," he murmured to the little horse, "it's time we got shut of here. Come along, *coo-ee, coo-ee*, little hoss. That's good, that's real good. Easy, easy. . . ."

They went in behind the creek falls, as the yellow ladino steer had done. The mustang pulled back a bit at the water but once it had hit him he steadied down and followed Canady's urging pull on the lariat as well and as obediently as any horse would have done in similar straits. Beyond the sheet of the falls, the left-hand trail went sharply but safely upward and around the trunklike bulge of the canyon's wall which had hidden it from Canady's view at the spring. Around the turn was the expected straight run at the leap-over. It was better, even, than Canady hoped. There was some actual soil in its track and, here and there, some clumps of tough wire grass to give footing and power for the jump.

"Steady, now," said Canady, and eased up onto the crouching mustang. The little mount flinched and deepened his crouch, but he did not break. Canady sighed gratefully and nodded upward to that power which clearly was helping now. He took his grip on the rope rein and put the pressure of his bowed knees to the mustang's ribs. Beneath him, he felt the little horse squat and gather himself. Then he touched him, just touched him, with his left bootheel. The wild stud uncoiled his tensed muscles, shot down the runway of the trail, came up to the jump-across as though he had been trained to it since colthood. Canady felt his heart soar with the mighty upward spring in the small brute's wiry limbs. He laughed with the sheer joy of it. He couldn't help it. He had never in his life felt a triumph such as this one; this sailing over that hell's pit of blackness down there beneath him; this gliding spring, this arching, floating burst of power that was carrying him high above those deadly rock fangs so far below, and was carrying him, too, up and away from those blood-hungry possemen and their winking, glaring, prying bull's-eye lanterns, which he could just see now, from an eye-corner, coming into view down-canyon of his deserted place at the spring above the pool and the peaceful grove of mountain ash and alder and willow there at the head of Rainbow Creek in Blind Canyon, sixty and more miles from the Second National Bank and that fool of a dead teller in Gray's Landing, Montana. Oh, what a wondrous, heady thing was life! And, oh! what a beholden and humble man was Frank Canady for this gift, this chance, this answer to his fumbling prayer. He would never forget it. Never, never, never.

They came down very hard at the far end of the jump. The concussion of the horse hitting the ground rattled Canady's teeth and cracked his jaws together as loud as a pistol shot. He saw lights behind his eyes and heard wild and strange sounds, but only for a second or two. Then all was clear again and he and the little horse were going together up the right-side cliff trail, Canady leading the way, the little horse following faithful as a pet dog behind him. It seemed no more than a minute before they were where it had taken the yellow steer half an hour to climb, and it seemed only a breath later that they had topped out on the rim and were free.

Canady cried then. The tears came to his eyes and he could not help himself. He didn't think that the little mustang would care, though, and he was right. When he put his arms about the shaggy, warm neck and hugged the skinny old stud, the mustang only whickered deep in his throat and leaned into Frank Canady and rested his homely jughead over the man's shoulder. They were of a kind. They belonged to each other, and with each other, and that was true; for that was the way that the possemen found them when they came probing carefully up the bed of the creek in its brief run from the deserted pool grove to the foot of the spring's waterfall. The horse had fallen with the man beneath him, and neither had known a flash or a spark or a hint of thought, in the instant their lives had been crushed out among the granite snags of the creek bed below the jumping place of the yellow ladino steer.

SEX IN THE SAGEBRUSH

Friends of the wild frontier, rovers of the fabled lands across the wide Missouri, fellow-keepers of our Western past — listen up. We are here to praise the Old West, not to bury it.

Our stated aim today is to so rope and tie-down tomorrow, that it can't drag us away from yesterday. In fee simple this means let us remember what the Old West was, and was not, then keep full trust with that memory in what we write of it.

Sex in the Sagebrush is not an idle title; it has to do with keeping the Western faith.

The keepers of anything of great value do not sit idly over it. They have to fight for it. Uphold its worth. Insist that its describers get it right. Either that, or go away and find something less good and grand to despoil. Something they can warp and torture to make fit their twisted images. That is just so long as they do not try to call what they do Western writing, and themselves, Western writers. And the same in shameful spades to their publishers.

Meanwhile, our Old West was never before so poisoned by its own storytellers, as by the present-day crop of so-called "adult Western" writers. We hold that truth to be self-evident. And we owe it our unforgiving opposition. Which is not to say it is to be censored or proscribed in any manner, whether open or covert. The Western is not sacred. We can see it funny, we can see it sad. We can show its picture narrow as a ferret's hips, or broad as the beam of a brockle-faced ox. The limits have yet to be drawn for our native literary treasure, the Western Story. Its definitions, even, are in argument.

Yet we are today moving destructively to re-define those limits which have been set by Western characters, geography and tradition of our frontier past, and doing so before ever that past is consulted or considered.

The game is easy to play.

If you can't win by the rules that apply, change the rules.

We had better understand this.

If we don't, if we fail to recognize and repel these perverters of our Western past, we won't have an Old West to worry about.

Some modern Torquemada or latter-day Marquis de Sade will take over in lizardskin cowboy boots and Izod La Coste jeans, and that will be that, for whatever last defenders may yet linger, crying out to know for whom tolls the bell of our vanished Western past.

These threateners of the Western Story are, of course, the kinky sex and butcherknife violence authors of the damnable *au courant* "dirty" Western novels. Softcore, mediumcore or granitecore porno; name the size of your stomach for such noxious fare and these novels will overfill it for you.

Still, a reasoned disclaimer: fair is fair.

Violence for the sake of violence is routinely condemned, yet violence in the expression of the frontier justice system is routinely practised by all of us in Western writing. The uniform code of swift and deadly retribution for the classic wrong, is inherent in Western fiction. In whatever medium — print, film, TV tape — it's *there*. It cannot be denied, or exorcized.

In example, and quite against the critical tide of my Western writing peer-group, I think the Clint Eastwood "Fistful of Dollars" movies were, on the whole, a mental invigoration for the Western story. This, despite their outrageous flummery and abattoirian body counts. Old Clint with his Sonora dog turd cigar, flinty stare and blanket poncho, was the mythic Western (good) Bad Guy come to settle *all* accounts, whether they needed it or not. Admittedly, his spaghetti-Western films were but grand *guignols* of the real thing. Absurd. Bawdy. Pantomimic. Crude. Brutal. Dumb. Yes, of course. They still fascinate and amuse. Particularly if taken with sufficient salt, as they were intended. The Old West was surely never the spaghetti-Western way, but Eastwood's character was, all the same, the sort of sagebrush High Executioner who won our secret fealty. The essential mysterious stranger. The quintessential man on horseback. Wearer of the mandatory black hat. Rider off, always, into the sunset. Don Quixote with two Colts and a '73 Winchester, leaving behind an entire generation of young readers shouting into the deepening gloam for Clint to come back, and never mind Shane.

The difference, in Eastwood's favor, between his theatrical violence and the gory print sex of our so-called "adult Western" authors, is inescapable.

Had dirty Western writing a scintilla the wit or camp of "For a Few Dollars More," or "High Plains Drifter," one might forgive it. But it does not have Clint's class. And it isn't humor or satire or high camp but just plain old unfunny fornication. There is in it no art, no quality, no socially redeeming significance, nothing save a straight-out pander shot full of sweat and salivation and moans and groans and cryings-out enough to win a year's subscription to *Creative Degeneracy* magazine.

But beware, there is a real problem with these dirty works.

It has nothing to do with your ire or my despisement.

They make money.

Lots of money.

The best-intentioned paperback houses in the country have been rightfully worried that they, too, must come to this lowlife literature, merely to stay solvent. Most of them publicly eschewed such trash. In private, they would tell you they were thinking the unthinkable: getting their own deviate series ready for the printer. The situation has since plateau'd. But so has it for the clean Westerns. The market is soft for all Western endeavor, books, films, television. But the economic lull has its dividends. This whole interlude of the pornographic Western novel will be looked back upon in time as a period apart in Western writing. It will be seen to have been an abberation unique in the consideration of popular literature genres. And what will now eventuate for it (the dirty Western) as the traditional Western market recovers, is roundly argued wherever Westerns and Western writing are critically reviewed today. The verdict has not yet been returned. The jury is reported deadlocked. It may still find for the Sex Western.

But guess what has happened outside the courtroom, back yonder at the plateau?

Dirty writing may be added to the other lost causes against the Old West. The slowdown has hurt the porno passion group. It has given the straight Western writers the opportunity to do something material about combating the sleaze dealers. And those dealers *are* worried. They don't want to talk about it. They are reluctant to make eye contact. Can it be that they are going to have to reckon at last with the power of the *real* American Western?

There comes that day, you know.

All about we see signs of an awakening consciousness of the Western as original American literature. A host of things small but exciting.

Here, the rebel academic breaking ranks to cheer us on. There, the insightful critic discovering the Western sunrise, greeting it bravely. Nothing major but the excitation will not go away. One simply senses that the Western Story is on the move.

And this is not merely cheer-leading. Not whistling in the false dawn. Not squinting to see the sun where it doesn't shine.

There *is* something inherently wrong about the "hardball" Westerns. They disfigure the humanity of our frontier times. They diminish and sicken the definitions of what should be a uniquely robust native literature. They make of the true Western an endangered species. They are in effect and in fact unclean.

There is no real alkali in such works, no burnt hair at the branding fire, no blue norther, no last of 5,000, no hackamore-broken green broncs, nothing in them, nothing at all.

Let them be away and finally gone.

Sic transit gloria the sexual frontier.

Still, we know the Sex Western will not be thus simply yearned away. Nor banished by our rightful indignation. Nor yet made to laugh less on its merry way to the bank, by our curses and outcries.

We still must protect and defend the sane, derivative Western, cherishing it before all others.

It is the weapon of rational choice in our war on the dirty Western. We must wield it with full valor.

Admittedly, it is a nerve-boggling joust to take lance against the requisite multiorgasmic *fin de tout* of the porno-Western. What can an honest old crooked sheriff, or hard working bumbler of a good-hearted bank robber, or simpering sweetcake of a bushwhacked rancher's dehymened daughter do for encores against the turgid wonders of the labia majorae and the meatus rampant?

Not a great deal, one despairs; sex is a tough act to critique.

The odds stand that if we persevere in our cause, the smutbrush sagas must wither, the poisoned waterholes of their sustenance seep away into the sands of those other, alien streambeds from whence they arose.

The interim problem is that the Western has been made such sport of for so long and with such relentless determination by both the critical and the academic media that it has been rendered the natural prey of every venal writer seeking a category in which it is safe to fail while still taking home a handy buck or three.

The Western, of course, is not alone in the sexual invasion. Virtually all mainstream fiction today is steamy with explicit sex. But the Western clearly remains the easiest game to all the subverters. And it will so remain until we act to save it from them by lifting it by its own original merits to the level of an accepted and equal literature.

Only when this has been done can the Western be called secured for posterity.

This happy ending will come about through the continued jealous guarding of our frontier heritage and its original source-material: our ancestors who went before us to open the West and to guarantee the American future in the doing.

That is the real thing, friends.

Let us hang onto it. Let us make certain we stay true to yesterday. If we do, tomorrow will take care of itself.

The Western will remain the Western.

A TIME TO TALK
OF HEROES

L et us agree it is time to talk of heroes. Specifically, let us speak to their importance in American Western literature. In that speaking let us agree that we address in fact a far broader literature, that of the screen, the television tube, the critical press, the academic community. Finally, let us concede that, within these fertile fields of communication, we are today whelmed over with a separate literature of misanthropy in which the leading characters are, by requisite definition, social losers.

These are not just societal misfits. Not merely the loners whom we have always had with us in honorable roles. Not simply honest citizens inundated by foul fortune and fighting the good fight to tilt the odds along with the windmill. No, we are talking genuine losers here. People, man, woman, child, who are just no damned good. The kind that once upon a time were called villains, but now are the new non-heroes. And, since this contemporary "leading loser" to coin a category, performs all the evil works of the oldtime villain, there is no proper personified villain in any of these sagas glorifying failure.

But, lo, there is no hero either.

There is only the anti or non-hero who, again, man, woman, child, is a psychotic nurd or just plain pathetic own-worst-enemy, whose grubby life and gray visions spell nothing but the degradation of the human spirit. Beginning with pathological dementia and descending to every intermediate form of ugly character disintegration to the final psychasthenia, society itself becomes the villain and government the enemy to the end that there is no hero but the loser, no social cause higher than the gutter, no land and no law save the twilight zone of the street.

This is the humanoid cipher so persistently raised up from the muck by the writers and packagers of today's all-media literature.

He is the same — mark you well — unclean creature emerging from the Pit to threaten the American Western Story, the last bastion of the oldtime straight arrow hero, the uncomplicated palladin of the Old West, the Man who does what he has to do, the underdog who knows forever that evil must fall where good stands, like Jackson at Bull Run, "like a stonewall."

This article of Western faith echoes the anger caged in the true believer's breast against those who minstrelize "the losers." And who, doing so, seek to decay the credo that no one wins where heroes lose.

What is this denial of man's mortal need for role idols? This calumny against his never-ending search for leaders he can follow, whether as a trooper of the Seventh, or a feathered cavalryman of Crazy Horse's Oglala? This suborning of perjury against the history of those who fought and died for their chance to begin again "out West"? This false railing against those others never named or known who fought as well and at the same supremest risk? This rottenness of spirit? This meanness of faith in the frontier and its heroic folklore? What can it be called but an inner sickness of those who suffer it, the mindless expunging of that one candle mankind has lit in all the millenia against the darkness of despair — hope.

Without heroes there can be no hope. That is the whole of it, the entire. Yet, hold, and behold — the sickness spreads.

Think about the current films and books and critiques thereof which feature and extol social pariahs as non-heroes and which thereby assume the customer will spend his $5 or his $15 for a theatre seat or hardcover copy of the book at today's outer-space prices, to what? Why, to watch these certified creeps bump and cohabitate along the bottom of the new Slough of Despond, that's what. They're making a statement, you see.

But listen to the bookkeepers.

It will restore your esprit.

Let us celebrate the factor-in-common shared by these products of the new non-hero. Put forth with ultimate fanfare, lauded automatically by the review media as works of a higher art than most of us are mentally equipped to appreciate, virtually without notable exception these outre films and sicko fiction have lost money, most of them a lot of money. And that particular specimen of a negative cash flow means one thing alone: the consumer who votes with his theatre ticket or his bookstore purchase has marvelously rejected these demeaning stories without heroes.

One job-aware critic has described the sales disasters of these "social sickie themes" with due servility as, "not enough people being in the mood for downers in America today."

That's putting it Ivory-mild; I would use a Brillo Pad myself, for I think they all reek unto heaven.

But if you are a calm person, more together than certain old devils, and well versed in the Western in all its forms, perhaps you would care to speak against the need for heroes. Particularly, if you are wont, or known, to harbor adamant doubts about the Good Guy ethic in the American West, and the American Western. Or anywhere for that matter. Salt sage and rabbit ear brush and belly-high Spanish grama are not at search nor issue here. We are after an idea. A tradition. An actual hunger shared around the world to believe in the American Western. So thunder forth, you stalkers of the legend, you slayers of the myth. We have cried a pox on all non-heroes. How cry you? And why?

You all know well the resolution: man must have heroes to go with his sweat and bread. Even so, wait along. Your position may have been misunderstood, something lost or twisted in the translation. Speak now, if we have taken you unfairly. Are we substantially correct that you contend there are no more heroes today? No more classic gladiators of humanitas? How about some just ordinary embattled human beings capable of rising above temptation and despair to fight on to victory. "Winners" in the simplest word.

Losers are anathema to the Western Myth. Underdogs are beloved of it. The biggest winners in the Western world come from underdog beginnings. Winning and losing, being a winner or a loser, is not merely a matter of victor and vanquished. Losing can be accomplished in all honor. Winning can be the sorriest of triumphs. The plaudits of the mob do not a hero make. Indeed, the dim-minded mesomorphic "champion" has been one of our favored lamentations since time remembered. All this being said, however, the so-called "sensitive" and "vulnerable" people — not charming losers but depressive and degraded cretins — still seem to be the preferred heroes of today's all-media writers, and the purchasers of their subhuman wares.

Yet remember that the irresistible misfit has always been a staple of every commercial writer's market-basket of profitable types. We are not talking of this wondrous weed in the literary garden when we assail the non-hero worshippers. We are aiming at the steady serpent's hatch of "downers" which, finally even unto the noble Western Story, has been foisted upon us by the media masters bowing down to the Pewter Calf of the quick and sleazy buck.

God, or Somebody Up There, please start helping us.

We are brought, North to South, and East to Western, to prize and celebrate a zoo of central and supporting types in our literature from whom, if met in the ordinary circumstances of real life, we would flee desperately. Or shun as the biblical plague. Or have up on charges of indecent exposure. Or, at very least, provide with court-ordered protective custody — theirs and ours.

So why are these menaces to our mental health idolized by the contemporary novelists, newswriters and film makers? Is this their idea of art mirroring life? One supposes regretfully that it is — or is sorrowfully content that this is the rude case — and so is led again, this time *a' toute force*, to cry out for higher aid. The purveyors of the "no hero" Western are riding free in our older, hard-bought saddles. And they are mean to catch. Fortunately, they leave a tell-tale trail; *entrailles* by any other name still smell bad. We will corral them in the end.

Until then, remember dear the Word: *vita sine litteris mors est;* if we must live without literature, we might as well be dead.

But remember also that literature without heroes is already dead. Heroes live. Non-heroes never did. Nor ever will.

This is a whang-leather lesson for the forces of the anti-hero to chew their ways through. Lip-reading is tough with a mouthful of saddle skirting. But it is incumbent upon us all who believe in the good that men do, to make sure that they keep chewing.

The lesson is that heroes are forever.

Let us keep after them until they get it right.

Here is a scary tale of a very small boy faced with a very large problem and needing adult help in a very great hurry to solve his quandary before it solves him. When children seek help from grownups they are frequently put off with short words, or not listened to at all. In the case of ten-year-old Chamaco Díaz, the author thought to see a lonely Mexican boy faced with the threat of death to his beloved Presidente of all Méjico, Benito Juárez. How would such a small boy react when given this chance to save the life of El Presidente by risking his own life? How many boys would even think to try? Chamaco Díaz would. And that is the story of the Tallest Indian in Toltepec. He knew if he did not do something, no one would. But he needed firepower to counter-attack the evil Colonel Ortega, who had sworn to kill El Presidente. And all he could find was a worn-out old American gunfighter, afraid even of his own shadow, but having one thing in common with Chamaco Díaz — when he saw a fellow human being in very great trouble, he would never look the other way.

— W.H.

THE TALLEST INDIAN
IN TOLTEPEC

W here the wagon road from the small town of Toltepec, in the
state of Chihuahua, came up to the Rio Grande, the fording
place was known as the old Apache Crossing. This was because the Indians used it in their shadowy traffic in and out of Texas from Old Mexico. It was not a place of good name, and only those traveled it who,
for reasons of their own, did not care to go over the river at the new
Upper Crossing.

This fact of border life was well understood by Colonel Fulgencio
Ortega. He had not forgotten the Indian back door to El Paso on the
American side. That is why he had taken personal charge of the guard
post of his troops at this point.

A very crafty man, Colonel Ortega.

And efficient.

It was not for nothing that the *descamisados*, the starving shirtless
poor, called him the Executioner of Camargo. Chihuahua had no more
distinguished son, nor another son half so well known in the ranks of
the irregular *rurales*, which was to say the stinking buzzards of the
border.

Now, with his men, a score of brutes so removed from decency and
discipline that only their upright postures stamped them as human beings, he lounged about the ashes of the supper fire. Some of the bestial
soldiers bickered over the cleaning of the mess kits. Others sat hunched
about a serape spread on the ground, belching and complaining of the

foulness of their luck with the cards and with the kernels of shelled corn
which passed for money among them. The heat of the evening was
stifling. Even with the sun now down at last beyond the Rio, it was still
difficult to breathe with comfort. The horseflies from the nearby picket
line still buzzed and bit like rabid foxes. It was a most unpromising
situation. In all of the long daylight they had wasted at the ford, no fish
had come to their net, no traveler from Toltepec had sought to pass the
crude barricade flung across the wagon road.

"*Válgame!*" announced Ortega. "God's name, but this is slow work,
eh, Chivo?"

The name meant "goat" in Spanish, and the bearded lieutenant who
responded to it seemed well described.

"True, jefe." He nodded. "But one learns patience in your service.
Also hunger. Hiding. Sand fleas. Body lice. How to use corn for money.
How to live on water with no tequila in it. Many things, Excellence."

Ortega smiled and struck him across the face with the butt of his
riding quirt. The blow opened the man's face and brought the bright
blood spurting.

"Also manners," said the Colonel quietly.

Chivo spat into the dirt. "*Si,*" he said, "also manners."

Presently, the man on duty at the barricade called to his leader that
someone was coming on the road.

"By what manner?" asked Ortega, not moving to rise.

"A burro cart."

"How many do you see?"

"Two. A man and a boy. Hauling firewood, I think."

"*Pah!* Let them go by."

"We do not search the cart, jefe?"

"For what? Firewood?"

"No, jefe, for *him;* these are Indians who come."

Instantly, Ortega was on his feet. He was at the barricade next moment, Chivo and the others crowding behind. All watched in silence
the approach of the small burro cart. Had they begun to pant or growl
it would have seemed natural, so like a half circle of wolves they appeared.

On the driver's seat of the cart, Díaz grew pale and spoke guardedly
to his small son.

"Chamaco," he said, "these are evil men who await us. Something
bad may happen. Slip away in the brush if there is any opportunity.
These are the enemies of our leader."

bad may happen. Slip away in the brush if there is any opportunity. These are the enemies of our leader."

"You know them, Papa, these enemies of our Presidente?"

"I know the one with the whip. It is Ortega."

"The Executioner?" The boy whispered the dread name, and Juliano Díaz, slowing the plodding team of burros, answered without moving his head or taking his eyes from the soldiers at the barricade.

"Yes, my son. It is him, the Killer of Camargo. As you value your life, do not speak the name of El Indio except to curse it. These men seek his life."

El Indio was the name of love which the shirtless ones had given the revolutionary President whom they had brought to power with their blood, but who now fought desperately for the life of his new government and for the freedoms which he sought to bring to the *descamisados* of all Mexico, be they Indians, such as himself and Juliano and Chamaco Díaz, or of the Spanish blood, or of any blood whatever. To the small boy, Chamaco, El Indio was like Christ, only more real. He had never seen either one, but he knew he would die for his Presidente and was not so sure about the Savior.

He nodded, now, in response to his father's warning, brave as any ten-year-old boy might be in facing the Executioner of Camargo.

As for Ortega, perhaps the sinister appelation was only a product of ignorance and rebelliousness on the parts of the incredibly poor Indians of the Motherland. He understood this for himself, it was certain. But being a soldier was hard work, and the people never comprehended the necessity for the precautions of military control. This did not mean that one of the Spanish blood could not be gracious and kind within the limitations of his stern duty. The Colonel waved his whip pleasantly enough toward the burro cart.

"Good evening, citizen," he greeted Díaz. "You are surprised to see us here, no doubt. But the delay will be slight. Please to get down from the cart."

"*¿Qué pasa?*, Excellence. What is the matter?" In his fear, Díaz did not obey the request to step down but sat numbly on the seat.

"Ah, you know me!" Ortega was pleased. "Well, it has been my work to get acquainted among the people of El Indio. Did you hear my order?"

"What?" said Díaz. "I forget. What did you say, Colonel?"

Ortega moved as a coiled snake might move. He struck out with his whip, its thong wrapping the thin neck of Juliano Díaz. With a violent

"I said to get down, *Indio*," he smiled. "You do not listen too well. What is the matter? Do you not trust your Mexican brothers?"

Díaz was small in body only. In heart he was a mountain.

"You are no brothers of mine!" he cried. "I am an Indian!"

"Precisely," answered Ortega, helping him up from the dirt of the roadway. "And so is he whom we seek."

Díaz stood proudly, stepping back and away from the kind hands of Colonel Fulgencio Ortega. He made no reply, now, but the boy on the seat of the burro cart leaped down and answered for him.

"What!" he exclaimed, unable to accept the fact anyone would truly seek to do ill to the beloved Presidente. "Is it true then that you would harm our dear — " Too late, he remembered his father's warning and cut off his words. Ortega liked boys, however, and made allowances for their innocence.

"Calm yourself, little rooster," he said kindly. "I said nothing of harming El Indio. Indeed, I said nothing of your great Presidente in any way. Now how is it you would have the idea that it is *him* we look for, eh?"

All of Mexico knew the answer to the question. For weeks the outlands had thrilled to the whisper that El Indio would make a journey to the United States to find gold and the hand of friendship from the other great Presidente, Abraham Lincoln. It was understood such a journey would be in secret to avoid the forces of the enemy en route. But from Oaxaca to the Texas border the *descamisados* were alerted to be on the watch for "the Little Indian" and to stand at all times ready to help forward the fortunes of his journey.

Chamaco Díaz hesitated, not knowing what to say.

His father, brave Juliano, broke into the growing stillness to advise him in this direction.

"Say nothing, my son," he said quietly, and stood a little taller as he said it.

Chamaco nodded. He, too, straightened and stood tall beside his father.

They would talk no more, and Ortega understood this.

"My children," he said, "you have failed to comprehend. We do not seek to harm the Presidente, only to detain him."

If standing tall, Chamaco was still but a small boy. He had not learned the art of dishonesty.

"Why do you stop *us*, then, Colonel? he demanded. "We are only poor wood gatherers from Toltepec, going to El Paso."

"Just exactly my problem," explained Ortega, with a flourish of the whip. "You see, *probrecito*, it is my order that every Indian going across the border must be measured against that line which you will see drawn on the dead oak tree." He pointed to the sunblasted spar with the whip. "Do you see the line on the tree?"

"Yes, Colonel."

"Well, it is drawn five feet from the ground, *chico*. That is just about the tallness of your great Presidente, not being too precise. Now the problem is that I, myself, am not familiar with this great man. I would not know him if I saw him. But we have his height reported to us, and I have devised this method of — shall we say? — ruling out the chance that El Indio shall get over the river into the United States and complete his journey."

"Colonel," broke in Juliano Díaz, going pale despite his great courage, "what is it you are saying?"

Ortega shrugged good-naturedly.

"Only that if you are an Indian not known to me, or to my men, and if your height is the same as that of El Indio, and if I detain you, then I have prevented a possible escape of your great Presidente, eh?"

"You mean that you think I, Juliano Díaz of Toltepec, am —" He could not finish the thought, so absurd was it to his simple mind. Could this rebel colonel truly believe such a thing? That he, Díaz, was the leader, the great El Indio? Díaz gave his first hint of a relieved look. It may even have been the trace of a smile. There was, after all, and even with the sore neck from the whip, something ironic about the idea. "Please, Excellence," Díaz concluded, forcing the small smile to widen for the sake of Chamaco's courage, "take me to the tree and put me against the mark, that my son and I may go on to El Paso. I have not been well, and we need the pesos from this wood to buy medicine in Texas."

"Chivo," snapped Ortega, no longer smiling, "measure this Indian!"

Chivo seized Díaz and dragged him to the tree. Pushing him against its scarred trunk, he peered at the line.

"He comes exactly to it, jefe. Just the right size."

"Very well. Detain him."

The matter was finished for Colonel Ortega. He turned back to the fire. He did not look around at the pistol shot which blew out the brains of Juliano Díaz. To a scrofulous sergeant, even with the startled, sobbing cry of Chamaco Díaz rising behind him, he merely nodded

irritably. "Coffee, Portales. Santa Maria, but it is hot! Curse this river
country."

What would have been the fate of Chamaco, the son, no man may
say. Chivo was hauling him to the fire by the nape of his neck, pistol
poised to finish him as well, with the Colonel's permission. Also, no
man may say if Ortega would have granted the favor. For in the instant of death's hovering, a thunder of hooves arose on the American
side of the river and a rider, tall sombrero proclaiming his Mexican
identity, dashed his lathered mount across the ford and to a sliding stop
by the fire of the Executioner of Camargo.

"Colonel!" he cried. "I come from El Paso! Great news is there. El
Indio is in the town. He has already been to see the American
Presidente and is on his way back to Mexico!"

Ortega stepped back as though cut in the face with his own whip.
The wolf pack of his men drew in upon him. Chivo, in his astonish-
ment that El Indio had gotten out of Mexico and was ready to come
back into it, dropped his rough hands from Chamaco Díaz. It was all
the signal from above that the quick-witted Indian youth needed. In
one scuttling dive he had reached the crowding growth of river brush
and disappeared, faithful, belatedly, to his dead father's instruction.

Chivo, pistol still smoking, led the yelping rush of the guerrilla band
after the boy. Ortega cursed on his men, raging about himself with the
lashing whip.

"Kill him, you fools!" he screamed. "He must not get over the river.
Shoot! Shoot! Stomp him out and shoot him. He must not warn the
Americans that we know they have El Indio! After him, after him, you
idiots!"

Deep in the brush, Chamaco wriggled and squirmed and raced for
his life. The rifle bullets of the renegades cut the limbs about him. The
cruel thorns of the mesquite and catclaw and black chaparral ripped
his flesh. He could hear the soldiers panting and cursing within a
stone's toss of his heels. He cried for his dead father as he ran, but he
ran! If God would help him, he would reach the other side of the river
and El Indio.

As the desperate vow formed in his mind, he saw ahead a clearing in
the tangled growth. Beyond it, the waters of the Rio Grande flowed
silver-red in the sunset dusk.

Riding through the twilight toward El Paso, the thoughts of Charlie

Shonto were scarcely designed to change the sunburned leather mold of his features — not, at least, for the happier.

A job was a job, he supposed, but it seemed to him that all the while the work got harder and the pay less.

Who the hell was he, Charlie Shonto? And what the devil was the Texas Express Company? And why should the two names cause him pain, now, as he clucked to his weary buckskin and said softly, aloud, "Slope along, little horse, there's good grass and water awaiting."

Well, there was an affinity betwixt the likes of Charlie Shonto and the Texas Express Company, even if it hurt. The latter outfit was a jerkwater stage line that had gotten itself about as rump-sprung as a general freight and passenger operation might manage to do and still harness four sound horses, and Shonto was a "special agent" for the stage company. But Charlie Shonto did not let the fancy title fool him. There was a shorter term, and a deal more accurate, for the kind of work he did for Texas Express. If a man said it with the proper curl of lip, it came out something awfully close to "hired gun."

Shonto didn't care for the label. He didn't especially relish, either, the risks involved in wearing it. But a "riding gun," be he on the driver's box with an L.C. Smith or Parker on his lap, or in the saddle with a Winchester booted under his knee, made good money for the better jobs. The better jobs, of course, were those in which the survival odds were backed down to something like, or less than, even money. So it was no surprise to Shonto to be sent for by Texas Express for a "special assignment." The surprise might lie in the assignment, itself, but the sun-tanned rider doubted it. It could be assumed that when Texas Express sent for Charlie Shonto, the "opportunity for advancement" was one already turned down by the Rangers and the U.S. Army, not to mention Wells Fargo, Overland Mail, or any of the big staging outfits.

Shonto clucked again to the *bayo coyote*, the line-backed buckskin dun, that he rode.

"Just around the bend, Butterball." He grinned dustily. "Billets for you and bullets for me."

Butterball, a gaunt panther of a horse which appeared wicked and rank enough to eat rocks without spitting out the seeds, rolled an evil eye back at his master and flagged the ragged pennant of his left ear. If he had intended further comment than this one look of tough disgust, the urge was short-circuited.

Scarcely had the comment about "bullets" left Shonto's lips than a respectable, if well-spent, hail of them began to fall around him in the thicket. Next instant, the sounds of the rifle shots were following the leaden advance guard in scattered volleys.

Instinctively, he ticked Butterball with the spurs, and the bony gelding sprinted like a quarter-mile racer for the near bend ahead. When he brought Shonto around that bend, the latter hauled him up sharply. Across the Rio Grande a tattered company of Mexican irregulars were target-practicing at a dark, bobbing object in midstream. Shonto's immediate reaction was one of relief that the riflemen had not been firing at him. The next thought was a natural curiosity as to what they had been firing at. It was then the third message reached his tired mind, and his mouth went hard. *That was a little kid swimming for the American side out there.*

The night was well down. In the Texas Express office in El Paso, three men waited. The drawn shade, trimmed lamp, the tense glances at the wall clock ticking beyond the way-bill desk, all spoke louder than the silence.

"I wish Shonto would get here," complained the express agent, Deems. "It ain't like him to be late. Maybe Ortega crossed over the river under dark and blind-sided him."

The second man, heavy-set, dressed in eastern clothing, calm and a little cold, shook his head.

"Shonto isn't the type to be blind-sided, Deems. You forget he's worked for me before. I didn't exactly pull his name out of a hat."

Deems stiffened. "That don't mean Ortega didn't pull it out of a sombrero!"

Sheriff Nocero Casey, last of the trio, nodded.

"Deems is right, Mr. Halloran. I don't care for Charlie being late either. It *ain't* like him. If Ortega did hear we had sent for Charlie Shonto —" He broke off, scowling.

Halloran took him up quickly. "It's not Shonto being late that is really bothering you, is it? I counted on you, Sheriff. I didn't dare import a bunch of U.S. marshals. I hope you're not getting cold feet."

"No, sir. It's common sense I'm suffering from. This job is way out of my bailiwick. The government ought to send troops or something to see it through. It's too big."

Again Halloran shook his head. "The U.S. government can't set one toe across that river, Sheriff. You know that. It's the law. That's why we've brought in your 'special agent.' Mr. Shonto is a man who understands the law. He appreciates its niceties, its challenges."

"Yeah, I've often wondered about that," said the Sheriff. "But I won't argue it."

"Ah, good. You see, there is no law which says Texas Express cannot ship a consignment such as our invaluable Item Thirteen into Toltepec. It will be done every day now that the new Mexican Central line has reached that city."

Agent Deems interrupted this optimism with a groan.

"Good Lord, Mr. Halloran, what's the use of talking about what we can ship when that cussed Mexican Central Railroad starts running regular between Toltepec and Mexico City? They ain't even run one work engine over that new line that I know of. Them blamed ties that are laid into Toltepec are still oozing greenwood sap!"

Halloran's heavy jaw took a defiant set.

"Are your feet feeling the chill, also, Deems? I thought we had the plan agreed to. Where's the hitch?"

Agent Deems stared at his questioner as if the latter had taken leave of whatever few senses government secret service opertives were granted in the beginning.

"Where's the hitch, you say? Oh, hardly anywhere at all, Mr. Halloran. You're only asking us to deliver this precious Item Thirteen of yours to railhead in Toltepec, Mexico, fifty miles across the river, tonight, with no one wise, whatever, right square through Colonel Fulgencio Ortega's northern half of the loyalist guerrilla army, guaranteeing to get our 'shipment' on the train at Toltepec safe and sound in wind and limb and then to come back a-grinning and a-shrugging and a-saying, 'Why, shucks, it wasn't nothing. It's done every day.' Mister, you ain't just plain crazy, you're extra fancy nuts."

"As bad as all that, eh?"

"Fair near," put in Sheriff Casey. "We don't know if that Mexican train will be in Toltepec. We don't even know if those wild-eyed coffee beans even *got* a train. All we know is that you government men tell us they got the train, and that it'll be in Toltepec if we get this Item Thirteen there. Now that's a heck of an 'if.'"

Halloran was careful. He knew that only these local people — Texans familiar with every coyote track and kitfox trail leading into Chihuahua — could bring off the delivery of Item Thirteen. Nothing must go wrong now.

"If we took Item Thirteen five thousand miles, Sheriff, surely Texas Express ought to be able to forward shipment the remaining fifty miles to Toltepec."

"Huh!" said Deems Harter. "You got one whack of a lot more faith in Texas Express than we have. In fact, about forty-nine miles more. As agent, I'll guarantee to get your precious shipment exactly one mile. That's from here to the Rio Grande. Past that, I wouldn't give you a nickel for your chances of making that train in Toltepec. *If* there's a train in Toltepec."

Halloran shook his head, unmoved.

"I'm not exactly thinking of my faith in terms of Texas Express, Harter. It's Charlie Shonto we're all gambling on."

"Yeah," said Harter acridly. "And right now Charlie Shonto looks like a mighty poor gamble."

"Well, anyways," broke in Sheriff Nocero Casey, who had drifted to the front window for another look up the street, "a mighty wet one. Yonder comes our special delivery man, and it looks to me as though he's already been across the river. He's still dripping."

Halloran and Harter joined him in peering from behind the drawn shade. It was the express agent who recovered first.

"Good Lord!" he gasped. "What's that he's toting behind him?"

Sheriff Nocero Casey squinted carefully.

"Well," he said, "the bright lights of El Paso ain't precisely the best to make bets by, but if I had to take a scattergun guess at this distance and in the dark, I'd say it was a sopping-wet and some-undersized Chihuahua Indian boy."

In the shaded office of the Texas Express Company, the silence had returned again. First greetings were over. Shonto and Halloran had briefly touched upon their past experiences during the war between the states, and the time had very quickly run down to that place where everyone pauses, knowing that the next words are the ones that the money is being paid for. Sheriff Casey, Agent Harter, Shonto, even little Chamaco Díaz, all were watching P. J. Halloran.

"Now, Charlie," said the latter, at last, "we haven't sent for you to review the squeaks you've been in before." He let the small grimace which may or may not have been a smile pass over his rough features. "But I did feel that some slight mention of our past associations might prepare you for the present proposal."

"What you're saying, Mr. Halloran, is that you figure your Irish blarney is going to soften up my good sense."

Shonto's own grin was a bit difficult to classify. It was hard as flint and yet warmed too, somehow, by a good nature or at least a wry appreciation of life as it actually worked out in the living.

"But you're wasting your talents," he concluded. "I've had a couple of birthdays since I was crossing the Confederate lines for you, and now I don't sign up just for a pat on the back from my fellow countrymen. I've learned since the war that a man can't buy a bag of Bull Durham with a government citation. Not that I regret my time in the 'silent service,' mind you. But a fellow just doesn't like to be a hog about the hero business. Especially when he did his great deeds for the North, then went back to earning his keep in the South. If you spend your time in Texas, Mr. Halloran, you don't strain yourself reminding the local folks that you took your war pay in Union greenbacks."

Halloran nodded quickly.

"Don't be a fool, Charlie," he said. "Harter, here, and Sheriff Casey were carefully sounded out before we ever mentioned your name. They are not still afire with the Lost Cause. We can forget your war work."

"I'm glad you told me, Mr. Halloran. Somehow, I still remember it every so often. Matter of fact, I still occasionally wake up in a cold sweat. Now I can put all that behind me. Isn't it wonderful?"

"Shonto" — Halloran's hard face had turned cold again — "come over here to the window. I want to show you something." He took a pair of binoculars from Harter's desk, and Shonto followed him to the drawn shade. There, Halloran gave the glasses to him and said quietly, "Look yonder on the balcony of the Franklin House. Tell me what you see. Describe it exactly."

From the other's tone, Shonto knew the talk had gotten to the money point. He took the glasses and focused them on the hotel's second-story *galería*, the railed porch so common to the southwestern architecture of the times. As the view came into sharp detail, he frowned uneasily.

"All right," he began, low voiced. "I see a man. He's short, maybe not much over five feet. He stands straight as a yardstick. Stocky build. Big in the chest. Dark as hell in the skin, near as I can say in the lamplight from the room windows behind him. He's dressed in a black Eastern suit that don't fit him, and same goes for a white iron collar and necktie. Black hat, no creases, wore square like a sombrero. Long black hair, bobbed off like it was done with horse shears." He paused, squinting more narrowly through the binoculars. "Why," he added softly, "that's a blasted Indian dressed up in white man's clothes!"

"That," said P. J. Halloran, just as softly, "is exactly what it is." They turned from the window. "Up there on that balcony," Halloran continued, "is the most important man, next to Lincoln, in North America. I can't reveal his identity, and you will have to know him as Item Thirteen, until you have him safely on that waiting train at Toltepec."

"What train at Toltepec?" Shonto frowned. "Since when have they built the Mexican Central on into that two-burro burg?"

"Since today, we hope," said Halloran. "The idea was that, precisely as you, no one knew the railroad had been laid on into Toltepec. Those last few thousand yards of track were to be spiked down today. The gamble is that not even Ortega and the *rurales* would hear about it in time. Or, hearing of it, not realize a train was waiting to be run over it."

"That's what I'd call house odds, Mr. Halloran. This Item Thirteen must be one heck of a table-stakes man."

"He's one heck of a man," answered the government operative. "Anyway, Charlie, the train is supposed to be waiting at midnight in Toltepec. If we can get Item Thirteen there, the train can get on down past Camargo by daybreak and out of Ortega's reach — *if* the train's waiting in Toltepec."

"Longest two-letter word in the world," said Shonto. "Go ahead, drop the other boot."

"Well, we know that powerful enemies lie between El Paso and Toltepec. There's no point explaining to you the type of enemy I mean. I believe you're familiar enough with Colonel Ortega and his loyal militia."

"Yes, just about familiar enough. In case you're still wondering how Chamaco and I got ourselves doused in the Rio, it was meeting Ortega's loyal army, or as big a part of it as I came prepared to handle. I'd say there was twenty of them. They were pot-shooting at the kid swimming the river. He got away from them while they were murdering his father. Butterball got excited at the rifle fire and ran away with me: bolted right into the river. Next thing I knew, I was in as bad shape as the kid, and, long as I figured two could ride as cheap as one, I scooped him up and we made it back to the American side by way of hanging onto Butterball's tail and holding long breaths under water on the way. I have got to get me another horse. In my business, you can't be fooling around with jumpy crowbaits like that."

"When you decide what you want for Butterball," put in Sheriff Nocero Casey, "let me know. I've been looking for just such a loco horse."

"Charlie," broke in Halloran, "are you interested or not? We've got to move soon."

Shonto nodded speculatively, a man not to be rushed.

"Depends. You haven't dropped that other boot yet."

"All right." Halloran spoke quickly now. "The small man in the black suit carries a letter of credit — a U.S. letter of credit — for an enormous amount of money. Some say as high as fifty million dollars. That's fifty million U.S., not Mexican. It's to bail out his revolution down there." Halloran gestured toward the Rio Grande and Mexico. "I don't need to tell you, Charlie, what men like Ortega will do to prevent that letter from getting to Mexico City. The money means the rebels are through — loyalists, they call themselves — and that the revolution will succeed and will stay in power. As you have already learned when your horse ran away with you, Colonel Ortega has been assigned the job of sealing off the border in Chihuahua State. Now, it becomes your job to unseal that border."

Charlie Shonto's grin was dry as dust.

"Shucks, nothing to that — nothing that I couldn't do with ten or twelve companies of Rangers and a regiment of regular Cavalry."

"Don't joke, Charlie." Halloran pulled out an official document and handed it to Shonto. "Here are my orders. You don't need to read them. But check that final postscript at the bottom of the page against the signature beneath the Great Seal of this country you and I fought for, when *he* asked us to."

Shonto glanced down the page, reading aloud slowly.

"'Any man who may aid the bearer of these orders in the business to hand will know that the gratitude of his government and my own personal indebtedness shall be his and shall not be forgotten. [Signed] A. Lincoln.'

"Well now," he said, handing back the document as gingerly as though it were the original of the Declaration of Independence. "Why didn't you say so, Mr. Halloran?"

"Like you" — Halloran smiled, and this time there was no doubt it was a smile — "I always save my best shot for the last target. What do you say, Charlie?"

"I say, let's go. For *him* I'd wrestle a bear, blindfolded. Who all's in it?"

"Just you, Charlie. I've brought our man this far. Sheriff Casey and Agent Harter have handled him here in town. But from here to Toltepec, he's your cargo — *if* you'll accept him."

Shonto winced perceptibly.

"There's that word again. You got anything extra to go with it this time?"

Halloran picked up a rolled map from Harter's desk.

"Only this chart of the area between here and Toltepec supplied by the Mexican Government. You know this ground as well as any man on this side of the Rio Grande. Take a look at this layout of it and tell us if you spot any way at all of getting past Ortega's patrols, into Toltepec."

He spread the map on the desk. Harter turned up the wick, and the four men bent over the wrinkled parchment. Behind them, the little Indian, Chamaco Díaz, had been forgotten. He stood silently in the shadows, wondering at the talk of these *Americans*. Chamaco had been to school some small time in El Paso and knew enough English to follow the conversation in the rough. Lonely and sorrowful as he was, he knew who that other little Indian in the black suit was, and his heart swelled with love and pride for these *American* men, that they would talk of risking their lives that El Indio might live and might reach *Mexico City* with the United States money which would save the Presidente's brave government of the *descamisados* and *pobrecitos* such as his father, Juliano Díaz, who had given their lives to establish it. Now, Chamaco watched the four big *Americans* bent over the map of Toltepec — his part of the beloved Motherland — and he waited with held breath what the verdict of the one tall man with the dried leather face would be.

For his part, the latter was having considerable last doubts. The map wasn't showing him anything he didn't already know. Presently, he glanced up at Halloran.

"There's no help here," he said. "I was hoping to see an old Apache route I've heard stories of. But this map shows nothing that wouldn't get me and the little man in the black suit stood up against the same tree that Chamaco's daddy was stood up against. Ortega knows all these trails."

"There's nothing, then? No way at all?"

"Yes, there's that Apache brush track. It was never found by the Rangers, but they know it exists. They've run the Chihuahua Apaches right to the river, time and again, then seen them vanish like smoke into midnight air. If we knew where that trail went over the Rio, we might have a coyote's chance of sneaking past Ortega's assassins." Shonto shook his head. "But there isn't a white man alive who knows that Apache track. . . ."

His words trailed off helplessly, and the four men straightened with that weary stiffness which foretells defeat. But into their glum silence a small voice, and forgotten, penetrated thinly.

"*Señores*, I am not a white man."

Shonto and his companions wheeled about. Chamaco moved out of the shadows into the lamplight.

"I am an Indian," he said, "and I know where the old trail runs."

The four men exchanged startled looks and, in their momentary inability to speak, Chamaco thought that he detected reproof for his temerity in coming forward in the company of such powerful friends of Mexico. He bowed with apologetic humility and stepped back into the shadows.

"But of course," he said, small-voiced, "you would not trust to follow an Indian. Excuse me, *Señores*."

Shonto moved to his side. He put his hand to the thin shoulder. Telling the boy to follow him, he led the way to the office window. He held back the drawn shade while Chamaco, obeying him, peered down the street at the Franklin House.

"Boy," he said, "do you know who that small man is standing up there on the hotel balcony?"

Chamaco's eyes glowed with the fire of his pride.

"Yes, patrón!" he cried excitedly. "It is *him!* Who else could stand and look so sad and grand across the river?"

Shonto nodded. "You think *he* would trust an Indian boy?"

Chamaco drew himself up to his full four feet and perhaps five inches. In his reply was all the dignity of the poor.

"Patrón," he said, "he once *was* an Indian boy!"

Charlie Shonto nodded again. He tightened the arm about the boy's shoulders and turned to face the others.

"Don't know about you," he said to them, "but I've just hired me an Indian guide to Toltepec."

The men at the desk said nothing, and again Chamaco misinterpreted their hesitation.

"Patrón," he said to Charlie Shonto, "do *you* know who it is up there standing on the *galería* looking so sad toward Mexico?"

"I could take an uneducated guess," answered Shonto, "but I won't.

You see, Chamaco, I'm not supposed to know. He's just a job to me. It doesn't matter who he is."

The Indian boy was astounded. It passed his limited comprehensions.

"And you would risk your life for a stranger to you?" he asked, unbelievingly. "For an Indian in a rumpled white man's suit? A small funny-looking man with a foreign hat and long hair and a dark skin the same as mine? You would do this, patrón, and for nothing?"

Shonto grinned and patted him on the head.

"Well, hardly for nothing, boy."

"For what, then, patrón?"

"Money, boy. Pesos. Muchos pesos."

"And only for that, patrón?"

At the persistence, Shonto's cynical grin faded. He made a small, deprecatory gesture. It was for Chamaco alone; he had forgotten the others.

"Let's just say that I was watching your face when you looked up at that hotel balcony a minute ago. All right, *amigo?*"

The dark eyes of Chamaco Díaz lit up like altar candles.

"Patrón," he said, "you should have been an Indian; you have eyes in your heart!"

Shonto grinned ruefully. "Something tells me, boy, that before we get our cargo past Ortega tonight we'll be wishing I had those eyes in the back of my head."

Chamaco reached up and took the gunman's big hand. He patted it reassuringly. "Patrón" — he smiled back — "do not be afraid. If we die, we die in a good and just cause. We lose only our two small lives. Him, up there on the *galería*, he has in his hands the lives of all of the poor people of Mexico. Is that not a very fair exchange, our lives for all of those others, and for his?"

Shonto glanced at the other men. "Well, Chamaco," he said, "that's one way of looking at it. Excuse us, gentlemen: we've got a train to catch in Toltepec."

He took the boy's hand in his and they went out into the street. Halloran moved to follow them. At the door he halted a moment, shaking his head as he looked back at the express agent and the sheriff.

"Do you know what we've just done?" he said. "We've just bet fifty million dollars and the future of Mexico on a Chihuahua Indian kid not one of us ever laid eyes on prior to twenty minutes ago. I need a drink!"

The coach bounced and swayed through the night. Its side lamps, almost never lit, were now sputtering and smoking. They seemed to declare that this particular old Concord wanted to be certain her passage toward the lower ford would be noted from the far side — and followed.

The idea was valid.

The lower crossing, the old Apache route, was the way in which a mind of no great deception might seek to elude examination by the *rurales* at the upper, or main, crossing. The driver of the old Texas Express vehicle, a canvas-topped Celerity model made for desert speed, held the unalterable belief that the Mexican mind was so devious as to be very nearly simple. It twisted around so many times in its tracks, trying to be clever, that in the end it usually wound up coming right back where it started.

The driver was banking on this trait. He was depending on Colonel Fulgencio Ortega to think that, when the planted rumor from El Paso reached him by avenue of his kinsmen in that city, he would say, "Aha! This stupid *American* stage-line company thinks that if they announce they will try to cross with El Indio at the old lower ford, that I shall at once conclude they really mean to cross at the new upper ford, and that I shall then be waiting for them at the new upper ford and they can cross in safety at the lower place. What fools! I shall quite naturally watch both crossings, and this they realize full well. What they are trying to do is see that I, personally, am not at the lower ford. They think that if they can contest the crossing with my men — without me — it will be a far easier matter. Well, now! ¡Ai, Chihuahua! Let them come. Let them find out who will be waiting for their disreputable stagecoach and its mysterious passenger at the old lower ford! Hah! Why will they attempt to match wits with the Executioner of Camargo?"

Of course, if Colonel Ortega did not reason thus, the driver of the coach would have made a grievous error, for the entire plan depended on meeting the Executioner.

The driver, a weatherbeaten, leathery fellow, wrapped the lines of the four-horse hitch a bit tighter. He spoke to his leaders and his wheelers, tickling the ears of the former and the haunches of the latter with the tip of his fifteen-foot coaching whip.

"Coo-ee, boys!" he called to the horses. "Just so, just so." Leaning over the box, he spoke to the muffled, dark-faced passenger — the only passenger — in the rocking stage. "*Señor*, it is all well with you in there?" He used the Spanish tongue, but no reply came in kind from the interior. Indeed, no reply came in any tongue.

A very brave fellow, thought the driver. His kind were not many in the land-below the Rio — or any land.

"You are a very small boy," said the somber-looking little man. "How is it that you are so brave?"

"Please, Presidente. I beg of you not to say more, just now. We are very near to the place, and there is great danger." Chamaco spoke with awed diffidence.

"I am not afraid, boy." El Indio patted him on the shoulder. "Do I not have a good Indian guide?"

"Presidente, please, say no more. You don't know Colonel Ortega."

"I have dealt with his kind. I know him, all right. They are all alike. Cowards. Jackals. Don't be afraid, boy. What did you say your name was?"

Chamaco told him, and the small man nodded.

"A good Indian name. It means what it says. How much farther now, boy, before we cross the river?"

They were moving on foot through a tunneled avenue in the river's brushy scrub of willow and rushes. It was the sort of thoroughfare frequented by the creatures of the night. None but very small men — or boys — might have used it at all, and then only very small Indian men or boys. If the Rangers had wanted to know one reason, just one, why the Apaches raiding up from Chihuahua had been able to disappear before their eyes on the American side of the Rio, it would have been that they were seeking some "hole" in the brush which would accommodate an ordinary mortal, not a Chihuahua Indian. But Chamaco Díaz was not alone a small Indian boy; he was a patriot.

"Presidente," he now pleaded, "will you not be quiet? *Por favor*, Excellence! We are coming to it this moment."

The small man in the black suit smiled.

"You dare to address me in this abrupt manner!" he said. "You, an Indian boy? A shirtless waif of the border? A brush rat of the river bottom? *Ai!*"

"Presidente," said the boy, "I will ask it one more time. I know that you do not fear the Executioner. I know that I am only a *pobrecito*, a *reducido*, a nothing. But in my heart you live with the Lord Jesus. I will die for you, Presidente, as I would for Him, even sooner. But I have sworn to guide you across the river and to the rendezvous. I have sworn to get you to Toltepec by midnight this night. Therefore, why should we die, when you must live for the people of our suffering land? I am taking you to Toltepec, Presidente. And if you continue to speak along the way, I will die for nothing and Mexico will never get the money you bear and she will not be saved. But mostly, Presidente, you will be dead. I cannot bear that. You are the life of all of us."

They had stopped moving. El Indio, in a streak of moonlight penetrating the arched limbs above them, could see the tears coursing down the dark cheeks of Chamaco Díaz. He reached quickly with his fingers and brushed away the tears.

"An Indian does not weep," he told the boy sternly. "Go ahead, now. I shall be still."

Chamaco swallowed hard. He dashed his own hand quickly at the offending eyes. His voice was vibrant with pride.

"It was the brush, Presidente, the small limbs snapping back and stinging me across the face. You know how it is."

El Indio nodded once more.

"Of course, boy. I have been in the brush many times. Go ahead, show the way. I have been an old woman, talking too much. We are both Indians, eh? Lead on."

Straight as a rifle barrel, Chamaco Díaz stood before him a moment. Then, ducking down again, he scuttled on ahead. El Indio watched him go. Just before he bent to follow, he glanced up at the patch of moonlight. The beams struck his own dark face. They glistened on something which seemed to be moist and moving upon his own coffee-colored features. But then of course in moonlight the illusions are many, and the lunar eye is not to be trusted. Had he not just said, himself, that Indians did not weep?

The coach of the Texas Express Company splashed over the old Apache Crossing and came to a halt before the flaring bonfire and wooden barricade across the Toltepec road. *¿Qué pasa?"* the tall driver called down to the leering brigand who commanded the guard. "What is the matter? Why do you stop me?"

"De nada. It is nothing." Lieutenant Chivo smiled. "A small matter which will take but a moment. I hope you have a moment. *Yes? Very well. Colonel,"* he called to the squat officer drinking coffee by the fireside, "the stage for Toltepec has arrived on time."

The Colonel put down his tin cup and picked up a long quirt. Uncoiling the whip, he arose and came over to the barricade. He stood a moment looking up at the coachman. With the pause, he nodded pleasantly enough and spoke in a friendly manner.

"Please to get down," he said.

"Sorry, I can't do it," replied the driver. "Company rules, Colonel. You understand."

"Of course," said the guerrilla chief easily. "Without rules nothing is accomplished. I'm a great believer in discipline. Did I introduce myself? Colonel Fulgencio Ortega, of Camargo. Now do you care to get down?"

"*The* Colonel Ortega?" said the American driver, impressed. "Jefe, this a great honor. And these are your famed *rurales?*" He pointed with unqualified admiration to the surly pack stalking up, now, to stand behind the colonel and his lieutenant. "My, but they are a fine-looking troop. Real fighters, one can see that. But then, why not? On the side of justice all men fight well, eh, Colonel?"

Ortega ignored the compliments.

"Did you hear what I said?" he asked. "I wish you to get down. I do not believe I have met your passenger, and I think you should introduce me to him. My men will hold your horses."

His men were already holding the horses, as the driver was keenly aware. Also, he did not miss the fact the soldiers were holding something else for him: their rifles — pointed squarely at him. But he was the steady sort, or perhaps merely stupid.

"Passenger?" he said. "I carry no passenger, Colonel. Just some freight for Toltepec."

Ortega stepped back. He looked again into the coach.

"Freight, eh?" he mused. "Strange wrappings you have put around your cargo, *cochero*. A black suit. Black hat with round Indian crown worn squarely on the head. And see how your freight sits on the seat of the coach, just as if it were alive and had two arms and two legs and might speak if spoken to. That is, if fear has not sealed its cowardly Indian tongue!" His voice was suddenly wicked with hatred, all the smile and the pretense of easiness gone out of it — and out of him. "Chivo!" he snapped. "Please to open the door of this coach and help El Presidente to dismount!"

The stage driver straightened on the box.

"El Presidente?" he said to Ortega. "Whatever in the world are you talking about, jefe?"

"We shall see in a moment." Ortega nodded, in control of himself once more. "Hurry, Chivo. This *cochero* does not understand the importance of his passenger. Nor is it apparent to him that jokes about 'freight' which walks and talks like an Indian are not laughed at in Chihuahua just now. *¡Adelante!* Get that coach door opened, you fool!"

Chivo, grinning as only a dog wolf about to soil the signpost of his rival may grin, threw open the door of the Concord and seized the lone passenger by the arm. With a foul-mouthed oath, he pulled the small figure from the coach and hurled it viciously to the ground.

His surprise was understandable.

It is not the usual thing for a victim's arm to come off at the shoulder and remain in the offending hand of its assaulter while the remainder of the torso goes flying off through the night. Neither was it the usual thing for the poor devil's head to snap off and go rolling away like a melon when the body thudded to earth.

"*¡Santísima!*" cried one of the brute soldiers of the guard. "You have ruined him, you dumb animal!"

But Lieutenant Chivo did not hear the remark, and Colonel Ortega, if he heard it, did not agree with the sentiment, except perhaps as to Chivo's intelligence. For what the guerrilla lieutenant had pulled from the Texas Express Company's Toltepec stage was quite clearly a dressmaker's dummy, clothed to resemble a very short and large-chested Mexican Indian man who always sat straight on his seat and wore his black hat squarely on his head.

Moreover, Colonel Fulgencio Ortega was given no real time in which to comment upon his soldier's awed remark or his lieutenant's amazed reaction to the arm in his hand and the head rolling free upon the firelit banks of the Rio Grande. For in the small moment of stricken dumbness which had invaded all of the *rurales* when El Presidente's body had come apart in mid-air, the American driver of the Toltepec stage had wrapped the lines of his four-horse hitch, stepped to the ground in one giant stride from the precarious box of the old Concord, and all in the same motion slid out a long-barreled Colt's revolver and buried its iron snout in the belly of the Executioner of Camargo.

"Jefe," he announced quietly. "if you make one false movement, your bowels will be blown out all over this riverbank," and this statement Colonel Fulgencio Ortega had no difficulty whatever in comprehending.

"Chivo!" he cried out. "In the name of María, hold the men. Let no one touch trigger!"

"Yes, Chivo." The leather-faced American *"cochero"* nodded, spin-ning Ortega around so that the muzzle of the Colt was in his spine. "And so that you do not in greed seek to replace your beloved jefe in command of the *rurales* of Camargo — that is to say, that you do not in this moment of seeming opportunity make some move deliberately to get me to shoot him — permit me to introduce myself."

"Ah?" queried Chivo, who truly had not yet thought of this obvious course of treachery to his leader. "And to what point would this be, *cochero?* Do you think that I am in fear of stagecoach drivers?"

The tall driver shrugged.

"Well, I think you ought to have the same break I give any other man I'm paid to get past."

There was something in the way that he spoke the one word "paid" which penetrated Chivo's wily mind. He hesitated, but two of the soldiers did not. Thinking that they stood well enough behind their companions to be safe, they moved a little aside from the pack to get a line of fire at the big *American.* The instant they were clear of their friends, however, flame burst from behind the back of Colonel Ortega — one lancing flash, then another — and the two soldiers were down and dying in the same blending roar of pistol shots.

"Shonto," said the stage driver to Chivo, the smoking muzzle of the Colt again in Ortega's spine. "Over there across the river, they call me Shonto."

"*¡Madre María!*" breathed Chivo, dropping his rifle, unbidden, into the dirt of the wagon road. "Carlos Shonto? *Por Dios, pistolero,* why didn't you say so?"

"I just did." Charlie Shonto nodded. "Now you better say something. Quick."

Chivo shrugged in that all-meaning way of his kind.

"What remains to die for?" he inquired. "You do not have El Indio in the stage. You have fooled us with the dummy on the ground over there. Somewhere, El Presidente is no doubt riding through the night. But it is not upon the stage for Toltepec. Another of our guards will get him. For us, the work of the day is over. Command me."

Shonto then ordered all the soldiers to drop their rifles and cartridge bandoleers. All knives, pistols, axes went into the common pile. This arsenal was then loaded into the stage along with Colonel Fulgencio Ortega, bound hand and foot by his faithful followers. The work went forward under Chivo's expert direction, the spirit of the *rurales* now totally flagged. With their chances of snaring El Indio had gone their interest in being heroes. Like soldiers everywhere, they were of no great menace in themselves. Deprived of leadership, they were just so many surly dogs quarreling among themselves. Shonto had gambled on this, and gambled exceeding well.

Yet, as in every risk, there lurks the element of the unknown, the thing that cannot be depended upon except in the name of "luck."

Shonto's luck ran out with the command he now issued to the scar-faced Chivo.

"All right, Lieutenant," he said. "Up you go. You'll be the *cochero* now. I'll ride shotgun. You savvy *'la escopeta?'*" With the question, he reached for the double-barreled Parker laid across the driver's box, and Chivo nodded hastily. He "savvied" shotguns very well. One did not argue with them at close range, not ever. But Shonto had made his basic mistake some time ago, when he had put the thought of succeeding to Ortega's place of power in Camargo in the mind of the brutal lieutenant. Such towering aspirations had never flooded his dark brain. True, he would have seen Ortega killed in a moment, should that suit his purpose. This much was exactly what Shonto had guessed. What the wary gunman had not foreseen, however, was that, until he, Shonto, had mentioned the matter, Chivo had never really thought about the possibility of promoting himself over his Colonel.

Now the prospect inflamed his jackal's mind.

"Whatever you say, jefe," he told Shonto, fanging a smirk which the latter hardly supposed was a grin of good nature. "You see, I climb to the seat gladly. I take the lines and am ready to drive for you. Come on. Let's go."

Shonto started to swing up after him. For one moment both hands were occupied. It was in that moment that the boot of Lieutenant Chivo drove into his face. Shonto fell backward, landing hard. The shotgun was still in his grasp but was useless from that angle. Above him, Chivo was shouting the horses into motion. The coach lurched forward. Shonto made it to his feet in time to leap for the trunk straps in the rear. He caught one of them, held on, and dragged behind the moving stage for fifty feet. He still had the shotgun in his right hand.

The soldiers, sensing his helplessness, ran toward him. They seized clubs and picked up rocks on the run. Chivo, in response to their yells, slowed the stage, thinking to allow them to beat and stone the dragging American.

Shonto held onto the trunk strap. When the snarling soldiers were near, he raised the shotgun and fired it with one hand into their faces.

The first barrel and the second blasted as one. The soldiers fell away, three to stagger and fall mortally wounded, two others clutching at their shredded faces, screaming in the agony of the immediate torture and the knowledge, even in their terrible pain, that they would never use their eyes again.

Chivo, on the driver's box, turned in time to see Shonto haul himself up over the rear of the Concord. He had no weapon, now, but neither did the *rurale* lieutenant.

Chivo knew the one way open to him and took it. Over the side he went, rolling to the ground and free of the speeding wheels, the excited teams running wild the moment he flung away the lines. Shonto, weaving precariously, made it to the driver's box and threw himself down between the straining horses to recover the lines.

His luck now returned. He was able to gather up the lines and return to the box, the coach under control and still upright on the wagon road to Toltepec.

But now he knew the wolf pack behind him had a leader again. He could guess how long it would take Chivo to mount the survivors and take up the pursuit.

"Coo-ee, coo-ee," he called to the snorting team. "Steady down, you beauties. You've not begun your night's work yet. Save that pep and vim for the last lap!"

Where he had said he would be waiting beside the wagon road to Toltepec with El Presidente, there Chamaco Díaz waited when, half an hour's loping run from the Rio, Shonto pulled up his panting horses and hailed the underbrush. The Indian boy had guided his charge without fail and on foot through the night and between the prowling soldiers of Colonel Ortega four miles south of the river. The ancient and secret Apache escape route from Texas, which the two had traveled to reach their rendezvous with Charlie Shonto and the stage for Toltepec, lay still unknown behind them. Shonto did not ask Chamaco where it ran, and the boy did not tell him. He was an Indian, even now, and Charlie Shonto was a white man.

Swiftly, then, the last part of the plan was put into operation. The four horses were unhooked from the coach. Four saddles and bridles were brought from the coach trunk, and the mounts were readied. Colonel Ortega was removed from the stage and hung over the saddle of one mount in the manner of a sack of grain. Shonto tied his hands to his feet under the horse's belly, halfway hoping the ropes would not hold.

Where the rutted track of the road bent to go past the rendezvous, an eighty-foot bluff rose above the Chihuahua plain. Over this drop, Shonto and his two Indian friends now tossed the Concord's load of firearms. There was no time for more effective disposal. Mounting up, the party set out, away from the road, Chamaco leading, Shonto bringing up the rear with the pack horse of the Executioner of Camargo. The goat path along which the small Indian boy took them disappeared into the desert brush within a pistol shot from the wagon road. Shonto had no more idea where the trail led than did Ortega or El Presidente. No options remained in any event. Behind them, along the road from the river, they heard now the shouts of men of Mexican tongue and the hammer of horses' hooves in considerable number. In a pause to listen, they all recognized the high yelping tones of Lieutenant Chivo, discovering the abandoned stage and guessing, amid a goat's beard of rotten curses, the manner of flight of his enemies. And more: from Chivo's murderous bleats, they made out that he had with him another patrol of Ortega's *rurales*, evidently encountered along the way. These new soldiers, whatever their number, would be armed and were clearly being commanded by the Colonel's good lieutenant. All might still have been well — yes, surely would have been so — considering the depth of the brushland and the blindness of its cover. But in the press of time and because he had not thought ahead to the complication of Chivo picking up more arms en route, Shonto had not taken the precaution he ordinarily would have of gagging the captive colonel.

He thought of it, now, as Ortega's galling shout echoed down the slope they were climbing.

¡Aquí, aquí, muchachos! I am here! I am here!"

His head was hanging on that side of the horse nearest Shonto. The shout for help was cut off by the toe of the gunman's boot knocking out four front teeth and knocking out, too, the owner of the teeth. But the price of poker had just gone up, regardless.

"Chamaco," he said, "we have one chance: to split up."

"Never, patrón."

"Listen, kid" — Shonto's voice went hard as quartz — "you do what I tell you. I'm running this show."

"No, my American friend, you are not." The denial did not come from the boy but from the small man in the black suit. "It is I who must say what will be. And I say we stay together. You are not with

Spaniards, my friend. You are not with traitors who call themselves
Mexicans. You are with Indians. Lead on, boy."

Shonto knew he was helpless. He knew, as well, that they were
helpless, that it would be but a matter of minutes before the *rurales*
would come up to them, blind brush or not. They were so close behind
that they could follow by ear the sounds of the stagecoach horses breaking through the brush. The rifle firing would commence any moment,
and a bullet, unaimed except by the noise of their ponies crashing
ahead, would soon enough find all and each of them. There was no
other end within reason.

Yet Chamaco Díaz was no victim of such knowledge.

He had been supported by his Presidente, had heard him with his
own ears say, "You are with Indians." What was not possible in the
service of such a man?

"¡Patrón!" he now called to Shonto, voice high and sharp with excitement. "There is a way. Follow me, and don't worry about making
noise. The Rangers from your *Tejas* side of the river did not always
obey the law!"

Their horses were plowing on up the slope now, and true to Shonto's
fear the guerrillas were beginning to fire blindly at the sound of their
progress. The bullets hissed and sung about them. But the boy's shout
had intrigued Charlie Shonto.

"What's that?" he yelled back.

"The Rangers of Texas," answered the boy, laughing for the first time
in Shonto's memory of him. "Many times they would run the Apaches
right on across the river, patrón. Then the Apaches had to have a way
on this side to 'lose' them. I know the way, patrón. Ride hard and jump
your horse when I demand it."

Shonto wanted to know more about that "jump" business, but the
guerrillas were too close now. All he could do was bend low in the saddle and hope the bullet with his name on it went astray. It did. They
came to Chamaco's "jumping place" without a wound. The place itself
was a declivity in the trail — dug by hand and centuries gone — where
no rider, not knowing that it waited beyond the steeply descending
hairpin turn which hid it from above, could ever lift his mount over it
in time. The animal's momentum, coming down the roof-steep pitch of
the decline, would have to carry it and its rider into the "Ranger trap."
And this is the way that it worked with the eager *rurales* of Chivo. All
of the horses of Chamaco's party, even the pack horse with Colonel
Ortega's unconscious form, cleared the break in the trail, leaping it like

deer because spurred to the effort by their desperate riders. But the mounts of the guerrillas, scrambling around the hairpin, snorting furiously under the urging of their savage masters — the scent of the kill hot in the nostrils now, so close were they — had no chance to see or to lift themselves and their riders over the yawning pit. Into the waiting blackness of the man-made chasm the first dozen horses and soldiers went screaming and kicking. Another dozen soldiers and their mounts piled up in the trail above and did not plunge into the abyss with the others. But neither did they seem to retain their previous eagerness for the blood of El Presidente and the elevation of Lieutenant Chivo to the rank of Executioner of Camargo.

As for Chivo, himself, Shonto never knew if he was among the first group of riders, or the second. All that he did know was that, following the first terrible spate of screamings from the fallen, he did not hear again the harsh yelping voice of the bearded lieutenant.

"*¡Madre!* Chamaco," he said to the Indian boy, in the first moment of stillness following the piteous cries from above, "what is in the Apache trench up there?"

"Tiger's teeth," said the youth, "their points burned to hardness of iron, their butts set in the cracks of the mother rock. I don't wonder at the screams, patrón. I've looked down in that hole."

"*¡Santísima!*" breathed Shonto. "A staked pit!"

"For a pack of animals, the death of a pack of animals." The Oaxacan accents of El Presidente seemed sad. "Let us go on and catch that train in Toltepec. There is so much work to do in Mexico. The people cry out to me, and there is little time, so little time, for me to answer them."

Shonto did not answer, feeling the moment belonged to another. Chamaco understood the courtesy.

"Yes, Presidente," he said softly. "Please to follow your humble servant."

At once the small man in the black suit spurred his horse up beside that of the Chihuahua Indian boy.

"You are no one's humble servant," he said sternly. "Remember that always. You are a citizen of Mexico, a free man, humble to no one. If you believe in a god, you can thank him for that. If you believe in a man, you can thank a man."

"Yes, Presidente, I thank you *and* God."

"In that order, eh, boy?" A trace of warm amusement crossed the dark Indian features. "But you are wrong about the man, *muchacho*. It is another Presidente whom I charge you to remember. See that you don't forget his name, citizen; you owe it your life. Burn it in your mind, if you are a true Mexican: *Abraham Lincoln.*"

It was all downhill from there. Some minutes short of midnight, Shonto rode into Toltepec with his charges. By a quarter past the hour, "Item Thirteen" was aboard the waiting train. Steam being up and the dawn all too near, the parting was abrupt. Camargo must be run past in the dark. Also, for the benefit of good health, those who must remain behind when the train pulled out would do well to be drawing in American air come sunrise of that risky day. El Presidente, surrounded by his faithful guard aboard the train, was virtually "taken away" from Shonto and Chamaco. So, as well, was the one-time Executioner of Camargo. In a last-second view, El Presidente seemed to spy the tall American and the tiny Indian boy sitting their horses in the lamplight spilling from his car's window. Shonto and Chamaco thought they saw him wave to them, and they returned the wave, each with his own thoughts. If the Texas gunman saw the bright tears streaming down the dark cheeks of Chamaco Díaz, he said nothing of the matter, then or later. Each man was permitted his own manner of farewell. But when the train had pulled away from Toltepec — before, even, its smoke had trailed into the Chihuahua night behind it — Charlie Shonto knew all he ever cared to know of the ending of the story. His big hand reached through the dark to touch the knee of his companion.

"Come along, Chamaco," he said. "We had better make long tracks. It's forty-nine miles to the river."

The boy nodded obediently, saying nothing. They turned their horses and sent them into a weary lope.

As they rode, Shonto's rawhide features softened. He was watching the proud set of the thin figure riding by his side. He was aware, surely, that the small Indian man in the ill-fitting black suit had been Benito Juárez, the libertor of Mexico, his people's Abraham Lincoln. But that part of it did not impress the big gunman unduly. For Charlie Shonto, the biggest Indian that he saw that night was always a little Chihuahua boy who barely reached to his gunbelt. History would not record, Shonto suspected, the secret fact that Juárez had been spirited to the Capitol in Washington, D.C. History would never record, he knew certainly, the added fact of the strange manner in which the legendary El Indio had been returned safely to his native land. But Charlie Shonto and Texas Express would know the way that it was done, and so would the tallest Indian in all of Toltepec!

When he thought of that, somehow even Charlie Shonto felt better. As the shadows of the Toltepec hills closed behind them, he was sitting as straight in the saddle as Chamaco Díaz.

But of course not as tall.

WHAT GODS ARE MINE

The Indian does not see the Earth as given to the People. He sees the people as given to the Earth. They are not its owners but its unsleeping tenant caretakers. The People are seen as no more important in the Indian Great Scheme of Things than any bird, fish, mammal, reptile or insect that shares the Mother Earth with them. Theirs was a religion, always, of Naturalism. There was not a shred of *humanitas* in the Indian view of Earth. He would never have thought that mankind comes first before all. The Mother Earth comes first. It did forever with the Indian. He says this over and over in his Memoirs. It was the Litany of his History. Recall only General O.O. Howard lecturing the Nez Perce as the white man failing utterly to understand this Indian theism:

> We do not wish to interfere with your religion, but you must talk about practicable things. Twenty times over you repeat that the earth is your mother, and about Chieftanship from the earth. Let us hear no more, but come to business at once.

"Come to business" — what a white man's phrase! And so, too, "at once." What a purblind white view of what the Indian saw in his Mother Earth!

In fact, the Indian religion says to the People, go thou forth and care for your Mother Earth. The Judeo-Christian religion instructs man to go forth and do what? Procreate, multiply, till, harvest, take possession, own, defend, use, seize, take, be fruitful, it is ALL YOURS.

When the White Eyes get it through their arrogant heads that the Indians were not humanists but animalists and naturalists, worshippers of nature, not humanity, then they will begin to understand about Indians, and why I love them so and write about them in all those books.

The Indian asked nothing of his fellow man.

He looked for everything to his Mother Earth.

Human life was not regarded as sacred.

There was nothing sacrosanct about "the People."

Not as a group, not as individuals.

The Indian saw the European white man who came to invade their wild free buffalo pastures as the Curse of the Earth. Not, mind you, as the Curse of the People. He correctly forecast what would become of his Mother, should the white man "take her." He said, "These People will not save our Mother as they say; they will violate her; they will kill her."

Well, good friends of *humanitas?*

What are those People doing today?

Can you tell me that *humanitas* is not killing *our* Mother Earth?

Ah! Just so.

It was Malthus who was right, not Marx.

There is a sovereign remedy for this dread fate the Indians dreamed for their Mother Earth from the white man's coming. It is a medicine to make your blood run chill, Horatio, and you shall not hear its name from my lips. Yet I say to you that it must be prescribed by whatever political physician we choose to summon, whether yours or my own or that of the man who is stranger to us both. The patient is dying. She cannot live except by heroic regimens. Our Terra, our Late Great Planet Earth, is being buried alive. And by what, God's Name? Aliens? Spacelings? Atomic dust? Not quite. She is being buried alive by *humanitas.* By the sheer uncaring overbreeding of more and more and forever more human beings, by other human beings, and we shall end this unspeakable cannibalizing of our own kind by all being the devourers of ourselves, literally copulating ourselves out of our last heritage, the fairest planet in the solar system, and by whom?

By ourselves!

Us.

You and me.

Humanitas.

The Indians foresaw it; he dreamed it rightly; the Indian knew.

We still don't know.

We do nothing to save ourselves from ourselves.

We deny the fact of Malthus.

We argue the fallacy of Marx, the folly of *laisse faire* capitalism, the rise of Mohammed, the return of the Nazarene, the litany of One World, the godliness of Man, the blather of being Born Again. There is no end to our snares, our delusions, our self-snorting of philosophical coke. We live by the Lotus and we shall die by it.

Man is running out of Earth.

I must die before that time, my friend, but you will live to starve in it. It will not be the nuclear holocaust, but the population bomb. You will not die from the finger on the trigger, but at the hand of your neighbor who will kill you for the last bite of food left in your cupboard. Then what of *humanitas?* What of this noble race you believe must come before everything?

For myself, I know what of *humanitas.* The Indians told us a long, long time of Vision Dreaming past. A man is only a human being. He does not come before anything. He is brother to the bear, the fox, the antelope, the deer, the buffalo, the eagle, the ant that is crushed, the spider that is stepped upon, nothing more than the least of these is man. In his time he will die as these brothers die in their times. His bones will molder as theirs. His flesh fall away. Only his spirit will be left, with their spirits, and in a little while no one will remember his name, or that he ever passed this way as a man, but only as a being brother to all the other beings put upon the Mother Earth by Wakan Tanka, Tiwara, Ussen, Maheo or Hunyewat.

Pressed to consider that man, unique among all living creatures, has an immortal soul — or deserves to have one — the Indian will fairly weigh the possibility in his mind, then ask from his heart, in sad wonder at the Wasicun, "You do not make holy the beast thy brother; why venerate thyself?"

It is a good question, Pale Eye brothers.

Do we have a good answer for it?

WILL HENRY AND
THE INDIANS

When an author of one race presumes to write books about another race, he must expect fire from both sides. When that author is white and that other race red, he had best be prepared to hit the sand and stay there, until the red brother has decided to give him back his life — which was usually the Indian way, regardless of the white man's history books.

It's a hard place for the white author to be.

He is trapped on a literary Beecher's Island. No matter which way he runs, he is going to run into Indians.

One would imagine this to be self-evident to the Anglo writer and anticipate that he would be braced to absorb the Indian fire from whatever direction. That would be the logical assumption. As a matter of working fact it isn't true. The fire does not come from the red brother; it comes from the white brother — in the back.

After 30 years and 23 novels on the fighting horseback Indians of the West, this author has yet to hear in anger from one Indian reader. The Indian reader seems to understand the white brother means well, is trying, in his awkward way, to make amends for the past, hold out some hopes for the future, and is using his books as the best way that he knows to render a personal tribute to the American Indian.

The Indian, gracious in his poet's way, sly and knowing in his unfailing good humor, seems to reason that it is all right if the white man wants to try. What possible harm? After all, even a gelding can try. Let the Wasicun have his say. The Shacun knows what he knows.

But what about the white brother?

How gracious, how good humored has he been in his judgments of his fellow white man's Indian novels?

On the whole, the cross-mix of readers has not been unkind. Those who seek to be entertained, who read judgmentally in critique, or who assess the books as American Western Literature from the tenured purview of Academia, all have tended to be fair; with an embarrassing exception in the latter group, a certain pundit/professor who thinks dim of Indians, dimmer still of white men who find wonderment and romance in Indians, dimmest of all of that one old white man who devoted those 30 years and 23 books to his love affair with the Amerind.

The writer does not feel sorry for either the Indian, or for the old white man in this case. He feels sorry for the isolated savant who does not really understand anything about old white men, and less than that about Indians. Let us leave him to his narrowed trail. Upon it, he meets only those who agree with him.

As for Will Henry, his books from *No Survivors* and *The Last Warpath*, to *From Where The Sun Now Stands*, *Maheo's Children* and *Chiricahua*, have honored and respected the Indian. If some wish to render that romanticized and glorified, even with the pejorative sniff, the writer has it direct from Old Will himself that he can live with such woundings. Indeed, prosper. Given his own choice of lives, as surely as vermilion and ochre are the paints of war, Will Henry would have been born a horseback Indian of the high plains, riding wild and free and forever far away from the haunts of the white man, racing the sun and the wind and the rain beneath the spotted eagle's cry until the day that Wakan Tanka called him home to Wanagi Yata.

Wonunicun tahunsa, forgive me, cousins: I would ask to speak a little now of the Red Brother as I have known him in the Will Henry books, and as I pray that the author will continue to write of him in this life; his gods and the Red Brother's permitting.

If Will Henry has made a useful contribution to the image of the American Indian with his books about the Western horseback tribes, it has not been in the serene arenas of higher education but out upon the rougher playing fields of popular humanity. Indians have always been larger than life to this author, far more important to him as fellow people than as, say, "Ethnological source/origins of Neo-Shoshoni menstrual prayer dancing," or as, "Hitherto-unrelated circumcisional rituals of the Hidatsa, their implications for the Athapascan Fertility Rites of the Dust and Dirt Blowing Moon."

Will Henry would be far more interested in what Tashunka Witko, Crazy Horse, said about Red Beard Crook after mauling him within an inch of losing his command on the Rosebud, nine days before Little Big Horn. Or what was the squaw's name who was bedded by Bobtail Bull in disobedience to his Medicine Dream the night before the death of the Seventh Cavalry "along the Greasy Grass"? Or what did Joseph really say to Yellow Wolf when Yellow Wolf told him he was going to flee the Bear Coat Miles surrender agreement made by Joseph? Did the noble Nez Perce bless or curse the wild-hearted Yellow Wolf's decision to dishonor Joseph's word there in the blind-gut night before the final sunrise at the Bear Paws?

Such tipi-level curiosa are the stuff of horseback Indian humanness. What were the Indian people like? What made them fearful, sad, angry, happy, restless? What did they want from society? Or not expect from it? How did they define cruelty? Honor? Dishonor? Loyalty, treachery, friendship, enmity, leadership, family, courage, shame, victory, defeat, success, godliness, laughter, tears, life?

And all of these questions, with endless others, filtered in the answering through the mind and mores of a white man. No non-Indian, of course, can see the Indians as an Indian would. But he can try. In fact, he must try. It is no good to write another book filled with the eternal white prejudices. To listen to any Indian litany of innocence unbroken is just as unrewarding. What he who would write Indian books must do is one of two available things; (1) he must strive to present a balanced view or (2), he must choose sides and, having done so, ride at wildest gallop in favor of the side he has chosen.

As to Will Henry, book in and book out, good reviews or bad, he rides with the Red Brother.

It follows that he must have made a conscious choice in the beginning. It would do him no good to deny it. He never would in any event. His fascination with the nomad tribesmen of Western desert, plain and mountain, is an article of original faith. He admits it fervently. "They were right and we were wrong; simple as that," he says. "You pick a dog in a fight, you don't pick the one on top. You start yelling for the one underneath. It's the American Way."

But all of this enthusiasm has not saved Old Will from his full share of unwanted lumps. He doesn't think his Indians are *ever* stereotypes, for instance. Yet both his friends in the book-writing business, and his enemies, assure him that they *are*. Oh, the friends do say only *sometimes*, and the enemies concede not *always*, but the charge stands. However, somewhere between best friend and worst enemy, several million readers (Bantam Books says) have voted for Will Henry's

Indians with their money. And Will knows this is the ultimate review. "Greater love hath no reader," Will adds, "than that he shall lay down his hard-earned two dollars for a paperback copy of your book."

And that is why Will Henry vows he will keep doing it his way — the Indian way as he sees it — in his books.

It must never be misunderstood, however, he cautions, that he is not serious beneath the ebb and flow of the fiction in his works. The history in the Will Henry books is always honored in its repeating or its use as foundation for related fiction. It is never altered or distorted or downrightly cheated — as it is by so many of our newer writers — to force it to fit the particular author's politics of today. His books are fiction built upon history, not fiction paraded as history.

Still, the lumps remain.

And they smart.

But a romantic has got to expect hard knocks. Especially when he attempts to claim, as Will Henry does, that, for all their romanticism, his books are better history than most which are sold as straight historicals. Indeed, most of Will Henry's Indian books *are* historical novels. To merit this definition the author has had to render his tributes to the Red Man effective by confining his stories to the best-known truths of those situations and people both red and white and, indeed, brown and black, with which and with whom he has dealt in fiction. He thinks this is what distinguishes him from other romanticist Indian writers, whether those to whom an Indian can do no wrong and a white man no right, or those to whom the Indian is a foolishly drawn caricature bearing no resemblance to real life, the so-called stereotypical Hollywood Indian portrayed to the point of exclusionary inanity.

Will feels his Indians are neither foolish nor inane. There are unquestionably a number of writers who know, or profess to know, far more about the textbook facts of Indian history than he does. Will points this out. He has never made any pretense, he says, to such eminent authority. What he has made bold to do is to recreate in his white man's mind the Indian as he, Will, has envied and admired him in his own imagination since early childhood. And as he has since followed him across many a Wide Missouri in his adult studies of the American Horseback Indian of the West, Southwest and Northwest. By this process, by the time he came to the writing of *No Survivors*, his first book and first Indian book, he had his place already chosen, his point of view adopted, his White Eye's camera of recreation ready to roll. This Indian fascinated him. He wanted to be his brother. To ride with him, to learn his story and then retell it in his own behalf, in tribute to his vanishing nomad Western kind — the last of the really free tribes of Man.

In the end, Will says, let his epitaph read: "To the Fighting Horseback Indians of the West, With Love — Will Henry."

Ad Notum, POV THE INDIANS: As I wrote this viewpoint piece on Will Henry and the Indians, I was confronted with the feeling that even the most faithful reader might not be able to decide finally where friend Will was coming from in re his unflagging regard for the Amerindian.

Well, let's see.

If one critic sits on stool A (the Indian can do no wrong and the white man no right) and the other critic perches upon stool B (the Indian is a bastard and must be so drawn in fairness to the noble settler), then it becomes evident to the author that Will Henry tumbles somewhere in betwixt the two stools.

He does not think the white man was universally wrong and the red man universally right. He thinks the unfriendly view that Will Henry's Indians are rote-carved figurines pared to fit his romantic notions of Horseback Hiawathas is patent nonsense. The same for the camp that holds him to be some sort of Caucasian communist/apologist for, Lo, the Poor Red Man. Such sidetrack allegations are not valid for a minute, nor supportable in court for ten seconds. He does think some commentators on the Indian scene suffer occupational blind spots in the unrelenting condemnation of the white man. And he does acknowledge those other critics who contend he too often romanticizes both Red Brother and White past the point of serious literary acceptance. But acknowledge is not agree with. Since when have romantics been barred from serious literary consideration? This would surely be news to Admiral of the Ocean Sea Horatio Hornblower, Billy Budd, Captain Ahab, Alan Quatermain, Lawrence of Arabia, Ben Hur and Chullandar Ghose. Not to mention Don Quixote, Gulliver, Long John Silver, Huck Finn and Madame Bovary.

Ah! how soon they forget.

Will has a "parting poser" for those he calls "the good burgomasters of the critical media." This as to the matter of who in the literary world of the West contributes more to the lasting honor of the Indian. Is it the writer who professes to be *the* Indian authority only to speak with ideologically forked tongue in the name of the vanished red man? Or is it

the writer who has no politics but his admitted affair with the horseback Indians of the past, and who pens an eulogy with every book he
writes of them?

Will Henry will take the eulogy every time.

And will expect it to be around a hundred years after the down-beat
truth-twisters are lain away and long forgotten.

Tracts, no matter how skillfully sold, do not live, Will says. Dreams
live; and the horseback Indians of the West had a dream: *freedom*.

The grandest illusion of them all.

And the greatest romance.

Will Henry with the famed Model 94 Winchester, last in the line of historic Winchester lever-actions — the gun that really won the West. (Photo by Arthur Knight, c 1957)

When I was a little boy dragooned against my will into attending both school and Sunday school, it did not set well with me. I resented it then and I still think ill of it that small children are simply sent off to both classroom and Bible classroom and expected to (1) put up with it, and (2) make sense out of it. I suspect rather strongly that this early prejudice of the author led him to consider the plight of Heyets, the Mountain Sheep, favorite nephew of the great Chief Joseph, when the Nez Perce lad was ordered by his own father, and by his beloved tribal chief, to march himself off to the Christian School at the Lapwai Agency and "learn to be a peaceful Christian." Heyets, as you shall see, had a deal of powerful difficulty understanding what the study of Choosuklee, Jesus Christ, had to do with interrupting his "peaceful" Nez Perce boyhood. He tried in deep earnest to "learn the ways of the white man" because he so loved Joseph, to whom he had given his word to study hard. But the Mountain Sheep, so named for his extraordinary powers of eyesight, still thought those ways were passing strange, and that Choosuklee was not too bright to ride a jackass, when he might have had a fine Nez Perce Appaloosa warhorse and been a real chief like Joseph.

— W.H.

LAPWAI WINTER

I recall the day as though it were but one or two suns gone. It had been an early spring in the northeast Oregon country, the weather in mid-April being already warm and clear as late May. I was on the hillside above our village on the Wallowa River when Itsiyiyi, Coyote, the friend of my heart in those boyhood times, came racing up from the lodge below.

Poor Coyote. His eyes were wild. His nostrils were standing wide with breath. His ragged black hair was tossing like the mane of a bay pony. I pitied the little fellow. He was always so alarmed by the least affair. Now I wondered calmly what small thing brought him dashing up from the village, and I awaited his news feeling very superior in the advantage of my fourteen summers to his twelve.

But Coyote had the real news that morning.

Joseph, our chief, had decided to accept the invitation of White Bird and Toohoolhoolzote to go to Montana and hunt the buffalo. Since White Bird and Toohoolhoolzote were the chiefs of the fierce White Bird and Salmon River bands — what we called the "wild" or "fighting Indians" as against our own more peaceful Wallowa people — no news could possibly have been more exciting to a Nez Perce boy. With a cry as high-pitched as Coyote's, I dashed off down the hill to catch up my pony and get ready.

Within the hour, the entire village was packed and our horse herd strung out on the Imnaha Trail to Idaho and the Salmon River country, where the wild bands lived. There was no trouble crossing the Snake late that afternoon, and early the following sunrise we were off up the Salmon to see the famous warrior tribes.

The prospects sent my heart soaring higher than a hawk on hunting wing. Even though my mother, who was a Christian and had gone many years to the white man's missionary school at Lapwai, talked very strongly against such "Indian nonsense" as going to the buffalo, and assured me with plenty of threats that I was going to spend that coming winter at Agent Monteith's reservation school whether Joseph and my father agreed to it or not, I still could not restrain my joy at the adventure which lay ahead. I knew this was a time of times for any Nez Perce boy to remember, and I certainly was not going to let my mother's stern beliefs in her Lord Jesus, nor any of her threats about the white man's school, spoil it for me. I was an Indian, and this was a time for Indians.

It was a beautiful spring day. A shower during the night had washed the sky clean as a river stone. The sun was warm and sweet. Above us on the steepening hillsides the pine jays scolded with a good will. Below us along the rushing green water of the river the redwing reedbirds whistled cheerily. Tea Kettle, my dear mouse-colored pony, tried to bite me in the leg and buck me off. Yellow Wolf, my young uncle, who was as fierce as any fighting Indian, jogged by on his traveling mare and gave me a friendly sign. Even Joseph, that strange, sad-eyed man who almost never smiled, brightened to nod and wave at me as I passed him where he sat his horse by the trail, watching and counting to be sure all of his people were safe across the Snake and settled right upon the trail up the Salmon.

I looked all about me at that lovely pine-scented country and at my handsome, good-natured Nez Perce people riding up the sparkling river carefree and noisy-throated as the mountain birds around them, and, doing that, I thought to myself that I might well take this moment to offer up some word of thanks to Hunyewat, our Indian god. There was, too, good and real reason for the gratitude. Owing to President Grant's good treaty of the year before, the trouble between our people and the white man was over for all time. The Wallowa, our beautiful Valley of the Winding Water, had been given back to us and surely, as of that moment there among the Idaho hills, there was nothing but blue sky and bird songs in the Nez Perce world.

Bobbing along on my little gray pony, I bowed my head to the morning sun and said my humble word to Hunyewat.

Indians are supposed to be very brave, even the little boys. I was not such a good Indian, I fear. When we got to White Bird Canyon where the first village of the wild bands was located, I am afraid I did great shame to my fourteen years. I certainly did not act like a boy only three summers away from his manhood.

White Bird — it was his village nestled there on the canyon floor — was not at home. Neither were his warriors. Only the old men, the women, the children were left in the silent village. Some of the old men rode out to 'tell us what had happened.

Word had come that the white settlers in Kamiah Valley had stopped our Nez Perce cattle herds at Kamiah Crossing of the Clearwater River. The white men had showed the Nez Perce herdsmen the rifle and told them they could not bring their cattle into the Kamiah any more. It was white man's grass now; the Indian was going to have to stay off of it. White Bird had gone that same morning to gather up Toohoolhoolzote and the Salmon River warriors to ride to the crossing. *Eeh-hahh!* Bad, very bad. There was going to be real trouble now.

The moment I heard this I knew our trip to the buffalo country was ruined. It was then the tear came to my eye, the sniffle to my nose. Fortunately no one saw me. There were graver things to watch. Joseph's face had grown hard as the mountain rock above us.

It was a wrong thing, he told the old men, for the settlers to have closed the historic Indian road to the Kamiah grass. The Nez Perce had used that trail and those pastures since the grayest chief could remember. But it would also be a wrong thing to let White Bird and Toohoolhoolzote come up to the river ready to fight. They were dangerous Indians.

"Ollikut, Elk Water, Horse Blanket, Yellow Wolf," said Joseph quickly, "you four come with me. Go get your best horses; pick your buffalo racers. We must go fast."

"Where are we going?" asked Ollikut, Joseph's tall young brother.

"To Kamiah Crossing. We must stop these angry men, or there will be shooting. We have given our word against that. Do you agree?"

"Yes," said Ollikut. "We will get our horses."

In bare minutes they had mounted up and gone hammering down the trail around Buzzard Mountain to the Clearwater River. I sat there feeling my heart tear apart within me. Suddenly I saw Coyote motioning to me urgently. I guided Tea Kettle over toward him. He was on his scrubby brown colt and he had a pudgy White Bird boy with him. The boy had his own horse, a spavined paint with feet like snowshoes. I drew myself up, looking haughty.

"Well," I challenged Coyote, "what do you want?"

"This ia Peopeo Hihhih," he replied, indicating his companion.

"Yes? What is so remarkable about that?"

"Not much. Only his father's name is Peopeo Hihhih, too."

"Coyote, what are you trying to say to me?"

"This much — this boy's father is Chief White Bird."

"No!"

I could not believe it. This small, ugly little animal the true son of White Bird? Impossible.

"Boy," I said, "is my friend's tongue straight? Are you the blood son of Chief White Bird?"

"No. Only the near son. My mother was his sister. But he raised me in his tepee and gave me his name. Everybody calls me Little Bird. You look like a nice boy, what's your name?"

"Heyets."

"Very fine name. It means Mountain Sheep."

"That's very smart of you, boy. And you only seven or eight summers. Imagine!"

"Seven summers." The pudgy boy smiled. "Ten more and I will be a warrior like you."

I watched him closely, but he was not bright enough to be flattering me. He actually thought I had seventeen summers. Clearly, although not clever, neither was he as stupid as I had believed. I began to feel better about my lot.

"Well," I said cheerfully, "what shall we do? Ride down the river and stone the potholes for mallard hens? Go for a swim in the Salmon? Hunt rabbits? Have a pony race?"

Instantly the fat White Bird Boy was frowning at Coyote. "I thought you said he would want to go over to the Clearwater and creep up on the fight at Kamiah Crossing," he said accusingly.

"I did! I did!" protested Coyote. "But with Heyets you can't tell. He changes his mind like a woman. You can't trust his mind. Neither can he."

I did not care to stand there listening to a simpleton like Coyote explaining the workings of my thoughts to a seven-year-old White Bird Indian. I grew angry.

"Be quiet!" I ordered. "Of course I would like to go to the Clearwater and see the fight. But what is the use of such talk? It will be all over before we could get these poor crowbaits of ours halfway around the mountain." I paused, getting madder. "Coyote," I said, "from here where I now say good-by to you, I will speak no more to you in this life. I warned you, now we are through. *Taz alago.*"

"Well, all right, good-by." Coyote shrugged. "Have it your way, Heyets. But I just thought you would like to beat Joseph and the men to Kamiah Crossing. That's why I wanted you to see Little Bird. He knows a way."

I spun Tea Kettle around. "He knows what way?" I demanded.

"The secret way of his people over the mountain, instead of around it. It's a way he says we can get our poor horses to the crossing before any of them. Before Elk Water, your father. Before Horse Blanket, Yellow Wolf's father. Before Ollikut, Joseph's brother. Before —"

"Enough! enough!" I cried. "Is this true, Little Bird?"

Little Bird lifted his three small chins. "I am the son of a war chief," he said. "Would I lie to a Wallowa?"

I made as though I did not understand the insult and said, "*Eeh-hahh*, there has been too much talk. Let's go."

"Yes, that's right," spoke up Little Bird. "We have a tall mountain to get over. Follow me. And when we get up high, let your ponies have their heads. There are some places up there you will not want to look over. *Eeh-hahh!*"

Coyote and I understand that kind of instruction. We gave a happy laugh, hit our ponies with our buffalo-hide quirts, and went charging off after Little Bird's splayfooted paint. We were gone as quickly as the men before us.

That was a wild track up over that mountain, but it was a good one. We got to the Clearwater before Joseph and before even the White Bird and Salmon River warriors.

Little Bird led us off the mountain down a creek bed which had a cover of timber all the way to its joining with the river. This was below the crossing, up near which we could plainly see the white men sitting around their campfire making loud talk and boasting of the easy way they had run off the Indian herders that morning.

The day was well gone now. Whippoorwills were crying on the mountain. Dusk hawks were about their bug hunting. The sun had dropped from sight beyond the western hills; only its last shafts were striking the face of the cliffs above us. North and east, heavy clouds were coming on to rain. The river was starting to drift a chilly mist.

I shivered and suggested to my companions that we circle the white camp and go on up the river to the village of Looking Glass, the Asotin Nez Perce chief. Up there we could get a warm sleep in a dry tepee, also some good hot beef to eat for our supper.

But Little Bird had not come over the mountain to visit the Asotin, who were even more settled than the Wallowa.

"No," said the fat rascal, "I won't go up there. My father says Looking Glass is strong but his people are weak. They take the white man's way. *Kapsis itu*, that's a bad thing."

"Well," I countered, "it's going to rain. We'll get soaked and lie here on the ground shaking all night. That's a bad thing, too."

"*Eeh!*" was all he would say to me. "I am a Nez Perce; you Wallowas are all women."

"Not this Wallowa!" cried Coyote. "I fear no rain. I fear no white man. I fear no fat White Bird boy. *Ki-yi-yi-yi-yi!*"

He threw back his head and burst into his yipping personal call before I could move to stop him. My stomach closed up within me like a bunching hand. Only one thing saved us from instant discovery: Coyote made such an excellent imitation of the little brush wolf for which he was named that the white men were fooled. One of them picked up his rifle and shied a shot our way. The bullet slapped through our cover at the same time my hand took Coyote across his yammering mouth. He gave a startled yelp and shut up. The white man laughed and put down his gun and said, "By damn, I must have clipped the leetle varmint. How's thet fer luck?"

We didn't answer him, letting him think what he wanted.

It got pretty quiet.

Presently Little Bird said respectfully to me, "What I suggest, Heyets, is that we creep up the river bed and listen to the white man's talk. Coyote said your mother has been to the school at Lapwai and has taught you their language. You can tell us what they are saying up there, eh?"

I started to give him some good reason why we should not attempt this riskful thing but was fortunately spared the need. Happening to glance up the river as he spoke, my eyes grew wide.

"*Eeh!*" I whispered excitedly. "It is too late. Look up there on the cliff!"

I flung out my arm, and my friends, following the point of my rigid finger to the mountainside above the white man's fire, became very still. Everything all around became very still. That was the kind of a sight it was.

On the crest of the last rise past the settler campfire, sitting their horses quiet as so many statues carved from the mountain granite, were two craggy-faced war chiefs and half a hundred unfriendly looking, eagle-feathered fighting Indians.

"*Nanitsch!*" hissed Little Bird, filling the silence with the fierce pride of his words. "Look, you Wallowas! See who it is yonder on the hillside. It is my father, White Bird, and his friend Toohoolhoolzote, come to kill the Kamiah white man!"

The fighting Indians came down the hill. They came very slow, giving us time to slip up through the river brush to be close to it all when it happened. As they rode forward, the white men left their fire and took up their rifles. They walked out on foot to meet the mounted Indians in the way such things were done. Both parties stopped about an arrow shot apart. For the Indians, White Bird and Toohoolhoolzote rode out. For the white men, it was a lanky fellow with a foxy eye and a square-built man with blunt whiskers. We knew them both. They were Narrow-Eye Chapman and Agent Monteith.

The talk began but did not go far.

Neither White Bird nor Toolhoolhoolzote spoke a word of English. Monteith knew our tongue a little yet had to wait for Chapman to explain many things for him. Chapman was a squaw man, living with a Umatilla woman up in White Bird Canyon. The Indians knew him from a long time and took him as their friend. Still the talk kept stopping because of Agent Monteith. Toohoolhoolzote, famous for his harsh temper, began to grow angry. He glared at the Lapwai agent, then growled angrily at Narrow-Eye Chapman.

"Curse you both," he said, "I will not stay here and listen to any more of this delaying. We know why we are here. You know why we are here. Why do we argue? I am going to ride back a way and return with my gun cocked for shooting."

"No, no," the squaw man pleaded. "Wait now, old friend, don't do that. You haven't heard the whole story yet."

Toohoolhoolzote looked at him. "Do you deny these men stopped our cattle?" he asked.

"No, I can't deny that. But —"

"Never mind, I only want to know if you stopped the cattle. Now I will ask it of you one more time. Can the cattle go over the river into the Kamiah grass?"

Chapman looked around like a rabbit caught by dogs in an open meadow. Then he spoke rapidly to Agent Monteith, telling him what Toohoolhoolzote had said. The agent got very dark in the face.

"You tell that Indian," he ordered, "to bring his cattle and come to live upon the reservation as the other Nez Perce have done. Tell him there is plenty of grass at Lapwai, and be done with him. Tell him I will send for the soldiers if he does not do as I say."

But Narrow-Eye knew better than that. He shook his head. "No," he said quickly, "we can't do that. I will ask him to wait until morning with his decision. That will give us time to send back for more men. We will need every gun in the Kamiah if we stay here. We wouldn't last five minutes if they started shooting now, and they're mortal close to doing it. Those Indians are mad."

Agent Monteith peered at the angry faces of the fighting Indians, and of a sudden his own stubborn face changed. Even from as far away as our river bushes we could see him get pale above his whiskers. At once he agreed to the squaw man's plan, and Chapman turned and told the big lie to the Indians.

Toohoolhoolzote was for war right then. But White Bird looked up at the sky and said no. The light was already too far gone for good shooting; the morning would be time enough. There were only a dozen white men, and by the good light of daybreak they could be sure they got every one of them. For a moment I let out my listening breath, thinking everything was going to rest quiet at that agreement, giving Joseph time to get up and perhaps prevent the fight. I finished translating what had been said for my two friends, not thinking how they might take the white man's treachery. I had still much to learn about fighting Indians, even very small fat ones.

Little Bird, the moment he heard of Chapman's deceitful words to Monteith, burst from our cover like a stepped-on cottontail. Bounding through the twilight toward the Nez Perce, he kept shouting in our tongue for them to beware, to fight right then, that Narrow-Eye Chapman was sending for more guns, maybe even for the Pony Soldiers, that all of them would be killed if they waited for the morning.

When Little Bird did that — jumped and ran — I didn't know what to do, but crazy Coyote, he knew what to do. He jumped and ran after him yelling, "Wait for me! Wait for me! Wait for me!"

One of the white men, a heavy one with yellow-stained red whiskers, cursed, using his god's name, and called out to the others, "Come on, boys, we had better beat through them willows. Might be a whole litter of them red whelps in thar!"

With the words he leaped on his horse and plunged him into the brush where I was running around in senseless circles trying to decide which way to go. He reached down, seized me by the back of my hunting shirt, and rode back with me dangling in one great hand.

"Here, by cripes!" he bellowed. "Lookit here what I found. Damn me if it ain't a leetle red swamp rat!"

Well, it was no little red swamp rat but the fourteen-year-old son of Elk Water, the Wallowa Nez Perce. Still, it was no time for false pride — nor anything else for that matter. Before the red-whiskered man could bring me back to the campfire and before the startled Indians could form their line to charge upon the treacherous whites, a single shot rang out upon the mountainside.

The lone bullet splashed a whining mark of lead on a big rock which stood midway of the meadow between the settlers and our angry people, and a deep voice rolled down from above saying, "Do not fight. The first man on either side to ride beyond the rock will be shot."

We all fell still, looking upward toward the cliff down which wound the Clearwater trail.

There, fiery red in the reflected light of the disappeared sun, tall as giants on their beautiful buffalo horses, were Joseph and Ollikut, with my father and Yellow Wolf's father and Yellow Wolf himself. All save Joseph had their rifles pointed toward the midway rock, and there was still smoke curling from Ollikut's gun, showing it was he who had fired the lone shot. For himself, Joseph did not even have a gun. He was commanding the stillness with his upheld hand alone. It was a strange thing. All the Indians and all the white men likewise did his bidding. Not one man made to move himself, or his horse, or his loaded rifle in all the time it took our Wallowa chief to ride down from the cliff.

It was the first time I had seen the power of Joseph's hand. It was the first time I knew that he possessed this *wyakin*, this personal magic to command other men. I think that many of the Nez Perce had not seen it or felt it before this time, either. It was as if they did not know this Joseph, like he was a stranger among them.

Joseph talked straight with the white men. The other Indians came into the settler fire and stood at the edge of its outer light and listened without moving. But they did not talk; only Joseph talked.

In his patient way he went back to the beginning of the agreements on paper between our two peoples. He reminded Agent Monteith of the Walla Walla Peace Council of 1855 in which only the Nez Perce had stood faithful to the white man, and in which all the other tribes, the Yakimas, Umatillas, Palouse, Spokanes, Coeur d'Alênes — all of them save the Nez Perce — spoke against the paper and would not sign it.

Always, Joseph said, the Nez Perce had abided by that treaty. Only when the Thieves Treaty took away their lands in 1863, after gold was discovered at Oro Fino, had the Nez Perce faltered in their friendship. Even then they had made no war, only stayed apart from the white man, asking nothing but to be let alone. Now there was President Grant's good paper returning the Wallowa country to the Nez Perce.

Now all should be as it was in the old friendly days. But here was the
white man trying to steal the Indian's grass again. The Kamiah was Indian country. There was no treaty keeping Nez Perce cattle away from
it, yet here was the white man standing at Kamiah Crossing flourishing
the rifle and saying hard things to Joseph, who was trying to keep the
peace.

Was it not enough, cried Joseph, throwing wide his arms, that the
white man had torn the gold from the Indian earth? That he had taken
the best farmlands for himself? That he had built his whisky stores
along the Indian trails? That he had lured the Indian children away
from their parents into his Christian schools, had taught them to pray
to Jesus Christ and to sneer at the old Indian gods, had made them
forget the ways of their own fathers and mothers and led them to think
their own people were lower than dogs and the white man the lord of
all on earth? That he had lied to, stolen from, cheated on the poor
trusting Nez Perce for seventy snows and more? Were not all these
things enough? Did he now also have to starve the Indian as well, to
stomp in his water and stale in it, too? Must he not only take what grass
he needs, alone, but also the small amount necessary to the Indian's
poor few cattle?

What did such a situation leave Joseph to say to White Bird and
Toohoolhoolzote? What could he tell his angry brothers to keep them
from fighting in the morning? If any of the white men had the answer
to that question, he had better give it to Joseph now.

There was a long silence then while the white men talked it over.
Then Agent Monteith showed his stumpy teeth and stood forth to talk
unfriendly.

It was time, he said, for the Nez Perce to realize they could no longer
move themselves and their cattle about the land as they pleased. They
were going to have to keep themselves and their herds in one place
from now one, even as the white man did. There was no choice. If they
would not do it, the soldiers would come and make them do it. Was
that perfectly clear to Joseph?

Joseph was a wise man. He did not say yes, just to make a good feeling. He shook his head and said no; he did not think he understood
what Agent Monteith was saying. It seemed there was possibly more intended than was stated. Would the agent try again, Joseph asked
Chapman, this time with his tongue uncurled?

Chapman winced and said to Joseph, "I hope you understand that

my heart is with you. I think much of my wife's people. But I am
white; what can I do?

"Do nothing," answered Joseph, "that you do not think I would do."

"Thank you, my brother," said Chapman, and went back to
Monteith. The latter proved quite ready to repeat his exact meaning.
He did not like Joseph because he could not fool him, so he took refuge
in hard talk.

"All right." Monteith scowled. "Here is precisely what I mean: you
and your people are not going to the buffalo any more; you are not
leaving your lands to do anything. Such moving around makes the
young men restless and wild. When you put your cattle out to grass and
go to the buffalo, you are away six months. The children are kept out of
school; they have no chance to learn the ways of the new life that will
let them live side by side with the white man. This is a wrong thing,
Joseph. We must start with the children. They must be put in school
and kept there. It is the only way to real peace between our people. We
must have a common God and common ways. Only through the
children may this be done."

When Joseph heard this, he asked only what putting the children in
school had to do with showing the rifle at Kamiah Crossing. Monteith
answered him at once. Peaceful Indians, he said, were Indians who
stayed in one place. Moving Indians were fighting Indians. And the
day of the moving Indian was done. From this time forward the Nez
Perce must do as Indian Agent John Monteith said, not as White Bird
said, not as Toolhoolhoolzote said, not as any other fighting chief said.
And what agent Monteith said was that the Wallowas must now stay in
the level valley, the White Birds in their deep canyon, the Salmon
Rivers behind their big mountain. To guarantee this obedience there
was but one sure way: put the children in the reservation school and
raise them as white boys and girls. It was up to Joseph to make this
clear to the other Nez Perce. Did Joseph understand?

Our chief nodded slowly. The hurt in his face would have made a
stone weep. Yes, he said, for the very first time he did understand. Now
it was revealed to him what the white man really wanted of the Indian.
It was not to live in peace with him, as brother with brother. When the
agent said that about not going to the buffalo, about the cattle not going into Kamiah, it was only an excuse. The white man knew that to
shut up the Indian in a small place was to destroy his spirit, to break his
heart, to kill him.

If that was what Agent Monteith now wanted Joseph to tell the other chiefs, he would do it. He would tell them that either they went home and stayed there or the Pony Soldiers would come and drive them upon the reservation. He would tell them that in any case their children must soon be sent into Lapwai School and made to live there. But he must warn the agent that he was asking a very dangerous thing.

With this low-voiced agreement, Joseph turned away from Monteith and told the fighting Indians what he had said.

I had a very good look at this part of it. I was being held in the camp tent. The red-whiskered man was in there with me, holding his bad-smelling hand across my mouth the whole time. But I could see between his fat fingers and through the slight parting of the tent flap. Of course, none of the Nez Perce knew I was in there. They all thought I had gotten away down the river and would come into their camp when I had a chance.

When Joseph told the others about not going to the buffalo any more, about the soldiers putting them on the reservation if they moved around, about Agent Monteith demanding the surrender of the children as the earnest of their good faith, the Indians did a strange thing. Their faces grew not angry but very sad, and when Joseph had finished the last word they turned and went back up on the mountainside without a sound. Only old Toohoolhoolzote stayed behind with Joseph, and with our Wallowa chief he now went toward the white men.

Coming up to Monteith, Joseph said, "I have told my people what you said. Now Toohoolhoolzote will tell you what my people say in return." He stood back, giving over his place to the older man. Toohoolhoolzote stared at all the white men for a moment, then nodded.

"I will be brief," he said in Nez Perce to Chapman, but fixing his gaze upon the Lapwai agent. "Tomorrow, if you are still here, there will be shooting. We are going to the buffalo. We will graze our cattle where we wish. We will not bring our children into Lapwai. Joseph is a good man and he is your friend. Toohoolhoolzote is a bad man and he is not your friend. When the sun comes up, remember that. *Taz alago*, Agent Monteith. Sleep light."

For a time the old man stood there, the firelight making a black spiderweb of the seams and dry canyons in his face skin. His mouth was set in a line as wide and ugly as a war-ax cut. His eyes burned like a wolf's eyes. His expression was unmoving. Suddenly I was as afraid of him as the white men. The sight of him braced there lean and dark and

strong as a pine tree for all his sixty-eight winters, staring down all that
bitter talk and all those menacing white rifles with nothing save his Nez
Perce *simiakia*, his terrible Indian pride, put a chill along my spine
from tail to neckbone. When he finally turned away to follow his warriors up onto the mountain, it was even more quiet than when Joseph
came down the cliff trail.

Now there was only my own chief left.

He told Chapman in Nez Perce that he was sad that Agent Monteith
had done this dangerous thing to the spirit of the wild band. He promised he would yet do what he could to prevent the shooting in the
morning but begged Chapman to try and get the white settlers to leave
the crossing when it was full dark, to be far from it when the sun came
over Buzzard Mountain next day. Then he, too, turned to go.

In the last breath, however, Agent Monteith requested him to wait a
moment. Wearily Joseph did so, and Monteith wheeled toward the
camp tent and said "Bates, bring that boy up here."

Redbeard Bates grinned and spat and shoved me stumbling out of
the tent. Outside, he pushed me forward into the fire's light to face my
chief.

Joseph's tired face softened as he saw me.

But Agent Monteith's face grew hard. "Joseph," he said, "tell your
people over on the mountain that I don't trust them. I will hold the boy
with us until we see there is no shooting and no following us away from
here. The boy will be perfectly all right. After a time you come into
Lapwai, and we will talk about him. I know this boy is of your own
blood, and I have an idea for him you would do well to listen to. It may
be that we can use him to lead in the others. Do you understand that?"

Joseph understood it.

But to Agent Monteith he merely nodded without words, while to
me he spoke ever so gently in his deep voice.

"No harm will come to you, little Heyets," he said. "Go with the
agent, and do not fear. I shall come for you. As you wait, think well
upon what you have seen here. Do you think you can remember it?"

I drew myself up. "Yes, my chief, I will always remember it."

"Good. It is a lesson about the white man that you will never learn in
his school at Lapwai." He smiled, touching me softly on the shoulder.
"*Taz alago*, Heyets," he said, and turned for the last time away from
this dark fire by the Clearwater.

"*Taz alago*, my chief," I called into the twilight after him, and was glad he did not look back to see the tears that stood in my eyes, no matter that I was fourteen summers and would be a warrior soon.

I had never been to Lapwai longer than one day — say, as on a Sunday, to watch the tame Indians pray, or on a Saturday when they drew their Agency beef and might favor a visiting "wild" relative with a bit of fat meat to take home at the white man's expense. Accordingly, as I now rode toward the mission school with the agent and the Kamiah settlers, I began to recover from my fright and to wonder how it might be to live on the reservation over here in Idaho for a longer while, perhaps two or three days, or even a whole week.

But I did not get to find out.

We had been riding most of the night, having slipped away from the crossing as Joseph advised. Now, as the sun came up, we stopped to boil water and make coffee. Before the water started to roll in the old black pot, five Nez Perce came out of a brushy draw nearby and rode up to our fire. We knew them all. They were Joseph, Ollikut, Horse Blanket, Yellow Wolf, and Elk Water, my own father.

"Well, Joseph," demanded Agent Monteith at once, "what is this? Have you tricked me? What do you want here?"

Joseph looked at him steadily. "It is not my way to play tricks," he said. "Last night I gave you the boy so there would be no trouble with those White Birds and Salmon Rivers. There was no trouble. Now I want the boy back, that is all."

"Give them the kid!" I heard Narrow-Eye Chapman whisper to Monteith, but the agent set his stubborn jaw and said no, he wouldn't do it.

Ollikut, great handsome Ollikut, pushed his roan buffalo racer forward. He cocked his gun. "Agent," he said, "we want the boy."

"For God's sake," said Chapman out of the side of his mouth to Monteith, "give them the kid and get shut of them. What are you trying to do, get us all killed? That damned Ollikut will tackle a buzz saw barehanded. Smarten up, you hear? These ain't Agency Indians you're fooling with."

Agent Monteith stuck out his stubby beard still father and bared his many small teeth like a cornered cave bat, but he gave in. "Joseph," he said, "I am charging you with this matter. I want this boy in school this winter. You know why. It is the only way he can learn the white man's way."

"Yes, but he should have his say what he will do."

"No, he should not. That is the trouble with you Indians. You let the children run over you. You never say no to them and you never punish them for doing wrong. Children must be taught to do as they are told."

"We teach them. But what has that to do with striking them and saying no to everything they want? There are other ways to show them wisdom."

"Joseph, I won't argue with you. I leave it to your own mind. Whether this boy is going to grow up Indian or white is up to you. You and I are grown men: we will not change our ways. I have one God: you have another. My father taught from the Holy Book; your father tore up the Holy Book. We are as we are, you and I, but the boy can be anything which you say he can be. You are the head chief of the Wallowas, the most powerful band of the Nez Perce. If you send this boy of your own band and blood to go to school at Lapwai this winter, you will have said to all the other wild bands that you intend to take the white man's way, to obey your agent, to learn to live the new life. It will be a powerful thing for peace, an important thing for your people. What do you say? The decision is your own. You alone can make it."

If was a hard talk. I could see that Joseph was thinking much on it. I held my breath, for I was frightened again now. Of a sudden I lost all my bravery about going to Lapwai for a few days. This was serious. They were talking about the whole winter, perhaps about several winters. This could be a sad thing. I had heard many stories of boys dying at the school, of broken hearts and bad food and lonesomeness for tepee smoke and boiled cowish and dried salmon and roast elk and the smell of horse sweat and saddle leather and gun oil and powder and all of the other grand things a wild Nez Perce lad grew up with around him in his parents' lodge, his home village, and his native hunting lands.

Joseph, too, knew of these poor boys. The thought of them weighed heavy on him and made him take such a long time that Ollikut threw him a sharp glance and said, "Come on, brother, make up your mind. I feel foolish standing here with this gun cocked."

Joseph nodded to him and sighed very deep. "All right," he said to Agent Monteith, "give us the boy now. When the grass grows brown and the smell of the first snow is like a knife in the wind, I shall bring him to you at Lapwai."

In May, in the land of the Nez Perce, the spring sun comes first to the southern slopes of the tumbling hills which guard the wide valleys and shadowed canyons. Here in the warm sandy soil the cowish plant breaks through the mountain loam even before the snows are all gone from the rock hollows and catch basins which hold it there to water this sturdy rootling of the upper hills. To these cowish patches in that month of May would go my people, hungry and eager for the taste of fresh vegetables after the long winter of dried camass and smoked salmon.

The juicy roots of the cowish baked in the Nez Perce way have a breadlike, biscuity flavor, giving the plant its white man's name of biscuitroot. We called it *kouse*, and from that the settlers sometimes called us the Kouse Eaters. My people loved this fine food which was the gift of Hunyewat, and the time of its gathering was a festival time for us. All we children looked forward through the winter to the May travel to the cowish fields. Yet in May of the year that we did not go to the buffalo, I sang no gathering songs, danced no thankful dances, ate no *kouse* at the great feast held at the traditional Time of the First Eating. I sat apart and thought only of September and of the first smell of snow in the sharpening wind.

June was the time of going to the camass meadows. In that month my people would take up the tepees and journey happily to the upland plateaus where, in the poorly drained places, large flats of snow-melt water would collect and stand. Up out of these meadow shallows, springing like green spears from the black soil beneath the water, would come the fabled blue camass plant, the lovely water hyacinth or Indian lily of the Northwest.

Even within a few days, the surfaces of the water flats would be bright-grown as new meadow grass with its spreading leaves. Then, short weeks later, the brilliant bells of its blue blossoms would stalk out for their brief flowering. As the swift blooming passed, all the nourishment of Hunyewat's warm sky and cool snow water would go from the faded flower down into its underground bulb to store up strength and hardy life for its fortunate harvesters.

All this glad time of waiting for the camass root to come ripe and dry up for the digging, my band was camped with the other Nez Perce bands in the shady pines above the meadow. There was much gay chanting and dancing the whole while, but I did not take part in any of it. Instead, I stayed out on the mountain by myself, thinking of September and the snow wind.

Under the mellow sun of July, the shallow waters of the camass fields evaporated, the rich muck dried, and the great Indian harvest began.

Now while the men sat at their gambling games or raced their famous Appaloosa horses, and while the children played at stick-and-hoop or fished and hunted the summer away, the women took out the digging tools with their stubby wooden handles and pronged elkhorn tips and pried up the ripened bulbs of the blue lily.

After that came the cooking.

As many as thirty bushels of the bulbs were covered with wet meadow grass and steamed over heated stones. Then the bulbs were mashed, shaped into loaves, and sun-baked into a nourishing Indian bread. This bread would keep easily six to eight moons. It was good and valuable food, having a flavor much like a sweet yam. With the flesh of the salmon and the meat of the elk, the deer, and the antelope, it fed us through the severest winter. Thus, the July camass harvest was a time of tribal joy and gratitude for the Nez Perce. But I did not join in the Thankful Sing. I only wandered afar with Tea Kettle, my small gray pony, and looked with aching loneliness out across the blue peaks, hazy canyons, lapping waters, and lofty pines of the homeland I would see no more after the grass was brown beneath the autumn wind.

In late summer, in August, after the high spring floodwater had fallen and all the rivers were running low and clear, it was the Time of Silver Waters, of the great Columbia salmon run from the sea to the headwater creeks of Nez Perce country. This was the end of the Indian year, the very highest time of thanks for my people, and the very hardest time of work for them.

When the flashing salmon came at last, the men would strain from dawn to dusk with spear and net at every leaping falls from the mighty Celio upward to the least spawning creeklet which fed the main forks of the Salmon, Snake, Clearwater, Grande Ronde, Wallowa, and Imnaha rivers. The sandy beaches would soon be heaped to a small child's waist with the great humpbacked fish. Then the women would work like packhorses to split, clean, rack, and smoke the bright-red slabs of the blessed flesh which provided nine of every ten Nez Perce meals around the year and which kept my people from the famine which periodically visited the other Northwestern tribes.

Yes, August and the Time of Silver Waters was the real time to offer final thanks to Hunyewat. Yet even then I could think of no gratitude, no contentment, no happiness, but only of Joseph and Agent Monteith, and after them only the brown grass and snow smell of September and of the long-walled prison waiting for me in the school at Lapwai.

At last the Moon of Smoky Sunshine, September, was but three suns away. In that brief space it would be Sapalwit, Sunday, and Joseph would ride up to the tepee of my father and call out in his soft deep voice, "Elk Water, where is the boy? Where is Heyets, our little Mountain Sheep? The grass is grown brown again; the skies have turned the color of gun steel. I smell snow in the wind. It is the time to keep our word to Agent Monteith."

I let two of those last three suns torture me. Then on the final night, late and when the chilling winds had blown out all the cook-fire embers and no one stirred in all that peaceful camp, I crept beneath the raised rear skins of my father's tepee.

Moving like a shadow I found my faithful friend Tea Kettle where I had tethered him in a dark spruce grove that same afternoon. He whickered and rubbed me with his soft nose, and I cried a little and loved him with my arms about his bony neck. It was a bad time, but I did not think of turning back. I only climbed on his back and guided him on into the deepening timber away from the camp of my father's people there beside the salmon falls of the Kahmuenem, the Snake River, nine miles below the entrance of the Imnaha.

I was bound for the land of our mortal foes, the Shoshone. My reasoning was that if I could take an enemy scalp I would no longer be considered a boy. I would be a man, a warrior, fourteen summers or no, and they would no more think of sending me to school with Agent Monteith than they would my fierce uncle Yellow Wolf.

For equipment I had Tea Kettle, who could barely come up to a lame buffalo at his best speed. I had a *kopluts*, or war club, which was no war club at all but a rabbit throwing-stick cut off short to make it look like a *kopluts*. Also I had a rusted camp ax with the haft split and most of the blade broken off; a bow-and-arrow set given me by Joseph on my tenth birthday; a much-mended Pony Soldier blanket marked "U.S." in one corner, which was stolen for me by my father from the big fort at Walla Walla; three loaves of camass bread and a side of dried salmon; and my *wyakin*, my personal war charm, a smoked baby bear's foot cured with the claw and hair left on. And, oh, yes, I had my knife, naturally. No Nez Perce would think of leaving his tepee without putting on his knife. He might not put on his pants but he would always put on his knife.

So there I was on my way to kill a Shoshone, a Snake warrior far over across the Bitterroot Mountains in the Wind River country. I might also, for good measure, while I was over there, steal a few horses. About that I had not entirely decided. It would depend on circumstances. Meanwhile, more immediate problems were developing.

I had left home in good spirit if weak flesh. Now, however, after a long time of riding through the dark forest, the balance was beginning to come even. It occurred to me, thinking about it, that I had ridden many miles. It might well be that I needed food to return my strength. Perhaps I had better stop, make a fire, roast some salmon, warm a slice of bread. When I had eaten I would feel my old power once more. Then, although I had already ridden a great distance that night, I would go on yet farther before lying down to sleep.

I got off Tea Kettle and gathered some moss and small sticks which I laid properly in the shelter of a windfallen old pine giant. With my flint I struck a tiny flame and fed it into a good little Nez Perce fire, say the size of a man's two hands spread together, and clear and clean in the manner of its burning as a pool of trout water in late autumn. I cut a green spitting stick and propped a piece of salmon and one of camass over the flames. Then I put the soldier blanket around my shoulders and leaned back against the big log to consider my journey plans. The next thing I knew, a shaft of sunlight was prying at my eyes and two very familiar Indians were crouched at my fire, eating my salmon and camass bread.

"Good morning." Chief Joseph nodded. "This is fine food, Heyets. You had better come and have some of it with us."

"Yes," said Elk Water, my father. "It is a long ride to Lapwai."

"What is the matter?" I mumbled, my mind bewildered, my eyes still spider-webbed with sleep. "What day is this? What has happened to bring you here?"

"This is Sunday," answered Joseph in his easy way. "And what has happened to bring us here is that we have come to ride with you to Agent Monteith's school. You must have left very early, Heyets. That showed a good spirit. Probably you did not wish to bother us to rise so soon. Probably it was in your heart to let us have a good morning's sleep."

"Yes," agreed my father. "Surely that was it. Heyets is a fine boy. He wanted to let us sleep. He wanted also to ride into the white man's school alone so that we would know it did not worry him, so that we would be certain his heart was strong and he was not afraid. Is that not so, Heyets?"

My eyes had grown clearer, and it was in my mind to lie to them, to say yes, that they were right about my thoughtful actions. Yet I could not bring myself to do it. To my father I might have lied, for he was a simple man and would not have guessed the difference, no, and would not have cared a great deal for it. But Joseph — ah, Joseph was completely another matter and another man. His great quiet face, soft deep voice, and sad brown eyes touched me with a faith and a feeling which would not let my tongue wander.

"No." I replied, low voiced. "That is not the way it was at all. I was running away. I was going to the Snake country to take a Shoshone scalp so that you would think I was a man and would not send me to Agent Monteith's school. My heart was like a girl's; I was weak and sore afraid. I wanted only to stay with my people: with my father and with my chief."

There was a silence then, and my father looked hard at Joseph. He turned his head away from both Joseph and me, but I could see the large swallowing bone in his throat moving up and down. Still, he did not say anything. He waited for Joseph to speak.

At last my chief raised his eyes to me and said gently, "I beg your pardon, Heyets. The wind was making such a stir in the pine trees just now that I do not believe I heard what you said. Did you hear him, Elk Water?"

"No," answered my father, "I don't think I did. What was it you said, boy?"

I looked at Elk Water, my father, and at Joseph, my chief. Then I looked beyond them up into the pine boughs above us. There was no wind moving up there, no wind at all. I shook my head and got to my feet.

"Nothing," I said, untying Tea Kettle and kicking dirt upon my little fire. "Let us go to Lapwai and keep the word with Agent Monteith."

It will not take long, now, to tell of that Lapwai winter. It was not a good thing. The memory of it turns in me like a badly knitted bone. Yet, like a badly knitted bone, it will not let me forget.

I was sick much of the time, homesick all of the time. It was a hard winter, very cold, with a lot of wet-crust snow and heavy river ice the whole while. Some of my little Indian friends who sickened at the school did not grow well again. They were not watched over by Hunyewat as Heyets was. They lay down in the night and did not get up again in the morning. When we saw them the others of us wept, even we big boys. It hurt us very much.

If they were Christian Indian children they were buried in the churchyard. Their mothers were there; their fathers were there. All their many friends of the reservation were there to stand and say good-by to them, and to sprinkle the handful of mother earth on them as was the old custom. Agent Monteith read from the Holy Book at the graveside, and the proper songs of Jesus were sung over them. They were treated like something.

But if they were wild Indian children, like myself, their little bodies were left to lie out overnight and freeze solid like dog salmon. Then they were stacked, like so many pieces of stovewood, in the open shed behind the schoolhouse. There they waited, all chill and white and alone, until such time as their parents could come in over the bad trails to claim them for the simple Nez Perce ceremony of the Putting to the Last Sleep.

It was not a happy or a kind place for a boy raised in the old free Indian way. It made my heart sad and lonely to stay there. In consequence, and although I knew I was being watched closely because of my kinship with Joseph, both by my own and the agency people, I grew all the while more determined against the Lapwai, or white man's, way.

Naturally I learned but little at school.

I already knew how to speak the white tongue from my mother. But I did not let this help me. I would not learn to write, and in reading I was like a child of but six or seven. This blind pride was my father's blood, the old Nez Perce blood, the spirit, the *simiakia* of my untamed ancestors, entering into me. I was not a wicked boy, but neither was I willing to work. I was like a young horse caught from out a wild herd. I knew nothing but the longing to escape. The only chance to teach me anything was to first gentle me down, and there was no chance at all to gentle me down. I thought, of course, and many times, about Joseph's faith in me. I wanted to do what was right for the sake of my chief's hope that I would serve as an example to the other wild bands that they might send their children in safety, and with profit, to the white man's school at Lapwai. But my own faith was no match for my chief's. Daily I grew more troublesome to Agent Monteith. Daily he grew less certain of my salvation.

When I had been with him five moons — through the time of Christmas and into that of the new year — it had at last become plain to Agent Monteith that I was not "settling down," as he put it, and Joseph was sent for. When my chief arrived, I was called in while the talk was made about me. Joseph began it with his usual quiet direction, getting at once to the point.

"This boy's mother," he said, "reports to me that she has visited him here at the school and you have told her that her son is a bad boy, that he will not work, and that he is as bad for the other children as for himself." He paused, looking steadily at Agent Monteith. "Now I do not remember that Heyets is a bad boy. Perhaps my memory has failed me. Since I am also of his blood you had better tell me what you told his mother."

Agent Monteith grew angry, his usual way. "Now see here, Joseph," he blustered, "are you trying to intimidate me?"

"Excuse me. I do not understand what you mean."

"Are you trying to frighten me?"

"Never. What I want is the truth. Should that frighten you?"

"Of course not! This boy simply will not buckle down and study as he should. He will not work with the others. The class is told to draw a picture of our Lord Jesus humbly astride a lowly donkey, and this boy draws a lurid picture of an armed warrior on an Appaloosa stallion. I ask him, 'What picture is that, Heyets?' and he says, 'Why, that is a picture of Yellow Wolf on Sun Eagle going to the buffalo.' Now I put it to you, Joseph, is that the right way for a boy to behave before the others? A boy upon whom we have all placed so much hope? A boy the other bands are watching to see how he fares at Lapwai? Answer me. Say what you think."

My chief frowned and pulled at his broad chin. "I don't know," he said carefully. "Does he draw well?"

"He draws extremely well, easily the best in the class."

"He draws a good horse? A proper Indian?"

"Very good, very proper." Agent Monteith scowled. "Perfect likenesses, especially of the horse. He puts all the parts on the animal, and when I reprimand him he offers to take me to the Wallowa and show me that Sun Eagle is, indeed, a horse among horses."

Agent Monteith blew out his fat cheeks, filling them like the gas-blown belly of a dead cow.

"Now, you listen to me, Joseph! You promised to bring this boy here and make him behave himself and work hard to learn the white man's way. This has since become a serious matter for the school. It can no longer be ignored. Heyets is creating a grave discipline problem for me,

I mean among the other older boys. Some of them are beginning to draw pictures of spotted Nez Perce ponies in their study Bibles. I insist to you that this is no way for this boy of your blood to carry out our bargain."

Joseph shook his head in slow sympathy. "You are right, Agent," he said, "if what you tell me is true. But before I make a decision I would like to have you tell me one special thing Heyets has done — show me some example of his evil ways that I may see with my own eyes — so that I shall know what it is you and I are talking about."

He hesitated a little, looking at the agent.

"Sometimes, you know," he said, "the white brother says one thing and really means several others. It becomes difficult for an Indian to be sure."

Agent Monteith's blunt beard jutted out, but he kept his voice reasonable. "Joseph you are the most intelligent Indian I know. You are a shrewd man by any standards, red or white. You have been to this very school yourself in the old days. You were the best pupil they ever had here before your father, Old Joseph, tore up the Bible and took you away. You understand exactly what I mean and you do not have to ask me for any examples."

Joseph only nodded again and said, "Nevertheless, show me one special bad thing the boy has done."

The agent turned away quickly and picked up a study Bible from the desk of James Redwing, a Christian Wallowa boy of my own age and my best friend among the reservation Indians. He opened the book and handed it to Joseph.

"Very well," he snapped. "Look at that!"

Joseph took the book and studied it thoughtfully. "Let us see here," he said. "Here is a picture of a young baby being carried in his mother's arms. She is riding a small mule led by her husband. They are leaving an old town of some sort in a strange land, and they are not going very fast with such a poor beast to take them. Nevertheless, they are in a great hurry. There is fear in their faces, and I believe the enemy must be pursuing them. Is there something else I have missed?"

Agent Monteith stamped his foot. "You know very well that is the Christ Child fleeing Bethlehem with Mary and Joseph!"

"Oh, yes, so it is. A fine picture of all of them, too. Better than in the book they had here before."

"You know equally well," Agent Monteith continued, very cold-eyed, "what else I am talking about, and what else it is you have missed. What is printed under the picture of the Christ Child?"

Joseph nodded and held the book up for me to tell him the words. I did so, and he turned back to Agent Monteith and said, "The words there are 'Jesus Fleeing the Holy City.'"

"Exactly. And what has some heathen pupil scrawled in by hand under that sacred title, with a Nez Perce arrow pointing to the donkey?"

My chief's face never changed. Again he held the book up to me, and again I whispered the words to him. Looking back at Agent Monteith, he shifted the Bible as though to get a better light on it and answered, "Oh, yes, there is something else, sure enough. It says, 'If he had used an Appaloosa pony, his enemies never would have caught up to him.' Is that what you mean?"

"That is precisely what I mean, Joseph."

The agent took time to get a good breath and let some of it puff back out of his cheeks.

"That added writing was done by James Redwing, a Christian Indian of your own Wallowa band and a very fine boy who, until these past months, has been our star pupil. James is fifteen years old and I have worked with him a long time, Joseph. He had become a white boy in his thoughts and in his actions. I had saved him. He prayed on his knees every day, and he had given over his life gladly to the service of his Savior. Now he writes such things as you see there, and the other boys all laugh."

"That is not right," said Joseph softly, "but they are only boys, all of them. Boys are full of tricks, Agent."

"Indeed they are!" cried Monteith, puffing up again. "And I will tell you about just one of those tricks!"

"Do that, my friend. My ears are uncovered."

"Well, this past Christmas we celebrated the birth of our Lord by making a little stable scene with the manger, and so forth, in Bethlehem. Of course there was the little pack mule tied as the faithful ass beside the sleeping babe. And do you know what some monstrous boy had done to the innocent brute?"

Joseph shook his head wonderingly. "I could never imagine," he said. "Tell me."

"He had taken — he had *stolen* — some of the mission's whitewash and dappled the rear of that animal to imitate a Nez Perce Appaloosa horse, and had marked in red paint on the two halves of his rump the name 'Sun Eagle.' Now what do you think of that for your fine boy? He admitted it, you know. It was his work."

My chief put his chin down to his chest. He seemed to be having some trouble with his swallowing. It was as though he had caught a fishbone crosswise in his throat and were trying to be polite about choking on it. But after a bit he was able to raise his head and continue.

"I think it is very unfortunate," he answered the agent. "It is true my own father tore up the Bible and that I have followed his way, but I will not tolerate Wallowa boys making laughs about your god. What do you suggest we do?"

"Heyets must be punished severely."

"In what manner?"

"He should be flogged."

"Have you flogged him before, Agent?"

"No. Frankly, I've been afraid to try it. The rascal told me that if I touched him he would have his uncle Yellow Wolf come in and kill me."

"His uncle Yellow Wolf is but a boy himself, Agent."

"You do not need to tell me of Yellow Wolf. I know him very well. He has the eye of a mad dog. I wouldn't trust him ten feet away."

"I see. How else have you thought to punish Heyets?"

"He must be made to say the school prayers, on his knees, in front of the other boys."

"Alone?"

"Yes alone."

"Has he prayed like this before, Agent?"

"Not once. He says he believes in Hunyewat. He says he did not come here to study Jesus Christ. He tells wild tales of the power of Hunyewat to the Christian boys and has them believing that anything Jesus of Nazareth did in 'ten moons' Hunyewat could do in 'two suns.' He asks them such sacrilegious questions as, 'Did you ever see a picture of Hunyewat riding a pack mule?' and he has the entire class so disorganized they spend more time learning the Brave Songs, Scalp Chants, and Salmon Dances from him than they do the Sunday-school hymns from me. I will not tolerate it a day longer, Joseph. I simply cannot and will not do it. The matter is your entire responsibility, and you must make the final decision on it right now."

Joseph moved his head in understanding and raised his hand for the agent to calm himself and wait while both of them thought a little while.

Presently he went on. "Very well, Agent," he said. "Do you know what my father, Old Joseph, told me about this same school many snows ago when he came to take me away from it?"

"I can very well imagine what the old heathen might have said," agreed Agent Monteith. "But go ahead and tell it your way. You will anyway. That's the Indian of it."

"It is," replied Joseph, "and here is the way my father told it to me. He said, 'My son, always remember what I am about to say. A school is a good thing when it teaches school thoughts from school books. But the place for God and for His book is in the church. Pray in the church if you wish, and choose the God which pleases you. But in the school, do not pray. In the school, work hard all the time at the printed thoughts of reading and writing and of the white man's way of figuring with numbers. Do that six days, and on the seventh day go to church and pray all you want.'"

"Your father was a very wise man," admitted Agent Monteith, "until he left the church."

"He was a wise man after he left the church, too," said Joseph. "And here is the rest of his wisdom which you did not allow me to finish. The old chief finally said to me, 'But, my son, when the time comes that they will not let you learn your lessons except at the price of kneeling to their god, when they demand of you to become of their faith before they will give you a schoolbook, or feed you your food, or allow you your decent shelter from the snow and cold, then that is the time to tell them that they do not follow the way of their own Lord Jesus which He taught in the Holy Land two thousand snows before our little time here upon our mother earth. I once believed in Jesus Christ the Savior,' said my father, 'and I know his words as well as any agent. It was not His way to ask for payment, neither before nor after He gave of Himself or of His goods.'"

"In heaven's name," fumed Agent Monteith, breaking in again, "what are you trying to say, Joseph?"

And Joseph answered him very quietly, "I am trying to say that it is not my way either," and after that both men stood a considerable time staring right at each other.

"Well," said Agent Monteith at last, and somewhat nervously, "that is scarcely anything new. You have not been in church since your father tore up the Bible on this same spot eleven years ago."

"That is not what I mean, Agent."

"All right, all right, what is it that you do mean?"

"I mean about the boy."

"What about the boy?"

"I am doing with him as my father did with me when they would not teach me unless I prayed first."

"Joseph, I warn you!"

"It is too late for warning. All has been said. It is you and I who have failed, Agent, not this child. There is nothing he can do here. In his way he is wiser than either of us. He knows he is an Indian and cannot be a white man. I am taking him back to his own people, Agent. You will not see him in this place again. *Taz alago.*"

I could not have been more stunned.

Since I knew the importance of my position at the school, I had been waiting to learn what kind of punishment would be agreed upon as the terms of my staying here. Yet, instead, here was my chief taking me proudly by the hand and leading me out of that log-walled schoolhouse there at Lapwai, Idaho, in the severe winter of 1875, without one more spoken word of parting, or rearward glance of consideration, for powerful Indian Agent John Monteith.

I will say that it was a strange and wonderful feeling.

Thrilling to it, I got up behind Joseph on his broadbacked old brown traveling horse, and we set out through the falling snow toward the snug tepees along the Imnaha River where, since the most ancient one could remember, our Nez Perce people had spent their winters.

In all the long way home Joseph and I said not a word to one another, and that, too, was the Indian way. As he himself put it, all had been said back at Lapwai. Now was the time for riding in rich silence and, if a grateful Nez Perce boy remained of the old beliefs, for offering up a final humble work to Hunyewat.

So it was I bowed my small head behind Joseph's great shoulders and said my first prayer in five moons.

So it was I ended my Lapwai winter.

A TEST OF WILLS

Authors are traditionally asked to name those (other authors) who most influenced them in their choice of a writing field. The writer who influenced me the most did his bull-of-the-woods best, not to encourage me to write of the West, but to *not* write of it.

He exhorted me.

Threatened.

Pleaded — with his karate-hardened hands embracing my throat.

Explained — that mercy killing by a Black Belt was an honor.

Cajoled — in a muted whisper to be heard in Anchorage, or at least Salinas, that he wouldn't let me suffer.

He was magnificent.

And he was, of course, the late great Will Cook, the Jack London of our times, the man who lived what he wrote, and then some. He it was who physically mirrored Captain Wolf Larsen, of the sealing schooner *Ghost*, and who so mentally whipsawed me to admit to the problem inherent in trying to make a writing reputation in the Western novel category.

Will said it could not be done. He argued that the history of the Western genre showed no single case of an author in that genre being accepted as a serious writer. He held resolutely to his contention and, to the day of his death, was continuing to say neither of us would ever "make it" as Western writers.

I never did disagree with him but lacked his conviction that all we need do, as writers who took ourselves seriously, was to get out of the Western trap and we would at once be seen as candidates for "serious" consideration. I made no early effort to test Will's urgent message, but *he* did with novels like *Sabrina Kane*. These original surges did not produce the acceptance Will had so fervently forecast, and he returned to the bitter sage. This, he contended, was the clear choice of survival as a writer, and not any demonstration that his anti-Western bias was wrong. I suggested it wasn't any overwhelming demonstration, either, of his argument that recognition awaited us both in the straight historical novel, or contemporary novel, did we but make the move resolutely away from the Western.

I am certain Will was still seeing this Evening Star of non-Western fame luring him over yon twilight horizon when the dreadful pain encompassed him, stilling both the fierce heart and the restless, scintillating mind in the same sad moment of Might Have Been.

Will Cook remains a landmark in my writing life, a rough-hewn, loyal and dead-true friend, and more, a constant believer in Will Henry, a man who would not quit either in his own behalf, or that of his friend who, like himself, he believed was betraying his gift of fine writing by squandering that gift upon the barren sands of the Western desert.

I believe Will Cook could have done anything he wanted in the commercial field in any genre. The sadness was, I think, that he had been born in a sense to write his superb Western stories (*The Peacemakers, Comanche Captives, Fort Starke, Last Command, The Outcasts,* many others) and this was his unwanted genius, but his genius nonetheless. In his foreshortened life, he wrote 57 novels, nearly all of the unwanted Western variety. He was correct in his assessment of the impenetrable wall of criticism and academic snobbery which, he vowed to the end, would *never* open to admit the Western to pass in with honors as serious literature of the American scene. That wall and that criticism and snobbery, despite a recent campus rush to discover the Western novel as a native art form, stands today as immovable as ever Will Cook predicted. It is the one aspect of the Western as serious American literature that has not been resolved. I myself see it as possible of that solution in our time, but doubtful. For his time, Will Cook had it nailed. If only he could have lived to see the present awakening of the academic community to the existence of Western writers and Western writing as *respectable!*

Had he done so, however, he would never have admitted he was wrong. He would only have clouded that wild dark face of his and slitted those obsidian eyes, to rumble, "Oh, horseapples! Nothing's changed. The forslugging bastards. They'll never let you in."

I never made the break old Will guaranteed would make me famous, and more, acceptable. I tried it, writing a Henry W. Allen contemporary adventure novel, *The Bells of Tayopa,* subsequently published as *Tayopa!* But the bells never rang on the cash registers, nor did the chapels on campus unleash their joyful carillons in herald of the tidings that Will Henry had just come through the wall with Seventh Cavalry guidon rampant in the literary wind.

Neither did academe, or the print critics, hail in noisy welcome such attempted hardcover escape works as *Genesis Five,* nor its follow-up paperback effort, *See How They Run,* the first a science fiction treatise of secret Soviet genetic engineering, the second a time-survival Black settlement in an old underground railroad sub-station in the heart of "the great Okemokee Swamp."

The rejections never delayed me. I did not see them as failures but only friendly warning notices to get at once back where I belonged, writing the best Western "serious" novels that I could manage, with old dear Will Cook jogging my elbow to tangle and stack the Hermes Keys.

You were right, Will. You still are.

But we're working on it.

Editor's Note: William Everett ("Will") Cook died in 1964 at the age of 42. A prolific pulp writer, Cook's first novel, *Frontier Feud,* appeared in 1954. In addition to his own name, he wrote under the pennames "Wade Everett," "James Keene," and "Frank Peace."

Will & Will, 1955. "This was taken at a Hereford auction in Santa Rosa, California, during a Western Writers of America convention. The convention was running all right but Will & Will weren't running with it."   (Photo by Arthur Knight)

Writers are a touchy lot. Sometimes we bristle and hair-up about our line of work. This is one of those times. I don't like the uppity scribes who sniff down their noses at the happy ending story. I don't appreciate such fancy dan smirkers for a minute. But in the case of Sundown Smith I make grateful exception; the uppities got me ired enough to write his story: I figure there wasn't a better way to let a little light into their heads than to put down these words about old Sundown's way of seeing the world. You see, you don't take the happy ender away from the Old West without a fight. The happy ender is gospel "out there." It never flinches. It always starts out with the very most dire of unhappy beginnings, struggles desperately through the darkest of middle-ings, winds up with just the rightful lightning bolt of frontier justice for its final endings. Which should hint to the reader about here that Sundown Smith is no ordinary unwashed cowboy drifter but a very different breed of hero who will be tested within moments of our meeting him upon the peaceful sunny mountainside, by forces of brute evil a hundredfold more wicked than most men dream to see or face in their entire frightened lifetimes.

— W.H.

SUNDOWN SMITH

I t was utterly still upon the mountainside, as befitted a Sierra sunrise. Beside the lovely little mountain stream in a forest glade seemingly as remote as the moon from human evil, stood a ragged, one-man tent. Before the tent the coals of last night's campfire drifted a lazy wisp of scented pine smoke. The scolding of bluejays and the cheery small talk of the rushing creeklet provided the only important sounds.

Presently the tent flaps stirred and a man came out.

He stood yawning and stretching and scratching, clearly a man in no hurry to rush on toward his destiny. He was dressed in his customary nightclothes — which were also his dayclothes — a combination of worn, but very clean, blue jeans, and threadbare long-handled underwear. His faded gray flannel shirt he bore in the crook of his left arm; his run-over workboots he carried dangling in his right hand. The manner in which he accomplished his yawning and stretching and scratching while still retaining possession of these items was not a thing — not an art — lightly come by. It had taken years of patient practice.

Directly, the man had satisfied the morning's demand to ease the body ache of ground-sleeping and minor epidermal disturbances set up by pine needles, small rocks, sand fleas and the other habitues of his mountain couch.

Taking pause, he contemplated his campsite. He was, in the act, surveying the new day, and his entire worldly wealth with it.

He did not see much. A weary, wise old saddlehorse. An ax with a broken haft stuck in a cedar stump. A battered black coffeepot beside the fire. A shard of shaving mirror hung on a branchlet of a nearby pine. A mug, a brush, a bar of soap and a granite washpan seated upon a stump beside the pine. Little things, of little value.

Back at the tent flaps the man pursed his lips, shook his graying head in a dolefully philosophic way at what he saw.

Everything that met his eye was much like himself: a little old, a

little worn, a little worthless. Yes, he told himself musingly, he was a
poor man. A very poor man, and, in the ordinary sense, homeless. Yet
he knew that, somehow, he was rich. And, somehow, more at home in
the world than most.

He nodded to himself with the thought, then looked over toward the
fire. It was not twenty feet away, still the decision to cross over to it
was not to be made hastily. After a suitable bit he nodded again and set
out upon the journey. Arrived at the fire, he reached to pick up the
coffeepot and set it upon the hook above the coals. But the moment that
he bent forward, the old horse whickered petulantly.

The man stopped and looked off at the old horse. His glance, if testy,
was alight also with some inner warmth, for this was a very special, a
very dear friend.

"Mordecai," he announced severely, "How many times I got to tell
you not to talk to me till I've had my morning coffee?"

The question put, and going unanswered by Mordecai, he huffed on
about the business of putting the coffee to boil — measuring and grind-
ing the precious handful of beans — pouring the cold creek water —
setting the pot on the hook over the coals — throwing onto the coals the
exactly three chunks of bone-dry cedar required to roll the water, just
so, wasting neither the man's time — which was worth nothing — nor
the forest's firewood — which existed in an abundance of supply sufficient to stoke all the coffee fires of his lifetime ten million times com-
pounded.

As he worked, he talked continually to himself in a lively twosided
conversation; this in the manner of the Western man who is much
alone and who, perforce, enjoys his own company, or none at all. The
man did not mind this for it reduced argument to the minimum and
guaranteed victory in any debate to the party of the first part.

At the moment he was discussing Mordecai's future.

"Dawgone horse," he grumped. "Acts like he'd been took off his maw
two weeks ago, 'stead of twelve years. I'm gonna get me another pony
soon's I find work." He paused, glaring off, or trying to glare off, at
Mordecai.

"You cain't stop and spin decent no more. You cain't cut, nor change
leads without stumbling. You cain't head a critter worth a Indian-head
nickel, and you cain't catch up to nothing over three months old, and
you —"

He broke off, stomping his foot and whistling sharply.

"You hear me?" he demanded grumpily.

Mordecai heard him and whickered politely in reply.

"Dawgone right you do!" said the man. "And I mean what I say, too. I'm a'going to do it. Someday —"

"Someday" meant another ten or twelve years from then, or twenty. The old horse knew it, if the man did not. He had heard the identical threat more times, already, than there were pine needles on the floor of the little mountain glade. He whickered once more, the sound coming as closely as a dumb brute might come, to saying, "huh!" and then subsided wisely.

At the fire, the man gave him a ferocious look and returned his attention to the coffeepot.

A wisping stringer of aromatic steam was issuing from the ancient vessel, now, and the man removed the lid to inspect the cause thereof. Poking a tentative forefinger down into the pot, he winced and withdrew the member in considerable haste, flipping it and putting it tenderly to his lips to demonstrate that, as usual, he had burned himself in the line of duty.

But he was a man of some character, not to be deterred by the mundane frustrations of life.

Straightening from the fire, he moved over to the pine tree which bore the shard of shaving mirror. He peered into the glass, examining the quality of his five-day beard. In the marvelous mountain stillness the sound of his calloused fingers scraping over the wiry stubble was clearly audible. The man grimaced and shook his head at what he saw in the mirror.

He was looking at the reflection of advancing middle years and was not encouraged thereby. But the mirror showed more than that. It showed the crowsfeet at the eye corners deeply cut from the many years of smiling more often than weeping when the river failed to wash his way. It showed a tenderness of mouth and eye which knew no age, a love of the world and all within it, which could no more grow old than the rocks of the mountain around him. Yet all that the man saw was Sundown Smith, graying cowhand, itinerant ranch worker, saddle tramp, drifter, failure; a creature of the long-viewed lonely places; a man without friends, family, or known next-of-kin.

Still, there was a certain light behind that aging eye.

Sundown tilted his jaw. He angled it here and there, judging the condition and harvesting readiness of his beard with the eye of a wilderness expert.

"I dunno, I dunno —" he said to the face in the mirror. "A man should truly ought to keep hisself slick-jawed in case of company."

He picked up the old-fashioned straight-edged razor, which lay upon the stump among the other shaving tools. He held it out from him, eying it askance and at arm's length, as though it might bite him, if provoked. Then, warily bringing it closer, he ran a testing thumb over its honed bevel. At once, he cried out sharply, wincing and sucking his thumb and shaking it to show, undeniably, that he had cut himself.

The performance was as predictable and invariable as that of burning himself to see if the coffee was hot. Sundown Smith was an inept man. A man who, in his entire life, had never learned a solitary thing — except how to be happy.

He now cocked a rueful eye at the injured thumb, then looked back at his reflection in the mirror. His grin, when it came, was as optimistic as the morning sun.

"Naw, shucks," he decided, touching the beard again and shaking his head. "I won't do it. I ain't 'specting no callers. Leastways, not this year." He refolded the razor, returned it to the stump, adding in explanation to the man in the mirror. "Besides, I got to pack up and move on this morning." He nodded to both his selves and stumped off toward the fire, mumbling to the original. "Yes, sir, got to be moving along. But I'll just have my coffee before I think about it. As for reaping that there stubblefield, I can shave any time. Maybe next February. Say, March at the earliest. Yes, sir, April, anyway. Or May. . . ."

In such deceiving ways are ordered the lives of us all. Sundown Smith had just made a decision which could cost him his life. He did not know that, of course, and believed that he had handled the situation with great firmness and determination — qualities he admired vastly and knew very well that he did not possess.

Returned to the fire, he pulled up a convenient rock and seated himself. He poured a cup of the asphaltic brew from the tarred pot and sampled it cautiously. With an effort he swallowed the preliminary taste, his reaction indicating that it had the zest of liquid carbolic. Yet, with the brew once down, he widened his pale blue eyes and exclaimed to the mountainside, "Wonderful!"

When he took a second, exploratory sip, however, he shook his head critically. "Might need just a touch of sweetening," he allowed, doubtfully, and reached into one of his many pockets — he had donned the tattered shirt now — and brought forth an ancient leather poke of the variety used to carry nuggets and gold dust.

Peering around to make sure he was not observed, he loosened the drawstring and extracted one lump of cane sugar.

The moment he did this, the old horse whickered aggressively from his picket pin on the grassy creek bank. Sundown glared over at him resentfully. Closing the poke, he restored it to its hiding place and complained his way over to the old horse. His mien was one of outright menace, but once at Mordecai's side, he again searched the clearing to make certain there were no spies about, then growlingly fed the sugar to the bony gelding.

Starting back to the fire, he stopped, wheeled around and said defiantly to the horse, "One of these days I'm going to find out what it tastes like with sugar in it! You see if I don't! Dawgone horse —"

At the fire, he seated himself, upon the ground this time, his back to a friendly, windfallen log. Reaching, he retrieved his coffee cup from the rock upon which he had left it. As he started it toward his lips a mountain jay scolded him with sudden sauciness from above.

Sundown scowled up at the jay and scolded him right back in a whistle-perfect imitation of the bird's rusty-throated comment. Then, winking broadly at the offender, he turned back to his coffee. Retasting it, he smiled as though it were the veritable nectar of the gods. He leaned back against the log, raised the cup on high, drank steadily.

All was right in the small, lonely world of Sundown Smith.

The little campsite beside the talkative stream was now as nature had made it. It was a rule of Sundown's existence that man was not created to improve upon the other works of the Lord. When he left a place, he tried to see that no stone lay differently from the way it had when he had come upon that place. It was, perhaps, his way of acknowledging, without presuming upon the relationship, that there was a Creator and that he, Sundown Smith, was mightly beholden to Him for such gifts of sunshine, pine smell, bluejay argumentation and creek-water small talk, which made of Sundown's life the blessing he considered it to be.

But now Sundown was tightening the last strap upon the ill-shaped bedroll behind Mordecai's saddle. Then, standing back to scan the campsite, he nodded, finally satisfied he had left no scar upon the sweet land.

For some reason he sighed. He always felt a little sad when he left a place which he knew he would never see again. It was like saying farewell to an old friend even though he had known that friend a mere brief night.

But it was time to go. Where, or why, Sundown Smith did not know. It was just time. Time, maybe, to look for that job that never got found. Time to seek out a new set of bluejays with which to argue. Time to climb a new mountain. To see a new sunrise. To hear a new stream laugh in some different, lonely place. It was just time to travel on.

Sundown waved his hand to the little glade and turned to mount up. As he did so, he stood, poised, one foot in the nearside stirrup, head cocked, listening intently.

Far and faint and thin with distance, he heard the baying of a pack of hounds. It was not a musical baying but a fierce and savage and an eager sound, and it made Sundown fearful. The least shadow of a frown crossed his face.

Leaving the old horse, he went up on a rocky ridge, nearby, which overlooked the entire slope of the mountain. It was the first time that morning he had moved faster than a contemplative amble, or muttering stomp, and it was evident he sensed some impending trouble.

His instincts had not betrayed him: he was about to learn that the question "to shave, or not to shave," could be a deadly one.

The previous night, down in the valley mining community of Carbide Wells, an unknown killer had struck at an isolated ranchhouse outside the main settlement. He had gotten away into the hills without being identified, save that he was a "kind of rough-looking, trampy man; a stranger with a 'stubbly' beard" — and that dangerous identification had been made by a small boy at the ranch.

The nature of the killer's crime had no bearing upon Sundown Smith's story, and, moreover, decent words could not be found to describe it for anyone's story. Suffice to say that when the townfolk and rough miners of Carbide Wells found the young widow Bromley, they voted the killer the rope — *whoever* he was, and *wherever* they should find him.

Now, having reached the rocky ridge, Sundown crouched poised atop it, peering down upon the slope below. The sight which met his anxious gaze fulfilled the fears put up in him by the angry baying of the hounds. Far down along the rocky shoulder of the mountain, a mounted posse was moving upward, single file. Ahead of this grim string of manhunters, held in leash by a man on foot, three cross-bred airedale-and-bloodhound trail dogs bawled fiercely, as they followed upon the track of their closely driven but still unseen quarry.

That was the manner in which Sundown Smith became aware of the presence of evil upon his mountainside; with the sighting of three vicious cross-bred hounds and a hanging posse only minutes behind the human brute who would come to have, in later years of mountain lore, a name remembered to this day on the eastern slope of the Sierra — the Beast of Carbide Wells. And it was the manner in which, seconds later, Sundown came to learn that there was nothing but himself, and his weary old horse, standing between that shadow of human evil and certain death at the end of the posse's rope.

As Sundown now straightened from his frightened look below and would turn to go back to Mordecai and remove both the old horse and himself from this climbing danger, a noiseless figure rose up from out the rocks behind him and felled Sundown with a single blow from the gnarled treelimb club which he bore in his hairy fist.

Sundown fell heavily and his assailant seized from his frayed belt-holster the old cap-and-ball Colt's Revolver, which had been Sundown's camp mate for perhaps longer than even old Mordecai. He turned its muzzle upon Sundown, as the latter now rolled over and made groggy effort to sit up. Succeeding in the effort, he squinted painfully up into the face of the man bending over him with the rusted gun.

When Sundown saw him, he knew that his first fearful feeling at hearing the hounds crying upon the mountainside had been a true premonition.

The face above him was the face of a madman. It peered at him from the form of a Neanderthal brute who cowered and crouched and snarled like the hunted beast he was. There was no similarity between the Beast and Sundown Smith save that both were born of woman. But, wait. There was one small sameness about them. No, two small samenesses. Both wore poor and rough and ragged clothing, and both wore a five-day bristle of heavy, graying beard. It was a singular similarity. And, swiftly, a lethal one.

"Get up!" ordered the Beast, jamming the Colt's muzzle into Sundown's temple. "Make one sound and I'll blow your head off." His voice was a rasping, throat-deep growl, and he certainly meant his command literally. But Sundown was compelled to advise him otherwise, out of honesty.

"Not with that old cannon, you won't, mister," he grinned painfully.

"Shucks, firing pin's been broke most fifteen year. I use her for hammering tent-pegs."

Instantly, the Beast slashed Sundown across the forehead with the long barrel of the weapon. The blow smashed him down onto the rock of the ledge.

"It will kill you all the same," snarled the fugitive. "You had better believe it!"

Sundown nodded his head with difficulty.

"I believe it, mister," he said. Then, with a jerk of the thumb which indicated the slope below, he added.

"They after you?"

The other's lips writhed in what was intended to be a smile, but came out a silent snarl. "They *were* after me," he said. Then, savagely. "Get out of them clothes! Boots and all! We're gonna switch duds, complete."

Sundown's blue eyes widened apprehensively.

"Now wait just a minute, fella," he protested. "That posse don't know me from Adam's off-ox!"

"Don't worry," leered his companion. "They don't know me either."

Sundown at first nodded, as though that were an information of some relief. Then, belatedly, he realized what had gotten past him. "That's what I meant!" he gasped. "If they don't know you and they don't know me, and they was to catch up to me in your clothes, they might —"

"Percisely," said his threatener. "Not only they might, I'm betting my life they will. Now you get out of them clothes. Boots, first!" He broke off, cackling in a wild sort of demon's laugh which put the goose bumps up Sundown's spine from tailpiece to clavicle bone. "Them hounds don't know me, personal, no more than the posse does. It's these here old workboots they're trailing —" As he talked, he was toeing off his low-heeled brogans and kicking them toward Sundown Smith. "They'll foller whoever's in them!"

He interrupted himself for another of the demoniacal laughs, then let Sundown in on the secret of the joke.

"I never did want to die with my boots on," he chortled, "so I'll just let you do it for me!"

As instantly as the crazy laugh had broken, it stopped. Sundown had been standing still, listening to the demented fugitive, forgetting to continue with the disrobing which the latter had ordered. Like a bolt, the long revolver barrel struck again. It caught Sundown across the bridge of the nose, driving him to his knees on the rock ledge and spinning the forested world about him. When he could hear again, it was to recognize the snarl of the Beast in his ringing ears. The words, *"Hop to it, you hear me? I'll lay your skull wide open next time!"* and Sundown nodded that he understood, and began pulling and tugging to get his boots off, so that he might exchange them for his life — and the foul footgear of the killer.

The two men stood by Sundown's aging mount, down at the abandoned campsite. They had now completed the transfer of clothing and the time, for both of them, was growing short. Upon the mountainside, beyond, the baying of the hounds was hoarsely near, and the voice of their handler could be heard shouting them on.

Staring off toward the renewed clamor of his pursuers the Beast growled like a cornered animal, then swung up on Sundown's old horse. He pulled Sundown's old Model '73 Winchester from the saddle scabbard and snarled down at its owner, "You use this for driving tent-pegs, too?"

Sundown put up his hands as though to ward off a possible shot, and answered hurriedly. "Oh, no — that's my camp meat gun. Be careful. She works."

"She better work!" rasped the Beast, and levered the Winchester in a sharp, hard way which showed that he knew the gun and how to use it for something deadlier than getting in camp meat. He stood in his stirrups, twisting to look off in the direction of the mountain slope.

"Listen to them hongry-bellied devils a'bawling for their breakfast," he muttered. "Ain't that sweet music to a man's ears? Especially, when he's got a good horse under him and a center-shooting gun in his hand?" He laughed the weird laugh again, then snapped at Sundown, "Get going. Walk toward them yonder trees. And walk nice and deep and straight. Stomp hard. Leave them hounds a sharp-edged set of prints to sniff out. March!"

Sundown threw up his hands, appealing to the other's human mercy.

"Listen, mister. This is cold-blood murder. That posse won't give me two seconds to explain. They won't even let me open my mouth." He paused, then concluded fearfully. "Mister, they won't give me a chance!"

The brutish rider leaned down, hissing the words at him.

"They won't give *you* a chance? Listen, you no-good saddle-bum, I killed a woman down there last night. She played the lady with me and I killed her for it. She called me an animal, you hear? *Me!* An *animal!* Well, she won't call nobody an animal now — not ever . . ."

He paused, a fiercely angry expression passing over his face. There was a sudden sort of fear in it, too, as though he had just remembered something about his crime. Something he had forgotten, and which was dangerous to him. He shook his head, talking now to himself.

"Nor that kid neither; the dirty, sniveling, little sneak!" He tailed it off, then went on. "Not by the time I get back down there, he won't. I'd ought to have got him before. I knowed there was something I forgot. If only them three cowboys hadn't of rode in on me just when they did. But the kid won't tell. Oh, no, he won't tell. He'll be just like his maw. Nice and quiet and with that funny, vacant-eyed look —" He uttered the cracked laugh once more, sat in the saddle staring off emptily. Recovering with a jerk, he whirled back to Sundown Smith.

"They won't give *you* a chance," he repeated hoarsely. "Mister, what chance you think they'd give *me?*"

Sundown looked up at him with quiet dignity, answering with a courage that neither of them recognized.

"Mister," he said, "what chance you think they ought to give you?"

The Beast kicked the old horse into Sundown and drove the steelshod butt of the rifle down into the cup of his shoulder, caving him to the ground.

"Now you get up, mister," he told Sundown in a dead level growl, "and you walk like you was told to walk."

This time Sundown obeyed him. He crossed the open ground of the glade, his enemy herding him from horseback, and behind. At the timbered edge of the clearing the latter hauled up the old horse and snarled down at Sundown, "That's far enough."

He hesitated, twisting in the saddle, again, to listen to an excited burst of yelping from the dogs. Then he turned back to Sundown Smith.

"Good luck, 'killer,'" he told him, uttering the crazy laugh in appreciation of his own grisly joke. "You oughtn't to have no trouble with that posse. Just tell them who you are. They'll understand." Then, wanderingly, and with the vacant look in his eyes once more. "We're all just strangers passing on the long, long trail. So long, 'stranger.'"

He broke forth into his wild laughter for the last time, and rode out, driving the old horse into the timber. They had disappeared in a matter of seconds.

Sundown stood stock-still for a long, held breath, staring after them. Then he wheeled and ran back toward the rocky ledge. There, he fell upon his stomach and peered over, tense and fearful of his pursuers as the true killer had been before him. What he saw below turned his saddle-tanned face pale as a clean-washed bedsheet, brought the beat of his frightened heart high and suffocating into his throat.

The hounds and the posse were nearly upon him. They were, in chilling fact, coursing the very ledge beneath the one where Sundown crouched — not thirty feet from his whitened face. They had one more switchback of the trail to negotiate and they would be upon the ledge with him.

Now the prospect of death was very near, and very clear, to Sundown Smith. Also the prospect of life.

On foot, unarmed, a man who had never raised either hand or voice in anger against a fellow man, he had, somehow, to run down and seize the real murderer for the Carbide posse, before the Carbide posse ran down and seized him for the real murderer. The odds against him were eleven to one — the number of men in the posse — plus three savage, cross-bred hounds and thirty feet of hemp rope.

Sundown wheeled blindly to flee, instinct his only guide.

He began sliding and slipping down the rocks toward his former campsite, and toward the cheery little mountain streamlet which formed its frothy skirt. At water's edge, he plunged in to his knees, and began stumbling and fighting his way up the green-foaming current. He made it to an upper bend of the small raceway, got around the bend and up and over a four-foot falls above it. There, he held up to regain his breath, looking back and downward upon his late camp, as he panted desperately, and thought, in the same vein, of some way in which he might extend his momentary advantage over the hounds and their hard-eyed master.

As he watched, the dogs came bawling into the clearing below. At mid-clearing they went into a mill, straightened out, ran Sundown's track to the streambank, milled again where he had entered the water. Their handler pulled them off the scent and returned, with them, to mid-clearing. The posse now came up on the gallop. Swinging down from their lathered mounts, its members went into gesturing discussion with the houndman. The delay, Sundown knew, would be brief.

He was now at the bend of another stream than the icy small one in which he presently crouched.

He had been lucky, had gotten a start on the dogs, had borrowed ten minutes on his life's saving account. He could, possibly, get away now if he thought only of himself. But in his entire life, Sundown Smith had never thought only of himself. And the habits of a lifetime do not alter, even in the face of death.

Sundown's mind was not on the hounds or the possemen. It was on the words of the Beast — the words he had snarled about that little boy left on the lonely ranch somewhere down in the valley — a very young, very innocent, very much alive little boy who would now be the only witness in the world who could identify the *real* killer. It was suddenly in the desperately reaching mind of Sundown Smith that the brute who had brought down the mother, would not hesitate to stalk the son; as, indeed, he had threatened to do.

The criminal will always return to the scene of the crime, was the thought which now framed itself in Sundown's mind. Well, Sundown did not know about that. But he did know about something else. He had spent a lifetime in the wild and he knew this: *that an animal will frequently return to its last night's kill* — and the man who had taken his old horse, Mordecai, and left him afoot in his murderer's filthy rags, was not a man but an animal.

Sundown's face mirrored the terror that thought brought up in him. He reached, again, to seize the pine root which would pull him out of the stream. Once upon the rocky bank, above, he resumed his flight, following the faint trail along the stream's edge. Soon he was out of the heavy timber, into a more open, boulder-dotted country on the very flank of the mountain that loomed above Carbide Valley. As he reached this exposed terrain, the baying of the hounds was renewed with a bursting clamor. Sundown knew what the change in the baying meant. They had found his exit-point above the waterfall and their handler, sensing the nearness of chase's end, had unleashed them.

With the speed of life urgency, but not panic, he wheeled and ran once more. He knew where he was going, now, and he ran with a strength he had not possessed before. He was running for two lives and somehow that idea lent him the will to outdistance the dogs to the objective that could mean the second, far more important, of those two lives.

He remembered, from the previous day's journey around this same mountain flank, an old logging flume standing stark and rickety upon the crest above the trail. From its vantage above the trail, it plunged down the mountain's side straightaway toward the valley so far below. If a man could reach that flume ahead of the hounds, and if it still ran with water, and if he still had the strength to climb up its underpinnings and plunge into its precipitous race —

The three questions drove Sundown onward. They drove him well. He did beat the hounds to the flume, he did clamber up its sunbleached timbers, he did find water in its weathered flume and he did summon the will to leap into that water and to be whirled away down the mountainside.

The hounds had come so close they had torn a strip of cloth from his trouser leg. The posse had galloped up so swiftly that they had seen him poised to plunge into the flume, and had fired at him from horseback, one of the richochetting bullets striking him across the bunched muscles of his right shoulder and staggering him almost off the high dizziness of the flume's trestle.

He was thus marked for the killing, should they ever come up to him, but Sundown did not care about that. He cared only about the one other question which still remained unanswered in his race to reach the valley: who would come first to the secluded ranch house outside Carbide Wells?

Would it be Sundown Smith, or the Beast?

The sun went, twilight came, lingered briefly and was gone. Full dark fell and still Sundown had not come to the ranchhouse. But as the moon rose far out across the misting fields of the long valley, he saw, close at hand, and hidden until now by some bouldered brush lands lying before him, the lamplight of a cheery kitchen window winking at him with warm hope. Gathering his tired limbs, he set out on the last of the hours-long trail.

The Rochester lamp on the red-checkered tablecloth in the kitchen of the Bromley ranch house guttered to a sudden draft stirring through the room. Both the small boy and the old woman seated over their supper in the kitchen, glanced up at the one window. But the window was closed, and so was the one door into the room from the front of the house, and the one door out of it to the back of the house; and Bobbie Bromley and his Aunt Martha Sonnenberg nodded to each other and matched pale smiles and bent again to their eating.

Outside the house, along the kitchen wall, a shadow rose up from the high grass and brown weeds ten feet past the window, toward the front porch of the house. The shadow moved along the wall, to the window, and stopped. Then it moved again, and its maker slid in beneath the window and stood up beside it to peer in side-glancingly, and swift.

It was Sundown Smith.

When he looked in, his first thought was to sigh and to smile, for the boy was all right, and he was in time. But the second thought came in on the heels of the first, and he glanced nervously toward the front porch.

Was he in time?

He had just sneaked past that front porch and seen, there, the shotgun guard posted by the posse. The guard had been propped up against the closed and bolted front door, tilted in his chair as though naturally dozed off at his post of duty. But now it seemed to Sundown that he had never seen a man sit so still — a breathing man — and, of a sudden, the chilling thought re-took him: *was he in time?*

He had feared to stop and alert that guard. The man, in the startlement of being awakened, and seeing him so roughly clad and unshaven, might fire before he asked any questions, or before Sundown could answer him any. The sawed-off 10-guage L. C. Smith in his lap had loomed awfully blunt and deadly-looking to Sundown, and he had not dared to move over the rail and announce himself, at the time. Now, that second chilling thought was telling him that perhaps he was not in time, that perhaps it was now too late to awaken the guard. A man had to know, however. He could not simply stand there beneath that window waiting for the killer to make himself known — if he *was* there ahead of Sundown.

The drifter shrank closer to the wall, returned again to the tall weeds, crawled swiftly to the front porch rail and over it to approach the guard on tiptoe and to touch him lightly on the shoulder and whisper aloud, "it's a friend — please don't move or make a sound."

The guard obeyed Sundown. He neither moved, nor made a sound. And it was then Sundown noticed something. The shotgun which had been in the guard's lap only moments before, was no longer there. The shotgun was gone. And around the guard's neck, as Sundown leaned fearfully forward to see, was a short piece of broken halter rope, tied and rove in a perfect imitation of a tiny hangman's noose.

The guard was dead. Sundown did not touch him and did not need to. A man senses these things when he has lived long alone among the wild creatures, learning their ways, acquiring their instincts. The guard was dead and the small boy and the old woman were alone in the Bromley ranch house.

Alone, except for Sundown Smith.

Sundown was at yet another bend of the stream.

He could flee, now, and save himself. The posse man's horse stood saddled and ready in the outer yard. Life lay only that short distance away, and life was still sweet to Sundown Smith. But he looked at the shadow of the horse under the cottonwoods in the outer yard, and shook his head.

There had been something in the little boy's face, a look of loneliness and longing, all too familiar to Sundown Smith. Sundown knew how it felt to be alone — and lonely.

He shook his head again, and turned and went back over the porch rail and toward the kitchen window and toward seven-year-old Bobbie Bromley. Sundown was terribly afraid but would not turn away now. He understood the terminal quality of his decision. It was Sundown Smith against the Beast of Carbide Wells.

The kitchen window glass shattered with an inward, nerve-wrenching crash. The boy gasped and the old woman cried out. By then Sundown was through the window, had leaped to the table, seized and blown out the smoking lamp. The inrush of total blackness was blinked away by all three in the handful of seconds which followed. In this stillness, Sundown's soft voice pleaded with the two at the table. "Boy," he said, "and you, lady, you must believe me. I am your friend. There is not time, now, to tell you who I am — but the other one, the one you may think I am — is outside the house. He is yonder, there, in the night, somewheres, and he has come back down off the mountain to kill the boy —"

He stopped, and he could hear their breathing, close and tense in the thinning darkness of the room.

"But mister —"

"No, boy, don't talk. Listen."

Sundown stopped, again, taking his own advice and listening for a sound outside the house. He heard only silence, and the stir of the wind wandering up the valley.

"Lady, are you kin of the boy?"

"No, not blood kin. He ain't any of that left."

"It makes him and me even," said Sundown softly. "Boy, do you think I killed your mother?"

"You look like the man — your clothes and all — but you don't sound like him."

"Believe your ears, boy. Will you do that for old Sundown? Lady, will you believe in me? And tell the boy to listen? A woman knows. A woman's not like a man. She feels. She senses things. I mean past her eyes and ears. You know what I mean, lady? You believe me?"

"Yes," said Aunt Martha Sonnenberg. "I believe you. We will do as he says, Bobbie. If that man who killed your poor dear mother is out there —"

Outside the broken window a dry weed scraped against the cracked sideboards of the house's wall. There was no wind moving at the moment, and Sundown finished quietly for her, "That man *is* out there, lady. Come on. Into the parlor. Go first, boy. Take my hand. Here, lady, you take my other one."

They went soundlessly, Bobbie leading the way, feeling the excitement and fear of the deadly game rise up within him. Sundown held up, listening at the door into the kitchen. Then he came away, quickly, and whispered to Aunt Martha. "He is out there in the kitchen. Just came through the broken window. Now, there is that horse of the shotgun guard's out under them cottonwoods. Can you ride?"

"Of course I can ride!"

Sundown eased open the front door, took her by the arm, forcing her out upon the porch.

"Then, lady," he said, "you get on that horse and you ride for Carbide Wells and you pray every jump of the way!"

Aunt Martha Sonnenberg was sixty-seven years old. She had been in that valley when the Paiutes were bad and when a woman took orders from her menfolk without talking back. "Lord bless you, cowboy!" she murmured. "I'll be back with help soon's the horse will let me." She was gone then, scurrying across the dust of the moonlit yard like an old hen running from a hawk shadow. She got the horse free, and made it up onto him and got him safely away in a snorting gallop.

But it had all taken time, and made noise, and now the door into the kitchen slammed open and banged back against the parlor wall, and Sundown could hear the brute breathing in the blackness. He had not let go of Bobbie Bromley's hand the whole while, and now he squeezed it hard. Bobbie squeezed back, firm and quick, and Sundown thanked the Lord above that the boy had gumption and innards enough to go around.

Sundown felt in the dark for the chair back near his left hand. Finding it, he changed the set of his feet, let go of the boy, swept up the chair and hurled it across the room toward the breathing of the Beast.

It was the luck of the innocent, then. The chair struck thuddingly and, as it did, Sundown seized up the boy and ran out the front door and dove, with him, over the porch rail into the tangled, windblown weeds. Behind him, he heard the Beast growl deep in his throat. He put his hand over Bobbie's mouth and whispered, "Lie quiet, boy. I don't think he seen us go over the rail. The chair must of took him, full-on, and that's God's luck as ever was."

Presently, they saw the silhouette of the killer come out and move around the porch. Then it disappeared back into the house and they saw the flare of the match spurt up in the kitchen, as the Beast found and lit the lamp. His figure, black and hulking against the lamplight, the guard's shotgun dangling from one long arm, the deepest eyes shining like a varmint's in the yellow glare of the coal oil put the shivers to the bone in Bobbie Bromley's thin body.

Sundown tightened his arm about him and said, "Boy, we cain't stay here, now. He means to come out and tromp us out with the light and the scattergun. He knows I ain't got no weapon. And less'n we can find one —"

He stopped, listening hard again.

A new sound — or, rather, an old one — had come to his straining ears. Just up the valley, near the rock-girt rise over which he had come to drop down on the Bromley ranch house, the baying of hounds in full tongue burst into sudden, startling clamor. Sundown shivered now. The odds in the game were going up. Now he had not alone the deadly stealth of the killer against him, but the lethal creep of the clock, as well. For if the posse should come up soon, with the men finding the murdered shotgun guard and the dogs finding him, Sundown Smith, then he would still hang. And hang so swiftly he would be given not even the chance to state his true name, let alone the nature of his defense, or state of innocence.

"Mister Sundown —" the boy had been thinking, and now whispered tensely to the old cowboy holding him. "You said something about us finding a weapon. I know where there's a turrible weapon. I seen Paw use it onct, when I was little, to near kill a proddy range bull that had wandered into the yard and cornered Maw 'twixt the barn and house."

"Boy," said Sundown Smith, "what are you talking about?"

The killer was moving through the house again, now, coming from the kitchen, through the parlor, with the lamp and the shotgun.

"The old hayfork," answered the boy, watching the killer, with Sundown, and keeping his voice down to a field-mouse rustle, "It's in the barn, where Paw left it. He broke it on the bull and bought hisself a new one next trip to town. Maw sold the new one when we auctioned off the equipment after Paw was took."

"You sure it's there where your Paw left it? You seen it lately, boy?" muttered Sundown.

"No, I ain't certain. But I know where he left it."

"Can you find it, you reckon?"

The boy was still watching the house. The killer had come out on the porch now and was standing holding up the lamp, throwing its light this way and that.

"I reckon I'd better *try*," he said to Sundown, and Sundown nodded and felt a lump come up in his throat. He patted the boy on the shoulder and whispered back, "me, too," and reached around in the grass until he found a rock the general size and heft of a Rocky Ford muskmelon. "When I pitch this rock over to the far side of the house, you be ready to evaporate like a broom-swatted cat, you hear?" he asked the boy. "I hear," replied the latter, and Sundown rose up and pitched the rock over the house.

The rock fell, just so, on the far side of the house. It made a good crackling noise in the matted-dry weeds over there and the killer was off the porch and crouching toward the sound like a big, dark-bearded cat walking down a covey of fledgling quail. He moved so quickly that Sundown had to remind the boy to run, before he might smell out the decoy rock and come for them, full tilt.

They made it to the barn, slipping in the rear through a broken wallboard the boy knew of. The doors were hasped and locked, and the killer had not heard them across the barn lot. They had, perhaps, five minutes to find the old hayfork, and to figure out what to do with it when — and if — they did find it.

"Boy," said Sundown Smith, "he'll be here soon. There ain't but just so many places he'll look before he *knows* where we are. Two sides, and back and front of the house, and that's it. He's been front and one side. We ain't no world of time."

"You wait here, Mister Sundown."

"No, we dassn't separate for a minute. Here's my hand."

The boy took his hand and, together, they went through the musty gloom of the empty barn to the front stall where the lad remembered his father putting the rusted head of the old hayfork. The fork was there; the fork and about two feet of the broken, spear-pointed, hickory haft which was all that remained of its once five-foot handle.

"She'll do," said Sundown Smith, taking the wicked tines from the boy, and feeling them, and the remnant of handle, in the darkness. Then, softly. "Boy, is there nothing else you can think of? Anything at all, we might use for — well, you know."

"No," said the boy, "nothing."

"She'll *have to do*, then," said Sundown, hefting the fork. "Let's go, boy."

"Mister Sundown, I got a name. It's Bobbie. Bobbie Bromley. Junior."

"All right, Bobbie Bromley Junior. We still got to go. Fast."

"You going to stab him with the fork? Hide behind the door, maybe, and get him when he comes in?"

"I wouldn't dast risk it. Not with his kind. He's like a wild critter, boy. He'd smell me out."

"Well, what you aim to do then? If you're afraid to use the fork on him, how's it to do us any good?"

"We got one chance, boy. Is that a loft ladder yonder?"

"Yes, sir."

"Is there a hay trap in the loft?"

Yes, sir; over this here front stall, right where we're at. Paw used this stall for hay storage."

"All right, boy. You skin up that ladder and you keep an eye peeled on the house. When you see him coming you knock twicst on the loft floor. You hear?"

"Sure. But we can see him coming from here. Them wallboard cracks is half an inch wide. They'll let the lamp shine through easy."

"Boy," said Sundown, "when he figgers we're out here in the barn, he ain't going to be coming after us with no lamplight to let us lay for him by. He'll be coming in the pitch dark, and all you'll see of him is his shadow floating 'crost the barn lot. Now you get!"

"Yes, sir!" gulped Bobbie Bromley, and got.

The earth in the bed of the stall was loamy and soft and deep with the working of many an unshod hayrig pony's hooves. Sundown was able to get the sharp-pointed stub of the handle well down into it. Almost, in fact, halfway down to the steel of the fork head itself. He set

it as precisely beneath the frame of the trapdoor in the loft floor directly above, as he was able to guess at in the nearly blind gloom of the
barn. He had only the slightly less black square of the opening to work
by, but that had to suffice. And to suffice fast.

Above him, now, he heard the two sharp raps on the floor, and his
heart came up against the base of his throat, cutting off his breath.

More than one sound came to him in the ensuing silence.

Up-valley, the hounds were drawing nearer, their belling taking on
a fierceness it had not held before. Sundown recognized it as the same
change in their cry he had heard upon the mountainside, just before
reaching the logging flume. They had been unleashed again, and were
running.

Time again: time was trying to kill him and the Bromley lad as surely as was that black shadow floating toward them across the barn lot. If
that posse took him, Sundown, now, the true murderer would need
only to shy off and hide out until the Carbide men had gone on. He
would then be free to continue his stalk of the boy. For whether the
men took Bobbie along with them or not, they would leave the ranch
convinced they had destroyed his mother's killer, and that he was thus
removed from danger. True, the lad might try to defend him. But no
convincing he had forced on the latter by knocking in that kitchen window and blowing out the lamp would hold up with those tight-jawed
men who had been running his track since early dawn and who, certainly, when they now came up to him, would be in no mood to listen
to the thin stories of either a homeless drifter, or a big-eyed, weanling
ranch boy. The old woman, now, Aunt Martha, she would have been a
different pot of pepper. Her word would have held off the rope long
enough for the men to fan out and put the dogs on the real killer's
track. And had her word been not enough, she likely would have taken
up a whiffletree or a churn handle and impressed the Carbide committee directly. But Aunt Martha was long gone, and the chances of her
getting back from town in time to take a stand in favor of Sundown
Smith were about equal to an Apache Indian's winning a popularity
contest in Yavapai County, Arizona.

No. It was still Sundown Smith against the Beast.

And soon.

Outside the locked barn doors, now, he heard the scrape of a boot.
Then the snuffling, exactly like that of an animal, at the three-inch
crack between the sun-warped doors. The Beast was trying to smell
him out.

The quality of the outer night's darkness was now being thinned by the climb of the moon. When the killer left the doors to slide around the barn wall, pausing every few steps to sniff anew at some new separation of the sliding boards, Sundown could clearly follow the blot of his shadow. In this way, he knew when he had reached, and glided through, the missing board at the back of the barn. Now it was up to Sundown.

Deliberately, he ran for the foot of the loft ladder. Having the jump on the killer, he beat him to the rickety steps, and up them, into the loft. At the foot of the ladder, the Beast stopped, staring upward into the absolute pitch-dark blackness of the haymow.

When Sundown heard the creak of the first rung, he moved two steps away from the ladder's head. And only two steps.

From then, he counted each rung creak until there was utter stillness again. The Beast was in the loft, at the ladder's head — holding his breath, waiting for his eyes to adjust to the greater darkness. Sundown held his own breath, praying he could outlast the other. He could. Presently, he heard the labored indrawing of the killer's heavy breath begin again. Instantly, he spun about and leaped away from the ladder head, toward the loft hay trap and Bobbie Bromley. As instantly, the Beast snarled and lunged after him.

Sundown counted his steps away from the ladder, as he had counted them running toward it in the barn below. When he had taken the same number, he jumped as hard as he could to clear the yawning hay trap. He alighted safely on the far side, colliding in the soft mat of hay beyond with the hidden boy. In the same instant he heard behind him the killer's startled gasp, as his reaching feet found, and treaded wildly, the empty air of the open trap.

There followed a silence that seemed interminable but could not, in fact, have lasted more than fractions of a second. The period to this dread pause was a single wrenching cry from below. After that, there was no sound at all in the old barn. None, that is, save for the whisper made by the lips of Sundown Smith moving in fervent thanks to Providence for a delivery from evil which could not, surely, or solely, be explained by his own small, desperate craft.

The hounds came up to Sundown, with the posse at their bawling heels, just as he and the boy emerged from the darkened barn. The exhausted posse men would not listen to any protest, either of Sundown's or Bobbie Bromley's. They had the evidence of their own eyes, and that of the hounds' noses. It was enough. They had the rope shaken out and flung up over the hay-winch beam almost before the drifter or his new friend could utter an intelligible word, and certainly before the ranch boy could comprehend that they truly meant to hang the gentle man who had saved his life. When they had rove the coarse noose about Sundown's neck and tightened it testingly over the hayloft beam, he understood, and then he rushed forward crying his outrage between choking sobs and blows of his small fists at the braced legs of the rope men.

Still, the leader of the posse would not listen. Signaling one of the men to subdue the boy, he brought from his saddlebag the piece of trouser-leg torn from Sundown's faded Levi's upon the mountainside above. He fitted it into place on the drifter's leg and said to the boy, "Bobbie, this is the man who hurt your mother. He has lied to you but you must not believe him. You must believe us. We know what we are doing."

"You don't! you don't!" cried the boy, but the leader made a grim sign to his men, and they stood back to make room for their fellows on the rope's end.

"Take the boy around the corner of the barn," ordered the leader, and the man who had Bobbie nodded and dragged him out of sight, as instructed.

But the boy would not quit; not any more than the drifter had quit when he had the opportunity. Once the barn's corner hid him and his captor from the other men, he kicked hard and sure through the darkness, and his sharp boot toe did not miss the mark. The posse man yelled out a curse and let go of the boy to grab his injured shin.

Bobbie shot away from him like a stomped-on cottontail. Scooting on around the barn, he found the broken board at the rear, slid in and dashed through the darkness toward the front stall. The shadow man had still had the shotgun when he had fallen through Sundown's trap. If Bobbie could find the weapon, now, maybe he could use it to make the posse men understand that seven year's old and all stirred up, did not disqualify a boy from knowing what he knew, and being able to testify to it. Yes sir, if they wouldn't listen to a little boy, maybe they would listen to a big gun.

It took a great deal of courage to go near that stall, and near what lay within it, impaled upon the broken hay fork. But Bobbie Bromley went into the stall, and found the guard's doublebarreled, full-choke, Ithica 10-guage shotgun. And, with the weapon, he returned to the barnfront scene, just as the ropemen lay back on the rough strand, and Sundown's boot toes lifted free of the ground.

With no time to do anything else, the boy shouldered the huge double and triggered the left barrel blasting upward into the night, and into the barn's winch beam and the Carbide posse's tautened rope.

The charge of Number 4 buckshot dissolved the rope and a foot and a half of the end of the winch beam. Sundown fell to earth, unharmed save for a chafing of his five-day beard, and the Carbide posse men swung about to face a seven-year-old ranch boy who still had one shell to go, and didn't hesitate to let them know it.

He devoted the gape of the 10-gauge's bores to the general vicinity of the posse leader's belt buckle, and directed his remarks to the latter in no uncertain terms.

"The other tube's for you, Mr. Hannigan —" he broke off the threat to cock the big outside hammer of the remaining barrel, and in the silence which ensued, he added tearfully, *"— less'n you 'gree to look in the barn like Mister Sundown asked you to. Now you git!"*

Mr. Hannigan was no fool. He did not care to argue points of proper procedure with a small boy and a very big shotgun on full cock. He got.

The rest of the posse men went with him. When they had pried off the hasp of the doors and had flung them wide and stomped inside, holding high the Rochester lamp fetched from where the killer had left it in the house, they all stopped, stark-staring, at what they saw in the first stall.

The leader quickly blew out the lamp and said to his men, "Boys, get out of here; we can come back in the morning with tools and a wagon."

Outside the barn, he put his heavy arm around Bobbie Bromley's shoulders and muttered, "Bobbie, I reckon you know we're sorry. You done a brave thing, boy, and we're all mightily proud of you. Yes," he said, looking up to nod at Sundown Smith, "and of your friend, yonder, too."

He stepped to Sundown's side and said in a low voice, "We mean it, mister. You got a home in Carbide Valley long as you want."

Sundown just smiled in his sad, slow way, and shook his head.

"Thank you, Mr. Hannigan," he said. "But when the boy is rightly settled, I reckon I'll just be drifting on."

In Carbide Wells, it was just a little after sunrise. It was a day shot full of sunshine and good cheer. In front of the local office of the Inter-

Pacific Stagelines, a Concord coach was drawn up and a small crowd gathered.

Here assembled were the good folk of Carbide Wells, town and countryside, gathered to say goodbye to little Bobbie Bromley. It ought to have been a happy time, but it was not. Like Sundown Smith, Bobbie Bromley was now without kith or kin in the whole broad world, and he was being sent on the morning stage to San Francisco, where the state authorities would find a home for him.

To one side of the crowd stood Sundown Smith and his wise old horse, Mordecai. Upon the seat box of the stage Bobbie Bromley was perched beside the grizzled driver, trying to be far braver than he was. Neither his heart nor his eyes was in the business. Both were bent across the heads of the crowd toward Sundown Smith. And it became suddenly very doubtful that Bobbie would ever get to San Francisdo. Or, indeed, that he would ever start for San Francisco. That last look at Sundown and old Mordecai said more, in silence, than all the noisy wishes of the crowd could ever render in out-loud farewells.

In the final, fateful second before the stage driver kicked off his brake and yelled, "Hee-yahh!" at his waiting horses, Bobbie slid down off the seat box and ran waving, from that high, unhappy perch, toward Sundown Smith. As he reached him, the drifter got down from old Mordecai and gathered the boy up in his arms and held him there, defying the closing crowd like an aging gray wolf brought to bay, bewildered and confused, but determined somehow to defend what was his, and the boy's.

There was some hot talk, then, and loud. But Mr. Hannigan, who was the mayor of Carbide Wells, shut it off pretty prompt. "The question is," he said, "whether the boy goes our way, or his own. We'll put it to a vote." He paused, spreading his thick legs and jutting his big jaw. "Hannigan," he said, "votes for the boy."

Sundown and the boy stood high upon the mountainside looking back and down upon Carbide Wells for the last time.

They were leaving the valley to go over the mountain and look for that job of Sundown's, which it was to be hoped they would never find. On the way, they would seek some new bluejays with which to argue. They would search for another sunlit glade on another lofty slope. They would listen for the laughter of some new, small stream, in some different and distant place. But this time it would not be a lonely place.

With this thought, Sundown nodded to himself, and plodded on up the trail, the boy coming gladly behind him.

On the last rise before the trail bent to hide the town, Sundown paused to wait for the boy, and for the old horse the boy was leading. When they came up, the three of them stood looking back, just for the least, grace note of remembering. Then, straightening, Sundown nodded for the final time.

"Indeed," he said softly to himself, and through force of lifetime habit, "the question comes naturally to a man's mind, if there will ever be another lonely place for Mordecai and me. . . ."

When he spoke, the boy smiled up at him and put his hand in Sundown's hand and the two friends turned and went over the last rise, the old horse following them like a faithful dog.

THE
HORSE PUCKEY
HUCKSTERS

O nce upon a very brief and wondrous time, there was a place
called the Old West. In it, men were men, women were
women, and children kept their places and shut their faces and did
what they were told to do and — miracle of miracles! — it worked.

During the present century, other men have been enthralled by this
star-bright time in our history and the very luckiest among them have
been permitted to tell the stories of its splendid flowering and swift
fading. This blessed breed has been called Western writers, and they
are us.

We chosen few have been charged with keeping alive both the fact
and the fiction of the way it was out there along the wild frontier. The
code word is both. It is never enough to keep the record by itself. It is
the translation of that record wherein tales are born, legends extended
and the truth made larger than it is, and thereby more lasting.

Lately, we have been betraying that legacy.

The Old West has become a battleground for the socio-political guerrillas of Today. Western novels are no longer merely Western novels.
They are political tracts for whatever contemporary "philosophy of the
people" the particular author wants to promote. His reasons may range
from ignorance to sedition, but the result is the same whether noble or
base of intent. The West has been re-engineered into a sort of sagebrush
urban sprawl, wherein all of today's injustices of the asphalt jungle
prevailed.

It was not a place where honest and brave folk struggled at life's risk
to secure and make fruitful a new and giant land. It was not a God-
given second chance where penniless emigrants prayed — and found

— that freedom could be reborn and old lives of repeated failure and despair made quick again, and brave with the hope for a better future.

Oh no, say the clear-eyed prophets of the New West, it was never anything like that.

It was, rather, a cauldron of colonialist exploitation, a kettle of rampant bigotry, race hatred, religious intolerance, inhuman and uncivil wrongs and rip-offs, corruptly set to boil by, you guessed it, the unspeakable Americans.

It was, one is left to gather, a Pale Face settler ghetto wherein the Anglo reigned not alone supreme but exceeding wicked.

Well, now, let's see.

Perhaps the choice of the words ignorance and sedition is overblown to describe these Western writers who use the category to peddle modern political cant which did not exist on the frontier. Did not and could not, one might add, since its promulgators were still safely in the Old Country. But for those who are uncomfortable with the tight collar of tough language, how about a kinder term? A compromise. Something that will fit better because not so publicly binding.

How about good old uncomplicated commerical pandering? Which, for the purposes of this paper, shall be taken to mean that writer who, in order to sell what he writes, has deliberately applied the current political tilt of our times, to the life and times of the 18th century and called his work a Western novel.

It is a temptingly successful recipe.

It sells.

It is also a sell-out, not only of the Old West but of the entire American past. This nation was not built by pacifist, unisex, utterly equal pioneer "persons." It was built by exceptional people. By men with their hair where it belonged. By women who knew they already ruled their men. By children who understood their place in the family pecking order and who pecked away nonetheless as happily as though they were as brilliant as we keep telling today's children they are.

Oh, yes, friends, this country was not founded and expanded by ordinary people. Hell, they were the most extraordinary people who ever built a nation anywhere. So let's quit applying to yesterday's wild and dangerous frontier today's social horse puckey. If you put enough manure on anything, you will get fungus and toadstools.

Certainly, the so-called little people are the saltlick of any land. But little doesn't mean ordinary. A man is not by any definition little because he is poor or uneducated or black or Latino or Amerind or striving under any racial, religious, physical or political handicap. A man is a little man only if he says he is, feels he is, and works hard at being a little man. If, on the other hand, he thinks big and works big and fights big for what he believes in, then he is a big man. He can be a nation builder, a frontier tamer. And I don't give a damn if he is otherwise poor as Job's Turkey, ignorant of formal schooling as a Barbary Ape, stands five-feet-one in his high-heeled boots, is black as rubber ink, white as a flounder's umbilicus, or red as Geronimo's bandana. If he stands tall, he is tall. Period.

As a somewhat writer on the Westward expansion, I have been a documented friend of the downtrodden. My track record reaches back into the 1950s, well before it became *avant garde* in Western fiction to champion the losers. My sources and my aims in so doing were, and still are, real. What interests me are the real sources and real aims of those Western writers who extoll indiscriminately the blanket cause of those losers as sacrosanct, while pressing their discriminatory attacks on the winners, both as individuals and by group.

These authors succeed in making a crime out of the fact that the average settler was not able to worry properly about universal brotherhood and social justice when he was dying of disease untreated, of thirst at the waterhole where there was no water, of friendly Indian lance and arrow wound, or raging flood or freezing blue norther or smothering dust storm, or just plain starving to death in an arid, hostile land where human rights and five cents would buy you a bad cigar, and where the sole political philosophy that worked was the oldest rule of the human race, survival.

And when it came to that, to staying alive, it was never the rightest or the leftest or the middle-est that survived, but the fittest.

So what, really, is today's Western story tract writer getting at?

If his idea is wholly the inspiration of his personal empathy with the historically-shorted human elements of the fronter, then he must be prepared to have his work examined, not as history, but as seen through the fact-bending prism of social emotion known as relevance.

That is the operative word, friends — relevance. And what does it mean?

Well, to you as a Western writer it means that if you cannot write your yarn so that Joe Reader, perusing it, cries out, "Yeah, Jeez, just like today!" then you aren't being relevant. You must get old Joe wound up so overtight that he rushes out to embrace the street people and man the barricades, all lathered to go forward in love (and the life-style of his choice) toward social justice with the brothers and sisters of peace and freedom.

Now if, this phony relevance issue aside, there exists bona fide proof for such historical grafting backward of today's political headlines upon those of the past, that's great. You will have the best possible of Western stories. But somehow a few of us creaky fundamentalists have missed this ready source of relevance. And, as it has served our competitors so well, we yearn to repair our ignorance and so share in the profits.

The reason this possible oversight of genuine sources worries us cave dwellers so, is that we have diligently searched the records for just such invaluable bits of real history and have, as the Westerners say, come up dry. Dig as we may for these historical incidents which mirror a precise reflection of today's ills upon the heretofore thought healthy body of the frontier past, we are still drilling dusters. Damn, but it does get discouraging.

To close the brief for those rebutters who may rush to breech the barbed wire against the author's troglodyte kind, let it be summed thusly for the court:

I deplore the trend toward imposing the political and social miasmas of our own moribund times upon the vital body of our frontier past. God knows the pioneer days were cruel enough to the Indian and other non-white groups competing in what was essentially a white man's world. There is no human need to transfuse today's exotic social diseases into the simpler bloodstream of yesterday. The very idea of depicting the Indian or black man of frontier times as the same Indian or black man who lives today is a *reductio ad absurdum*. It is spurious and wrongful to both black and Indian history. And it is, as implemented by those Western writers who practice it, an act of love and friendship which, being given, the black man and the red need no other foe to harm them.

Oppositely, for the writer who attempts historical responsibility in his efforts to grant the black man, the Indian, the Mexican and the indentured Chinese, his rightful and long overdue place in the frontier sun, these blatant ideological transplants are anathema.

Moreover, there seems no surcease from them, no justice against their continued false testimony.

Yet we shall prevail.

And our credo will **remain**; Tell it like it was.

If we cannot do that, we can at least try to do it. If it evolves that the relevance is inherent to our theme, developing as the effect of our tale rather than its cause, we will have gone the distance honorably and be blessed accordingly. But if we start out with the relevance and *then* twist and wrench and contort our story to make it fit that relevance, why shucks, Ma'am, all we will wind up with is a best seller.

And who needs *that?*

Will in 1972, at the National Cowboy Hall of Fame and Western Heritage Center, accepting the "Wrangler" award for best historical novel — *Chiricahua*.

I first heard this story when I was working in a sheep camp. It was so long ago that I truly forget if that camp were in Wyoming or Utah or Colorado. I'll say it was Wyoming. But the fact is maybe I don't want to remember. That was my first, last and forever sheep camp. Then as now, whiteface cattle were my abiding breed. Them, and the little fourteen-hand mustang cowponies that showed the tossing fine head and hightail pride of their Spanish-blood ancestors. But loving cows and cowhorses only reminded old-time cowboys like Tom Isley how mortally they detested the bleating "woolies" that razor-grazed and ruined the grand Wyoming pastures that God had meant for the eternal use of range cattle. Love and hate, you see. The oldest story since the Lord rounded up and branded the earth in six days, then couldn't rest on the seventh for worrying about what He had wrought. But that small matter attended to, and nobody needing a renewal of his faith more than wandering, out-of-work cowhand Tom Isley, so then did appear to him a stranger out of the black and freezing night, asking nothing of Isley but to share his fire as man had done with man since palest dawn of human time. How the weary cowboy's fortunes were altered by what he learned from stranger Eben — of war and peace and bleating woolies — forms the surprise ending of this story remembered from so very long ago in faraway Wyoming, when both Will Henry and the Old West were half-a-century younger.

— W.H.

ISLEY'S STRANGER

He rode a mule. He was middling tall, middling spare, middling young. He wore a soft dark curly beard. His bedroll was one thready army blanket wound round a coffee can, tin cup, plate, razor, camp ax, Bible, copy of the *Rubáiyát*, a mouth harp, some other few treasures of like necessity in the wilderness.

Of course, Isley didn't see all those things when the drifter rode up to his fire that night on Wolf Mountain flats. They came out later, after Isley had asked him to light down and dig in, the same as any decent man would do with a stranger riding up on him out of the dark and thirty miles from the next shelter. Isley always denied that he was smote with Christian charity, sweet reason or unbounding brother love in issuing the invite. It was simply that nobody turns anybody away out on the Wyoming range in late fall. Not with a norther building over Tongue River at twilight and the wind beginning to snap like a trapped weasel come full dark. No, sir. Not, especially, when that somebody looks at you with eyes that would make a kicked hound seem happy, and asks only to warm his hands and hear a friendly voice before riding on.

Well, Isley had a snug place. Anyway, it was for a line rider working alone in that big country. Isley could tell you that holes were hard to find out there in the wide open. And this one he had was ample big for two, or so he figured.

It was a sort of outcrop of the base rock making a three-sided room at the top of a long, rolling swell of ground about midway of the twenty-mile flats. It has been poled and sodded over by some riders before Isley, and was not the poorest place in that country to bed down by several. Oh, what the heck, it wasn't the Brown Hotel in Denver, nor even the Drover's in Cheyenne. Sure, the years had washed the roof sods. And, sure, in a hard rain you had to wear your hat tipped back to keep the drip from spiking you down the nape of your shirt collar. But the three rock sides were airtight and the open side was south-facing. Likewise, the old grass roof, seepy or not, still cut out ninety-and-nine percent of the wind. Besides, it wasn't raining that night, nor about to. Moreover, Isley was a man who would see the sun with his head in a charcoal sack during an eclipse. It wasn't any effort, then, for him to ease up off his hunkers, step around the fire, bat the smoke out of his eyes, grin shy and say:

"Warm your hands, hell, stranger; unrope your bedroll and move in!"

They hit if off from scratch.

While the wanderer ate the grub Isley insisted on fixing for him — eating wasn't exactly what he did with it, it was more like inhaling — the little K-Bar hand had a chance to study his company. Usually, Isley was pretty fair at sizing a man, but this one had him winging. Was he tall? No, he wasn't tall. Was he short, then? No, you wouldn't say he was exactly short either. Middling, that's what he was. What kind of face, then? Long? Thin? Square? Horsey? Fine? Handsome? Ugly? No, none of these things, and all of them too. He just had a face. It was like his build, just middling. So it went; the longer Isley looked at him, the less he saw that he could hang a guess on. With one flicker of the fire he looked sissy as skim milk. Then, with the next, he looked gritty as fish eggs rolled in sand. Cock your head one way and the fellow seemed so helpless he couldn't drive nails in a snowbank. Cock it the other and he appeared like he might haul hell out of its shuck. Isley decided he wouldn't bet either way on him in a tight election. One thing was certain, though. And that thing Isley would take bets on all winter. This curly-bearded boy hadn't been raised on the short grass. He wouldn't know a whiffletree from a wagon tongue, or a whey-belly bull from a bred heifer. He was as out of place in Wyoming as a cow on a front porch.

Isley was somewhat startled, then, when his guest got down the final mouthful of beans, reached for a refill from the coffeepot and said quietly.

"There's bad trouble herebouts, is there not, friend?"

Well, there was for a fact, but Isley couldn't see how this fellow, who looked like an out-of-work schoolteacher riding a long ways between jobs, could know anything about *that* kind of trouble.

"How come you to know that?" he asked. "It sure don't look to me like trouble would be in your line. No offense, mind you, mister. But around here — well, put it this way — there ain't nobody looking up the trouble we got. Most of us does our best to peer over it, or around it. What's your stake in the Wolf Mountain War, pardner?"

"Is that what it's called?" the other said softly. Then, with that sweet-sad smile that lighted up his pale face like candle shine, "Isn't it wonderful what pretty names men can think up for such ugly things? *'The Wolf Mountain War.'* It has alliteration, poetry, intrigue, beauty—"

Isley began to get a little edgy. This bearded one he had invited in out of the wind was not quite all he ought to be, he decided. He had best move careful. Sometimes these nutty ones were harmless, other times they would kill you quicker than anthrax juice.

He tried sending a return smile with his reply.

"Well, yes, whatever you say, friend. It's just another fight over grass and water, whatever you want to call it for a name. There's them as has the range, and them as wants the range. It don't change none."

"Which side are you on, Isley?"

"Well, now, you might say that —" Isley broke off to stare at him. *"Isley?"* he said. "How'd you know my name?"

The stranger looked uncomfortable, just for a moment. He appeared to glance around as though stalling for a good answer. Then, he nodded and pointed to Isley's saddle propped against the rear wall.

"I read it on your stirrup fender, just now."

Isley frowned. He looked over at the saddle. Even knowing where he had worked in that *T-o-m I-s-l-e-y* with copperhead rivets and a star-nose punch, he couldn't see it. It lay up under the fender on the saddle skirt about an inch or so, purposely put there so he could reveal it to prove ownership in case somebody borrowed it without asking.

"Pretty good eyes," he said to the stranger. "That's mighty small print considering its got to be read through a quarter inch of skirting leather."

The stranger only smiled.

"The skirt is curled a little, Isley, and the rivets catch the firelight. Call it that, plus a blind-luck guess."

The small puncher was not to be put off.

"Well," he said, "if you're such a powerful good blind-luck guesser, answer me this: how'd you know to call me Isley, instead of Tom?"

"Does it matter. Would you prefer Tom?"

"No, hell no, that ain't what I mean. Everybody calls me Isley. I ain't been called Tom in twenty years." His querulously knit brows drew in closer yet. "And by the way," he added, "while it ain't custom

to ask handles in these parts, I never did cotton to being put to the
social disadvantage. Makes a man feel he ain't been give his full and
equal American rights. I mean, where the other feller knows who you
are, but you ain't any idee who he might be. You foller me, friend?"

"You wish me to give you a name. Something you can call me.
Something more tangible than friend."

"No, it don't have to be nothing more tangle-able than friend.
Friend will do fine. I ain't trying to trap you."

"I know you aren't, Isley. I will tell you what. You call me Eben."

"Eben? That's an off-trail name. I never heard of it."

"It's an old Hebrew name, Isley."

"Oh? I ain't heard of them neither. Sounds like a southern tribe.
Maybe Kioway or Comanche strain. Up here we got mostly Sioux and
Cheyenne."

"The Hebrews weren't Indians exactly, though they were nomadic
and fierce fighters. We call them Jews today."

"Oh, sure. Now, I knowed that."

"Of course you did."

They sat silent a spell, then Isley nodded.

"Well, Eben she is. Eben, what?"

"Just Eben."

"You mean like I'm just Isley?"

"Why not?"

"No good reason." Isley shrugged it off, while still bothered by it.
"Well," he said, "that brings us back to where we started. How come
you knowed about our trouble up here? And how come you got so far
into the country without crossing trails with one side or the other? I
would say this would be about the onhealthiest climate for strangers
since the Grahams and Tewksburys had at it down in Arizony Territory. I don't see how you got ten miles past Casper, let alone clear up
here into the Big Horn Country."

Eben laughed. It was a quiet laugh, soft and friendly.

"You've provided material to keep us up all night," he said. "Let us
just say that I go where trouble is, and that I know how to find my way
to it."

Isley squinted at him, his own voice soft with seriousness.

"You're right; we'd best turn in. As for you and finding trouble, I got
just this one say to say: I hope you're as good at sloping away from it as
you are at stumbling onto it."

The other nodded thoughtfully, face sad again.

"Then, this Wolf Mountain War is as bad as I believed," he said.

"Mister," replied Isley, "when you have put your foot into this mess, you have not just stepped into *anybody's* cow chip; you have lit with both brogans square in the middle of the granddaddy pasture flapjack of them all."

"Colorful," smiled Eben wryly, "but entirely accurate I fear. I hope I'm not too late."

"For what?" asked Isley. "It can't be stopped, for it's already started."

"I didn't mean too late to stop it, I meant too late to see justice done. That's the way I was in Pleasant Valley; too late, too late —"

He let it trail off, as Isley's eyes first widened, then narrowed, with suspicion.

"You was *there?*" he said, "in that Graham-Tewksbury feud?"

"I was there; I was not in the feud."

"Say!" said Isley enthusiastically, curiosity overcoming doubt, "who the hell won that thing, anyways; the sheepmen or the cattlemen? Naturally, we're some interested, seeing how we got the same breed of cat to skin up here."

"Neither side won," said Eben. "Neither side ever wins a war. The best that can be done is that some good comes out of the bad; that, in some small way, the rights of the innocent survive."

Isley, like most simple men of his time, had had the Bible read to him in his youth. Now he nodded again.

"You mean 'the meek shall inherit the earth'? he asked.

"That's close," admitted his companion. "But they never inherit anything but the sins of the strong, unless they have help in time. That's what worries me. There's always so much trouble and so little time."

"That all you do, mister? Go around looking for trouble to mix into?"

"It's enough, Isley," smiled the other sadly. "Believe me it is enough."

The little cowboy shook his head.

"You know something, Eben," he said honestly. "I think you're a mite touched."

The pale youth sighed, his soft curls moving in assent.

"Do you know something, Isley?" he answered. "I have never been to any place where the men did not say the same thing. . . ."

Next morning the early snow clouds were still lying heavy to the north, but the wind had quieted. Breakfast was a lot cheerier than last night's supper, and it turned out the newcomer wasn't such a nut as Isley had figured. He wasn't looking for trouble, at all, but for a job the same as everybody else. What he really wanted was some place to hole in for the winter. He asked Isley about employment prospects at the K-Bar, and was informed they were somewhat scanter than bee tracks in a blizzard. Expecially, said Isley, for a boy who looked as though he had never been caught on the blister end of a shovel.

Eben assured the little rider that he could work and Isley, more to show him to the other hands than thinking Old Man Reston would put him on, agreed to let him ride along in with him to the homeplace. Once there, though, things took an odd turn and Isley was right back to being confused about his discovery.

As far as the other hands went, they didn't make much of the stranger. They thought he looked as though he had wintered pretty hard last year, hadn't come on with the spring grass. Most figured he wouldn't make it through another cold snap. To the man, they allowed that the Old Man would eat him alive. That is, providing he showed the gall to go on up to the big house and insult the old devil's intelligence by telling him to his bare face that he aimed to hit him for work. A cow ranch in October is no place to be looking for gainful employment. The fact this daunsy stray didn't know that, stamped him a real tinhorn. Naturally, the whole bunch traipsed up to the house and spied through the front room window to see the murder committed. Isley got so choused up over the roostering the boys were giving his protégé that, in a moment of sheer inspiration, he offered to cover all Reston money in the crowd. He was just talking, but his pals decided to charge him for the privilege. By the time he had taken the last bet, he was in hock for his wages up to the spring roundup. And, by the time he had gotten up the the house door with Eben in tow, he would have gladly given twice over that amount to be back out on the Wolf Mountain flats or, indeed, any other place as many miles from the K-Bar owner's notoriously lively temperament.

He was stuck, though, and would not squeal. With more courage than Custer's bugler blowing the second charge at the Little Big Horn, he raised his hand and rapped on the ranchhouse door. He did bolster himself with an underbreath blasphemy, however, and Eben shook his head and said, "Take not the name of the Lord thy God in vain, Isley. Remember, your strength is as the strength of ten." Isley shot him a curdled look. Then he glanced up at the sky. "Lord, Lord," he said, "what have I done to deserve this?" He didn't get any answer from above, but did draw one from within. It suggested in sulfuric terms that they come in and close the door after them. As well, it promised corporal punishment for any corral-mud or shred of critter-matter stomped into the living-room rug, or any time consumed, past sixty seconds, in stating the grievance, taking no for an answer, and getting the hell back outside where they belonged.

Since the offer was delivered in the range bull's bellow generally associated with H.F. Reston, Senior, in one of his mellower states, Isley hastened to take it up.

"Mr. Reston," he said, once safe inside and the door heeled shut, "this here is Eben, and he's looking for work."

Henry Reston turned red, then white. He made a sound like a boar grizzly about to charge. Then, he strangled it, waited for his teeth to loosen their clamp on one another, waved toward the door and said, "Well, he couldn't be looking for it in better company, Isley. Good luck to the both of you."

"*What?*" said Isley in a smothered way.

"You heard me. And don't slam the door on your way out."

"But Mr. Reston, sir —"

"Isley." The older man got up from his desk. He was the size of an agey buffalo, and the sweetness too. "You remember damned well what I told you when you drug that last bum in here. Now you want to run a rest camp for all the drifters and sick stock that comes blowing into the barnyard with every first cold spell, you hop right on it. I'm trying to run a cow ranch, not a winter resort. Now you get that pilgrim out of here. You come back in twenty minutes, I'll have your check."

Isley was a man who would go so far. He wasn't a fighter but he didn't push too well. When he got his tail up and dropped his horns, he would stand his ground with most.

"I'll wait for it right here," he said.

"Why, you banty-legged little sparrowhawk, who the hell do you think you're telling what you'll do? *Out!*"

"*Mr. Reston* —" The stranger said it so quietly that it hit into the angry air louder than a yell. "Mr. Reston," he went on, "you're frightened. There is no call to take out your fears on Isley. Why not try me?"

"*You?*"

The Old Man just stared at him.

Isley wished he was far, far away. He felt very foolish right then. He couldn't agree more with the way the Old Man had said, "you." Here was this pale-faced, skinny drifter with the downy beard, soft eyes, quiet voice and sweet smile standing there in his rags and tatters and patches and, worst of all, his farmer's runover flat boots; here he was standing there looking like something the cat would have drug in but didn't have the nerve to; and here he was standing there with all that going against him and still telling the biggest cattleman in Big Horn basin to wind up and have a try at *him!* Well, Isley thought, in just about two seconds the Old Man was going to tie into him with a list of words that would raise a blood blister on a rawhide boot. That is, if he didn't just reach in the desk drawer, fetch out his pistol and shoot him dead on the spot.

But Isley was only beginning to be wrong.

"Well," breathed Henry Reston at last, "try you, eh?" He rumbled across the room to come to a halt in front of the slight and silent mule rider. He loomed wide as a barn door, tall as a wagon tongue. But he didn't fall in on the poor devil the way Isley had feared. He just studied him with a very curious light in his faded blue eyes, and finally added, "And just what, in God's name, would you suggest I try you *at?*"

"Anything. Anything at all."

Reston nodded. "Pretty big order."

The other returned the nod. "Would a man like you take a small order?"

The owner of the K-Bar jutted his jaw. "You ain't what you let on to be," he challenged. "What do you want here?"

"What Isley told you — a job."

"What brought you here?"

"There's trouble here."

"You like trouble?"

"No."

"Maybe you're a troublemaker."

"No. I make peace when I can."

"And when you can't?"

"I still try."

"You think me giving you a winter's work is going to help you along that path?"

"Yes. Otherwise, I wouldn't be here."

Again Henry Reston studied him. Reston was not, like Tom Isley, a simple man. He was a very complicated and powerful and driving man, and a dangerous man, too.

"I make a lot of noise when I'm riled," he said to the drifter. "Don't let that fool you. I'm a thinking man."

"If you weren't," said the other, "I wouldn't be asking to work for you. I know what you are."

"But I don't know what you are, eh, is that it?"

"No, I'm just a man looking for work. I always pay my way. If there's no work for me, I travel on. I don't stay where there's no job to do."

"Well, there's no job for you here in Big Horn basin."

"You mean not that you know of."

"By God! don't try to tell me what I mean, you ragamuffin!"

"What we are afraid of, we abuse. Why do you fear me?"

Reston looked at him startled.

"I? Fear you? You're crazy. You're not right in the head. I'm Henry F. Reston. I own this damned country!"

"I know; that's why I'm here."

"Now, what the devil do you mean by that?"

"Would the men in the valley give me work? They're poor. They haven't enough for themselves."

"How the hell do you know about the men in the valley?"

"I told you, Mr. Reston. There's trouble here. It's why I came. Now will you give me work, so that I may stay?"

"No! I'm damned if I will. Get out. The both of you!"

Isley started to sneak for the door, but Eben reached out and touched him on the arm. "Wait," he said.

"By God!" roared Reston, and started for the desk drawer.

But Eben stopped him, too, as easily as he had Isley.

"Don't open the drawer," he said. "You don't need a pistol. A pistol won't help you."

Reston came around slowly. To Isley's amazement, he showed real concern. This white-faced tumbleweed had him winging.

"Won't help me what?" he asked, scowlingly.

"Decide about me."

"Oh? Well, now, you ain't told me yet what it is I've got to decide about you. Except maybe whether to kill you or have you horse-whipped or drug on a rope twice around the bunkhouse. Now you tell me what needs deciding, past that."

"I want work."

Henry Reston started to turn red again, and Isley thought he would go for the drawer after all. But he did not.

"So you want work?" he said. "And you claim you can do anything? And you got the cheek to hair up to me and say, slick and flip, 'try me.' Well, all right, by God, I'll do it. Isley —"

"Yes, sir, Mr. Reston?"

"Go put that Black Bean horse in the bronc chute. Hang the bucking rig on him and clear out the corral."

"Good Lord, Mr. Reston, that outlaw ain't been rode since he stomped Charlie Tackaberry. He's ruint three men and —"

"You want your job back, Isley, saddle him."

"But —"

"Right now."

"No, sir," Isley began, hating to face the cold with no job, but knowing he couldn't be party to feeding the mule-rider to Black Bean, "I don't reckon I need your pay, Mr. Reston. Me and Eben will make out. Come on, Ebe."

He began to back out, but Eben shook his head.

"We need the work, Isley. Go saddle the horse."

"You don't know this devil! He's a killer."

"I've faced them before, Ilsey. Lots of them. Saddle him."

"You, a bronc stomper? Never. I bet you ain't been on a bucker in your whole life."

"I wasn't talking about horses, Isley, but about killers."

"No, sir," insisted the little cowboy stoutly, "I ain't a'going to do it. Black Bean will chew you up fine. It ain't worth it to do it for a miserable winter's keep. Let's go."

Eben took hold of his arm. Isley felt the grip. It took him like the talons of an eagle. Eben nodded.

"*Isley*," he said softly, "*saddle the horse.*"

The K-Bar hands got the old horse in the chute and saddled without anybody getting crippled. He had been named Black Bean from the Texas Ranger story of Bigfoot Wallace, where the Mexican general made the captive rangers draw a bean, each, from a pottery jug of mixed black and white ones; and the boys who got white beans lived and the boys who got black ones got shot. It was a good name for that old horse.

Isley didn't know what to expect of his friend by now. But he knew from long experience what to expect from Black Bean. The poor drifter

would have stood a better chance going against the Mexican firing
squad.

The other K-Bar boys *thought* they knew what was bound to take
place. This dude very plainly had never been far enough around the
teacup to find the handle. He was scarce man enough to climb over the
bronc chute to get on Black Bean, let alone to stay on him long enough
for them to get the blindfold off and the gate swung open.

But Isley wasn't off the pace as far as that. He knew Eben had
something in mind. And when the thin youth had scrambled over the
chute poles and more fallen, than fitted, into the bucking saddle, the
other hands sensed this too. They quit roostering and hoorawing the
pilgrim and got downright quiet. One or two — Gant Callahan and
Deece McKayne, first off — actually tried helping at the last. Gant
said, "Listen, buddy, don't try to stay with him. Just flop off the minute
he gets clear of the gates. We'll scoop you up 'fore he can turn on you."
Deece hung over the chute bars and whispered his advice, but Isley,
holding Black Bean's head, heard him. What he said was, "See that top
bar crost the gateposts? Reach for it the minute Isley whips off the
blind. Hoss will go right on out from under you, and all you got to do is
skin on up over the pole and set tight. You'll get spurred some by the
boys, but I don't want to be buryin' you in a feedsack, you hear?"

Fact was, that, between Gant and Deece giving him last-minute
prayers, and the other boys getting quiet, the whole operation slowed
down to where the Old Man yelled at Isley to pull the blind, and for
Wil Henniger to jerk the gate pin, or get out of the way and leave
somebody else do it — while they were on their way up to the big house
to pick up their pay. Being October and with that early blizzard
threatening, he had them where the hair was short. Wil yelled out,
"Powder River, let 'er buck!" and flung wide the gate. Isley pulled the
blind and jumped for his life.

Well, what followed was the biggest quiet since Giggles La Chance
decided to show up for church on Easter Sunday. And seeings that Giggles hadn't heard the preacher, wore a hat, or been seen abroad in
daylight for six years, that was some quiet.

What Black Bean did, sure enough deserved the tribute, however.
And every bit as much as Giggles La Chance.

Moreover, there was a connection between the two; the Devil
seemed involved, somehow, with both decisions.

That old horse, which had stomped more good riders into the corral
droppings than any sun-fisher since the Strawberry Roan, came out of

that bucking chute on a side-saddle trot, mincy and simpery as an old maid bell mare. He went around the corral bowing his neck and blowing out through his nostrils and rolling back those wally-mean eyes of his soft and dewy as a cow elk with a new calf. He made the circuit once around and brought up in front of the chute gate and stopped and spread out and stood like a five-gaited Kentucky saddlebred on the show stand; and that big quiet got so deep-still that when Dutch Hafner let out his held wind and said, "*Great Gawd Amighty!*" you'd have thought he'd shot off a cannon in a cemetery four o'clock of Good Friday morning.

Isley jumped and said, "Here, don't beller in a man's ear trumpet thataway!" and then got down off the chute fence and wandered off across the ranch lot talking to himself.

The others weren't much better off, but it was Old Man Reston who took it hardest of all.

That horse had meant a lot to him. He'd always sort of looked up to him. He was a great deal the same temperament as Old Henry. Mean and tough and smart and fearing neither God nor Devil nor any likeness of either which walked on two legs. Now, there he was out there making moony-eyes at the seedy drifter, and damn fools out of Henry F. Reston and the whole K-Bar crew.

It never occurred to Old Henry, as it later did to Isley, that Eben had done about the same thing to him, Reston, in his living room up to the ranch house, as he'd done to Black Bean in the bucking chute: which was to buffalo him out of a full gallop right down to a dead walk, without raising either voice or hand to do it. But by the time Isley got this figured out, there wasn't much of a way to use the information. Old Henry, cast down by losing his outlaw horse and made powerful uneasy by the whole performance, had given Isley his pay, and Eben fifteen dollars for his ride — the normal fee for bronc breaking in those parts — and asked them both to be off the K-Bar by sunset. Eben had offered the fifteen dollars to the Old Man for Black Bean, when he had heard him order Deece and Gant to take the old horse out and shoot him for wolf bait. Old Henry had allowed it was a Pecos swap to take anything for such a shambles, by which he meant an outright steal. But he was always closer with a dollar than the satin over a Can-Can dancer's seat, and so he took the deal, throwing in the bucking saddle, a good split-ear bridle and a week's grub in a greasy sack, to boot. It was maybe an hour short of sundown when Isley riding Eben's mule, and Eben astride the denatured killer, Black Bean, came to the west line of the K-Bar, in company with their escort.

"Well," said Dutch Hafner, "yonder's Bull Pine. Good luck, but don't come back."

Isley looked down into the basin of the Big Horn, sweeping from the foot of the ridge upon which they sat their horses, as far as the eye might reach, westward to Cody, Pitchfork, Meeteetse and the backing sawteeth of the Absoroka Range. The little puncher shook his head, sad, like any man, to be leaving home at only age forty-four.

"I dunno, Dutch," he mourned, "what's to become of us? There ain't no work in Bull Pine. Not for a cowhand. Not, especially, for a K-Bar cowhand."

"That's the gospel, Isley," said Deece McKayne, helpfully. "Fact is, was I you, I wouldn't scarce dast go inter Bull Pine, let alone inquire after work."

Gant Callahan, the third member of the honor guard, nodded his full agreement. "You cain't argue them marbles, Isley. Bull Pine ain't hardly nothing but one big sheep camp. I wisht there was something I could add to what Dutch has said, but there ain't. So good luck, and ride wide around them woolies."

Isley nodded back in misery. "My craw's so shrunk it wouldn't chamber a piece of pea gravel," he said. "I feel yellow as mustard without the bite."

"Yellow, hell!" snapped big Dutch, glaring at Deece and Gant. "These two idjuts ain't to be took serious, Isley. Somebody poured their brains in with a teaspoon, and got his arm joggled at that. Ain't no sheepman going to go at a cowboy in broad day, and you'll find work over yonder in the Pitchfork country. Lots of ranches there."

"Sure," said Isley, "and every one of them on the sharp lookout for a broke-down line rider and a pale-face mule wrangler to put on for the winter. Well, anyways, so long."

The three K-Bar hands raised their gloves in a mutually waved, "So long, Isley," and turned their horses back for the snug homeplace bunkhouse. Isley pushed up the collar of his worn blanket coat. The wind was beginning to spit a little sleet out of the north. It was hardly an hour's ride down the ridge and out over the flat to Bull Pine. Barring that, the next settlement — in cow country — was Greybull, on the river. That would take them till midnight to reach, and if this sleet turned to snow and came on thick — well, the hell with that, they had no choice. A K-Bar cowboy's chances in a blue norther were better than he could expect in a small-flock sheeptown like Bull Pine. Shivering, he turned to Eben.

"Come on," he said, "we got a six-hour ride."

The gentle drifter held back, shading his eyes and peering out across the basin. "Strange," he said, "it doesn't appear to be that far."

"Whoa up!" said Isley, suddenly alarmed. "What don't appear to be that far?"

"Why, Bull Pine, of course," replied the other, with his sad-soft smile. "Where else would we go?"

Isley could think of several places, one of them a sight warmer than the scraggly ridge they were sitting on. But he didn't want to be mean or small with the helpless pilgrim, no matter he had gotten him sacked and ordered off the K-Bar for good. So he didn't mention any of the options, but only shivered again and made a wry face and said edgily:

"I'd ought to know better than to ask, Ebe; but, why for we want to go to Bull Pine?"

"Because," said the bearded wanderer, "that's where the trouble is."

Eben was right. Bull Pine was where the trouble was.

All the past summer and preceding spring the cattlemen had harassed the flocks of the sheepmen in the lush pastures of the high country around the basin. Parts of flocks and whole flocks had been stampeded and run to death. Some had been put over cliffs. Some cascaded into the creeks. Others just plain chased till their hearts stopped. Nor had it been all sheep. A Basque herder had died and five Valley men had been hurt defending their flocks. So far no cattleman had died, nor even been hit, for it was they who always made the first jump and mostly at night. Now the sheepmen had had all they meant to take.

Those high country pastures were ninety percent government land, and the sheep had just as much right to them as the cattle. More right, really, because they were better suited to use by sheep than cattle. But the country, once so open and free and plenty for all, was filling up. Even in the twenty years since Isley was young, the Big Horn basin had grown six new towns and God alone knew how many upcreek, shoe-string cattle ranches. The sheep had come in late, though, only about ten years back. Bull Pine was the first, and sole, sheep town in northwest Wyoming, and it wasn't yet five years old. The cattlemen, headed by Old Henry Reston, meant to see that it didn't get another five years older, too. And Isley knew what Eben couldn't possibly know: that the early blizzard threatening now by the hour, was all the cattlemen had been waiting for. Behind its cover they meant to sweep down on Bull Pine in a fierce raid of the haying pens and winter sheds along the river. These shelters had been built in a community effort of the valley sheep ranchers working together to accomplish what no two or three or ten of them could do working alone. They were a livestockmen's curiosity known about as far away as Colorado, Utah and Montana. They had proved unbelievably successful and if allowed to continue uncontested, it might just be that the concept of winter feeding sheep in that country would catch on. If it did, half the honest cattlemen in Wyoming could be out of business. On the opposite hand, if some natural disaster should strike the Bull Pine feedlots — say like the fences giving way in a bad snowstorm — why then the idea of winter-feeding sheep in the valley would suffer a setback like nothing since old Brigham Young's seagulls had sailed into those Mormon crickets down by Deseret.

Knowing what he knew of the cattlemen's plan to aid nature in this matter of blowing over the sheepmen's fences during the first hard blizzard, Isley followed Eben into Bull Pine with all ten fingers and his main toes crossed.

By good luck they took a wrong turn or two of the trail on the way down off the ridge. Well, it wasn't exactly luck, either. Isley had something to do with it. But, no matter, when they came into Bull Pine it was so dark a man needed both hands to find his nose. Isley was more than content to have it so. Also, he would have been well pleased to have been allowed to stay out in front of the General Store holding the mounts, while Eben went within to seek the loan of some kind soul's shearing shed to get in out of the wind and snow for the night. But Eben said, no, that what he had in mind would require Isley's presence. The latter would simply have to gird up his courage and come along.

Groaning, the little K-Bar puncher got down. From the number of horses standing humpback to the wind at the hitch rail, half the sheepmen in the basin must be inside. That they would be so, rather than home getting set to hay their sheep through the coming storm, worried Isley a great deal. Could it be that the Bull Piners had some warning of the cattlemen's advance? Was this a council of range war they were stepping into the middle of? Isley shivered.

"Ebe," he pleaded, "please leave me stay out here and keep our stock company. Me and them sheepmen ain't nothing in common saving for two legs and one head and maybeso a kind word for motherhood.

Now, be a good feller and rustle on in there by yourself and line us up a woodshed or sheep pen or hayrick to hole up in for the night."

Eben shook his head. "No," he insisted, "you must come in with me. You are essential to the entire situation."

Isley shivered again, but stood resolute. "Listen, Ebe," he warned, "this here blizzard is a'going to swarm down the valley like Grant through Cumberland Gap. We don't get under cover we're going to be froze as the back of a bronze statue's lap. Or like them poor sheep when Old Henry and his boys busts them loose in the dark of dawn tomorry."

"It's Old Henry and the others I'm thinking of," said Eben quietly. "We must be ready for them. Come along."

But Isley cowered back. "Ebe." he said, "I know that kicking never done nobody but a mule no good. Still, I got to plead self defense, here. So don't crowd me. I'm all rared back, and I ain't a'going in there conscious."

He actually drew up one wrinkled boot as though he would take a swing at the drifter. But Eben only smiled and, for the second time, put his thin hand on Isley's arm. Isley felt the power of those slender fingers. They closed on his arm, and his will, like a Number 6 lynx trap.

"Come on, Isley," said the soft voice. "I need your testimony." And Isley groaned once more and put his head down into his collar as deep as it would go, and followed his ragged guide into the Bull Pine General Store.

"Friends," announced Eben, holding up his hands as the startled sheepmen looked up at him from their places around the possumbelly stove, "Brother Isley and I have come from afar to help you in your hour of need; please hear us out."

"That bent-legged little stray," dissented one member immediately, "never come from no place to help no sheepman. I smell cowboy! Fetch a rope, men."

Eben gestured hurriedly, but it did no good. A second valley man growled, "Ain't that Tom Isley as works for Henry Reston?" And a third gnarled herder rasped, "You bet it is! Never mind the rope, boys; I'll knock his head open, barehanded."

The group surged forward, the hairy giant who had spoken last, in the lead. Eben said no more, but did not let them beyond him to the white-faced K-Bar cowboy.

As the burly leader drew abreast of him, the drifter reached out and took him gently by one shoulder. He turned him around, got a hip into his side, threw him hard and far across the floor and up against the drygoods counter, fifteen feet away. The frame building shook to its top scantling when the big man landed. He knocked a three-foot hole in the floor, ending up trapped in a splintered wedging of boards from which it took the combined efforts of three friends and the storekeeper's two-hundred-pound daughter to extract him.

By the time he was freed and being revived by a stimulant-restorative composed of equal parts of sheepdip and spirits of camphorated oil, the rest of the assemblage was commencing to appreciate the length and strength of the drifter's throw. And, realizing these things, they were politely moving back to provide him the room he had requested in the first place. Eben made his address direct and nippy.

They had come down out of the hills, he said, bearing news of invading Philistines. They were not there to become a part of the Wolf Mountain War, but to serve in what small way they might, to bring that unpleasantness to a peaceful conclusion, with freedom and justice for all. Toward that end, he concluded, his bowlegged friend had something to say that would convince the sheep raisers that he came to them, not as a kine herder bearing false prophecies, but as a man of their own simple cloth, who wanted to help them as were too honest and God-fearing to help themselves at the cattlemen's price of killing and maiming their fellowmen by gunfire and in the dead of night when decent men were sleeping and their flocks on peaceful, unguarded graze.

This introduction served to interest the Bull Pine men and terrify Tom Isley. He was not up on kine herders, Philistines and false prophets, but he knew sheepmen pretty well. He reckoned he had maybe thirty seconds to fill the flush Eben had dealt him, before somebody thought of that rope again. Glancing over, he saw Big Sam Yawkey — the fallen leader of the meeting — beginning to snort and breathe heavy from the sheepdip fumes. Figuring Big Sam to be bright-eyed and bushy-tailed again in about ten of those thirty seconds, it cut things really fine.

Especially, when he didn't have the least, last notion what the heck topic it was that Eben expected him to take off on. "Ebe!" he got out in a strangulated whisper, "what in the name of Gawd you expect me to talk about?" But the Good Samaritan with the moth-eaten mule and the one thin army blanket wasn't worried a whit. He just put out his bony hand, touched his small companion on the shoulder and said, with his soft smile, as the sheepmen closed in:

"Never fear, Isley; you will think of something."

And, for a fact, Isley did.

"Hold off!" he yelled, backing to the hardware counter and picking himself a pick handle out of a barrel of assorted tool hafts. "I'll lay you out like Samson with that jackass jawbone!"

The sheepmen coagulated, came to a halt.

"Now, see here," Isley launched out. "Ebe's right. I'm down here to do what I can to settle this fight. There's been far too much blood spilt a'ready. And I got an idee, like Ebe says, how to stop this here war quicker'n you can spit and holler howdy. But it ain't going to be risk-free. Monkeying around with them cattlemen is about as safe as kicking a loaded polecat. They're touchier than a teased snake, as I will allow you all know."

Several of the sheepmen nodded, and one said; "Yes, we know, all right. And so do you. You're one of them!"

"No!" denied Isley, "that ain't so. Mr. Reston thrun me off the K-Bar this very day. Ebe, here, made him look some small in front of the boys, and the Old Man ordered us both took to the west line and told to keep riding. I got included on account I drug Ebe in off the range, and Old Henry, he said I could keep him, seeing's I'd found him first."

His listeners scowled and looked at one another. This bowlegged little man had been punching cattle too long. He had clearly gone astray upstairs and been given his notice because of it. But they would hear him out, as none of them wanted to be flung against the dry-goods counter, or skulled with that pick handle.

"Go ahead," growled Big Sam Yawkey, coming up groggily to take his place in front of the Bull Piners. "But don't be overlong with your remarks. I done think you already stretched the blanket about as far as she will go. But, by damn, if there's a sick lamb's chance that you *do* have some way we can get back at them murderers, we ain't going to miss out on it. Fire away."

"Thank you, Mr. Yawkey," said Isley, and fired.

The idea he hit them with was as much a surprise to him as to them. He heard the words coming out of his mouth but it was as though somebody else was pulling the wires and making his lips flap. He found himself listening with equal interest to that of the Bull Pine sheepmen, to his own wild-eyed plan for ambushing the cattlemen in Red Rock Corral.

It was beautifully simple:

Red Rock Corral was a widened-out place in the middle of that squeezed-in center part of Shell Canyon called the Narrows. If you looked at the Narrows as a sort of rifle barrel of bedrock, then Red Rock Corral would be like a place midways of the barrel where a bullet with a weak charge had stuck, then been slammed into by the following, full-strength round, bulging the barrel at that spot. It made a fine place to catch range mustangs, for example. All you had to do was close off both ends of the Narrows, once you had them in the bulge. Then just leave them there to starve down to where they would lead out peaceful as muley cows.

Isley's idea was that what would work for tough horses would work for tough men.

The sheepmen knew for a fact, he said, that the hill trail came down to the basin through Shell Canyon. Now, if added to this, they also knew for a fact, as Isley did, that Old Henry and his boys were coming down that trail early tomorrow to knock over their winter feed pens and stampede their sheep into the blizzard's deep snow, why then, they would be catching up to the first part of the Isley Plan.

Pausing, the little cowboy offered them a moment to consider the possibilities. Big Sam was the first to recover.

"You meaning to suggest," he said, heavy voice scraping like a burro with a bad cold, "that we bottle them cattlemen up in Red Rock Corral and starve them into agreeing to leave us be? Why, I declare you're balmier than you look, cowboy. In fact, you're nervier than a busted tooth. You think we need you to tell us about ambushing? That's the cattlemen's speed. And you can't go it without people getting hurt, kilt likely. Boys," he said, turning to the others, "some deck is shy a joker, and this is him. Fetch the rope."

"No! Wait!" cried Isley, waving his pick handle feebly. "I ain't done yet."

"Oh, yes you are," rumbled Big Sam, moving forward.

Yet, as before, he did not reach Tom Isley.

Eben raised his thin, pale hand and Big Sam brought up short as though he had walked into an invisible wall.

"What the hell?" he muttered, rubbing his face, frightened. "I must be losing my marbles. Something just clouted me acrost the nose solid as a low limb."

"It was your conscience," smiles Eben. "Isley has more to say. Haven't you, Isley?"

The little cowboy shook his head, bewildered.

"Hell, don't ask me, Ebe; you're the ventrillyquist."

"Speak on," nodded his friend, "and be not afraid."

"Well," said Isley, "I'll open my mouth and see what comes out. But I ain't guaranteeing nothing."

Big Sam Yawkey, still rubbing his nose, glared angrily.

"Something better come out," he promised, "or I'll guarantee you something a sight more substantial than nothing; and that's to send you out of town with your toes down. You've got me confuseder than a blind dog in a butcher shop, and I'm giving you one whole minute more to hand me the bone, or down comes your doghouse."

"Yeah!" snapped a burly herder behind him. "What you take us for, a flock of ninnies? Jest because we run sheep don't mean we got brains to match. And you suggesting that we set a wild hoss trap for them gunslingers and night riders of Old Man Reston's is next to saying we're idjuts. You think we're empty-headed enough to buy any such sow bosom as holding them cattlemen in that rock hole with a broomtail brush fence on both ends?"

"*No*," said Isley calmly, and to his own amazement, " *but you might trying doing it with blasting powder.*"

"What!" shouted Yawkey.

"Yes, sir," said Isley meekly, "a half can of DuPont Number 9 at each end, touched off by a signal from the bluff above. When all of them have rode into Red Rock Corral, down comes the canyon wall, above and below, and there they are shut off neat as a newborn calf, and nobody even scratched. I'd say that with this big snow that's coming, and with the thermometer dropping like a gut-shot elk, they'd sign the deed to their baby sister's virtue inside of forty-eight hours."

There was silence, then, as profound as the pit.

It was broken, presently, by Big Sam's awed nod, and by him clearing his throat shaky and overcome as though asked to orate in favor of the flag on Independence Day.

"Great Gawd A'mighty boys," he said, "it might work!"

And the rush for the front door and the horses standing back-humped at the hitch rail, was on.

As a matter of Big Horn basin record, it did work.

The Bull Piners got their powder planted by three A.M., and about four, down the trail came the deputation from the hills. The snow was already setting in stiff, and they were riding bunched tight. Big Sam Yawkey fired his Winchester three times when they were all in the middle of Red Rock Corral and Jase Threepersons, the storekeeper, and Little Ginger, his two-hundred-pound daughter, both lit off their respective batches of DuPont Number 9 above and below the Corral so close together the cattlemen thought it was one explosion and Judgement Day come at last.

Well, it had, in a way.

And, as Isley had predicted, it came in less than forty-eight hours.

The sheepmen were mighty big about it. They lowered down ropes with all sorts of bedding and hot food and even whiskey for the freezing ranchers, as well as some of their good baled sheep hay for the horses. But they made it clear, through Big Sam's bellowed-down advice, that they meant to keep their friends and neighbors from the hills bottled up in that bare-rock bulge till the new grass came, if need be. They wouldn't let them starve, except slowly, or freeze, unless by accident. But they had come out from Bull Pine to get a truce, plus full indemnity for their summer's sheep losses, and they were prepared to camp up on that bluff — in the full comfort of their heated sheep wagons — from right then till Hell, or Red Rock Corral, froze over.

That did it.

There was some hollering back and forth between the two camps for most of that first day. Then it got quiet for the better part of the second. Then, along about sundown, Old Henry Reston yelled up and said: "What's the deal, Yawkey? We don't get back to our stock, right quick, we won't have beef enough left to hold a barbecue."

Big Sam read them the terms, which Isley wasn't close enough to hear. Reston accepted under profane duress and he and Big Sam shook on the matter. Naturally, such a grip had the force of law in the basin. Once Old Henry and Big Sam had put their hands to an agreement, the man on either side who broke that agreement might just as well spool his bed and never stop moving.

Realizing this, Isley modestly stayed out of the affair. There were other inducements toward laying low and keeping back from the rim while negotiations went forward and concluded. One of these was the little cowboy's certain knowledge of what his fellow K-Bar riders would think of a cowman who sold out to a bunch of sheepherders. Even more compelling was the cold thought as to what they would *do* to such a hero, should they ever catch up to the fact he had plotted the whole shameful thing. All elements, both of charming self-effacement and outright cowardice, considered, Isley believed himself well advised to saddle up and keep traveling. This he planned to do at the first opportunity. Which would be with the night's darkness in about twenty minutes. It was in carrying out the first part of this strategy —

rounding up Eben and their two mounts — that he ran into the enter-
tainment committee from the Bull Pine camp; three gentlemen
sheepherders delegated by their side to invite Isley to the victory
celebration being staged in his honor at the Ram's Horn Saloon later
that evening.

Isley, confronted with this opportunity, refused to be selfish. He
bashfully declined the credit being so generously offered, claiming that
it rightfully belonged to another. When pressed for the identity of this
hidden champion, he said that of course he meant his good friend
Eben. "You know," he concluded, "the skinny feller with the white face
and curly whiskers. Ebe," he called into the gathering dusk past the hay
wagon where they had tied Black Bean and the mule, "come on out
here and take a bow!"

But Eben did not come out, and Jase Threepersons, the chairman of
the committee, said to Isley, "What skinny feller with what white face
and what curly whiskers?"

He said it in a somewhat uncompromising manner and Isley retorted
testily, "The one that was with me in the store; the one what thrun Big
Sam acrost the floor. Damn it, what you trying to come off on me,
anyhow?"

Jase looked at him and the other two sheepmen looked at him and
Jase said, in the same flat way as before, "*You* thrun Big Sam agin that
counter. There wasn't nobody in that store with you. What *you* trying
to come off on *us*, Tom Isley?"

"Blast it!" cried Isley, "I never laid a finger on Big Sam. You think I'd
be crazy enough to try that?"

The three shook their heads, looking sorrowful.

"Evidently so," said Jase Threepersons.

"No, now you all just hold up a minute," said Isley, seeing their pity-
ing looks. "Come on, I'll show you. Right over here ahint the hay
wagon. Me and Ebe was bedded here last night and boilt our noon
coffee here today. I ain't seen him the past hour, or so, and he may
have lost his nerve and lit out, but, by damn, I can show you where his
mule was tied and I'll fetch *him* for you, give time."

They were all moving around the wagon, as he spoke, Isley in the
lead. He stopped, dead. "No!" they heard him say. "My God, it cain't
be!" But when they got up to him, it was. There was no sign of a double
camp whatever. And no sign of the bearded stranger, nor of his moth-
eaten mule. "He was right here!" yelled Isley desperately. "Damn it,
you saw him, you're just funning, just hoorawing me. You seen him

and you seen that broke-down jackass he rides; who the hell you think I been talking to the past three days, *myself?*"

"'Pears as if," nodded Jase sympathetically. "Too bad, too. Little Ginger had kind of took a shine to you. Wanted me to see you stuck around Bull Pine a spell. But, seeing the way things are with you, I reckon she'd best go back to waiting out Big Sam."

"Yes sir, thank you very much, sir," said Isley gratefully, "but I still aim to find Ebe and that damn mule for you." He bent forward with sudden excitement. "Say, lookit here! Mule tracks leading off! See? What'd I tell you? Old Ebe, he's a shy cuss, and mightily humble. He didn't want no thanks. He'd done what he come for — stopped the trouble — and he just naturally snuck off when nobody was a'watching him. Come on! we can catch him easy on that stove-up old jack."

The three men came forward, stooped to examine the snow. There were some tracks there, all right, rapidly being filled by the fresh fall of snow coming on, but tracks all the same. They could have been mule tracks too. It was possible. But they could also have been smallish horse tracks. Like say left by Pettus Teague's blue-blood race mare. Or by that trim Sioux pony belonging to Charlie Bo-peep, the Basque half-breed. Or by Coony Simms's little bay. Or Nels Bofors' slim Kentucky-bred saddler. Or two, three others in the camp.

Straightening from its consideration of the evidence, the committee eyed Tom Isley.

"Isley," said Jase Threepersons, "I'll tell you what we'll do. All things took into account, you've been under considerable strain. Moreover, that strain ain't apt to get any less when word gets back up into the hills that you come down here and hatched this ambush idea. We owe you a'plenty, and we ain't going to argue with you about that there feller and his mule. But them cowboys of Old Henry's might take a bit more convincing. Now suppose you just don't be here when Big Sam and the others come up out of the corral with the K-Bar outfit. We'll say you was gone when we got here to the hay wagon, and that you didn't leave no address for sending on your mail. All right?"

Isley took a look at the weather.

It was turning off warmer, and this new snow wouldn't last more than enough to cover his tracks just nice. The wind was down, the sun twenty minutes gone and, from the rim of the bluff above the corral, sounds were floating which indicated the roping parties were pulling up the first of the K-Bar sheep raiders. To Isley, it looked like a fine night for far riding. And sudden.

He pulled his coat collar up, his hat brim down, and said to Jase Threepersons, "All right."

"We'll hold the boys at the rim to give you what start we can," said Jase. And Isley stared at him and answered. "No, don't bother; you've did more than enough for me a'ready. Goodbye, boys, and if I ever find any old ladies or dogs that need kicking, I will send them along to you."

Being sheepherders, they didn't take offense, but set off to stall the rescue party at the rim, true to their word.

Isley didn't linger to argue the morals of it. He got his blanket out from under the hay wagon, rolled it fast, hurried to tie it on behind old Black Bean's saddle. By this time he wasn't even sure who *he* was, but didn't care to take any chances on it. He just might turn out to be Tom Isley, and then it would be close work trying to explain to Dutch and Gant and Deece and the rest, what it was he was doing bedded down in the sheep camp.

He had the old black outlaw swung around and headed in the same direction as the fading mule tracks — or whatever they were — in something less than five minutes flat. The going was all downhill to the river, and he made good time. About eight o'clock he came to the Willow Creek Crossing of the Big Horn, meaning to strike the Pitchfork Trail there. He was hungry and cold and the old black needing a rest, so he began to look around for a good place to lie up for the night. Imagine his surprise and pleasure, then, to spy ahead, the winky gleam and glow of a campfire, set in a snug thicket of small timber off to the right of the crossing. Following its cheery guide, he broke through the screening bush and was greeted by a sight that had him bucked up quicker than a hatful of hot coffee.

"Ebe!" he cried delightedly. "I knowed you wouldn't run out on me! God bless it, I am that pleased to see you!"

"And I likewise, Isley," smiled the gentle-voiced drifter. "Alight and thrice welcome to my lowly board."

Well, he had a wind-tight place there. It was nearly as warm and shut in from the cold as the old rock house out on Wolf Mountain flat, and he had added to it with a neat lean-to of ax-cut branches, as pretty as anything Isley had ever seen done on the range. And the smell of the rack of lamb he had broiling over the flames of his fire was enough to bring tears to the eyes of a Kansas City cow buyer.

Isley could see no legitimate reason for declining the invitation.

Falling off Black Bean, he said, "You be a'saying Grace, Ebe, whilst

I'm a'pulling this hull; I don't want to hold you up none when we set down —"

While they ate, things were somewhat quiet. It was very much the same as it had been when Eben came in cold and hungry to Isley's fire out on the flats. Afterward, though, with the blackened coffeepot going the rounds, Isley rolling his rice-paper smokes and Eben playing some of the lonesomest pretty tunes on his old mouth harp that the little cowboy had ever heard, the talk started flowing at a better rate.

There were several things Isley wanted to know, chief among them being the matter of the Bull Pine men letting on as if he had jumped his head hobbles. But he kept silent on this point, at first, leading off with some roundabout inquiries which wouldn't tip his hand to Eben. These were such things as how come he didn't recognize any of the tunes Eben was playing on the harp? Or how did Eben manage to evaporate from the sheep camp at Red Rock Corral without any of the Bull Piners seeing him. Or why didn't he let Isley know he was going? And how come him, Eben, to have lamb on the fire in October, when there wasn't any lamb?

To this tumble of questions, Eben only replied with his soft laugh and such put-offers as that the tunes were sheepherder songs from another land, that the fresh snowfall had hidden his departure from the hay wagon bed spot, that he knew the Bull Piners planned a party for Isley and didn't wish to stand in his way of enjoying the tribute due him, and that for him, Eben, lamb was always in season and he could put his hand to some just about as he pleased.

Well, Isley was a little mystified by this sort of round-the-barn business. But when Eben made the remark about the Bull Pine party being due him, Isley, he quit slanting his own talk, off-trail, and brought it right to the bait.

"Ebe," he said, "I'm going to ask you one question. And you mighten as well answer it, for I'm going to hang onto it like an Indian to a whiskey jug."

"Gently, gently," smiled the other. "You'll have your answer, but not tonight. In the morning, Isley, I promise you."

"Promise me what?" demanded the little cowboy. "I ain't even said what I wanted."

"But I know what you want, and you shall have it — in the morning."

Isley eyed him stubbornly.

"I'll have what in the morning?" he insisted.

Eben smiled that unsettling sad-sweet smile, and shrugged.

"*Proof that I was with you all the while*," he said.

Isley frowned, then nodded.

"All right, Ebe, you want to save her for sunup, that's fine with me. I'm a little wore down myself."

"You rest, then," said the drifter. "Lie back upon your saddle and your blanket, and I will read to you from a book I have." He reached in his own blanket, still curiously unrolled, and brought forth two volumes; one a regular-sized black leather Bible, the other a smallish red morocco-bound tome with some sort of outlandish foreign scripting on the cover. "The Book of the Gospel," he said, holding up the Bible; then, gesturing with the little red book, "the *Rubáiyát* of Omar Khayyám: which will you have, Isley?"

"Well," said the latter, "I can tell by some of your talk, Ebe, that you favor the Good Book, and I ain't denying that it's got some rattling-tall yarns in it. But if it's all the same to you, I'll have a shot of the other. I'm a man likes to see both sides of the billiard ball."

Even nodded soberly, but without any hint of reproval.

"You have made your choice, Isley," he said, "and so be it. Listen. . . ."

He opened the small volume then and began to read selected lines for his raptly attentive companion. Lazing back on his blanket, head propped on his saddle, the warmth of the fire reflecting in under the lean-to warm and fragrant as fresh bread, Isley listened to the great rhymes of the ancient Persian:

". . . And as the Cock crew, those who stood before
The Tavern shouted — 'Open then the Door!
 'You know how little while we have to stay
'And once departed, many return no more! . . .'"

". . . Come, fill the Cup, and in the fire of Spring
Your winter-garment of Repentance fling:
 The Bird of Time has but a little way
To flutter — and the Bird is on the Wing. . . ."

". . . A Book of Verses underneath the Bough,
A Jug of Wine, a Loaf of Bread — and Thou
 Beside me singing in the Wilderness —
Oh, Wilderness were paradise enow! . . . "

". . . Yesterday this Day's Madness did prepare,
Tomorrow's Silence, Triumph, or Despair:

Drink! for you know not whence you came, nor why:
Drink! for you know not why you go, nor where. . . ."

". . . The Moving Finger writes; and, having writ,
Moves on: nor all your Piety nor Wit
    Shall lure it back to cancel half a Line,
Nor all your Tears wash out a Word of it. . . ."

The poetry was done, then, and Eben was putting down the little
red book to answer some drowsy questions from Isley as to the nature of
the man who could write such wondrously true things about life as she
is actually lived, just on a piece of ordinary paper and in such a shriv-
eled little old leather book.

Eben reached over and adjusted Isley's blanket more closely about
the dozing cowboy, then told him the story of Omar Khayyám. But
Isley was tired, and his thoughts dimming. He remembered, later,
some few shreds of the main idea; such as that Old Omar was a tent-
maker by trade, that he didn't set much store by hard work, that he
didn't know beans about horses, sheep or cattle, but he was a heller on
women and grapejuice. Past that, he faded out and slept gentle as a
dead calf. The sun was an hour high and shining square in his eye when
he woke up.

He lay still a minute, not recalling where he was. Then it came to
him and he sat up with a grin and a stretch and a *"Morning, Ebe,"* that
was warm and cheerful enough to light a candle from. But Eben didn't
answer to it. And never would. For, when Tom Isley blinked to get the
climbing sun out of his eyes, and took a second frowning look around
the little campsite, all he saw was the unbroken stretch of the new snow
which had fallen quiet as angel's wings during the night. There was no
Eben, no mule, no threadbare army blanket bedroll. And, this time,
there were not even any half-filled hoofprints leading away into the
snow. This time there was only the snow. And the stillness. And the
glistening beauty of the new day.

Oh, and there was one other small thing that neither Tom Isley, nor
anybody else in Big Horn basin, was ever able to explain. It was a little
red morocco book about four-by-six inches in size, which Isley found in
his blanket when he went to spool it for riding on. Nobody in Northwest Wyoming had ever heard of it, including Tom Isley.

It was called the *Rubáiyát* of Omar Khayyám.

JESSE JAMES
AND
WYATT EARP

If you, the reader, have ever dared imagine Will Henry might alter the accepted image of a famed real-life Western persona, the better to present him or her in what the author believes to be the contrary truth, there is no doubt you have struck paydirt in what follows.

Yes, I have consciously tried to revise images we have of people of the first order of Western fame. That is to say, I am conscious that I don't agree with what is thought of the particular famed personage and I want to alter that impression to what my studies have shown me was more nearly the truth of that person. That's whether the truth made the person less or more admirable, or despicable.

Jesse James, for example, has been entirely too well thought of by past Western and frontier historians and fictioneers. It was my conscious intention to redraw him with the darker, bloodier pen used in *Death of a Legend*. He was not a Robin Hood but a documented murderer. Without sensationalizing his homicidal side, while granting him his fair due of good acts, or civil intentions, or simply his earned credits as a member of the human race, my aim was to draw him to the life as lustily as to the inevitable death-by-betrayal. Above all, I wanted not to pretty him up to fit the false picture of "The Robin Hood of the Little Blue" which previous writers succeeded in doing, even against their better judgements. Hence the "death" in *Death of a Legend*. Jesse James will always be a legend, and a fascinating one. Evil is always of a more fatal charm than good. But, curiously, even controvertibly, Will Henry readers will know that the author has always shown this fascination with Jesse James and his fellow outlaws of the James and Younger gangs, has written of him and them more than two or three times, and will again, little doubt. His readers will also remember that Will does not ploddingly insist, in these other stories of "Dingus and his Friends," on drawing only Jesse's bleak or tragic side. He gives Jesse occasional marks for loyalty, decency, even humor. In doing so, equity and indeed truth is served. And what emerges in the end is a better picture of the man, and his followers, than is given in the distorted "good guy" image of Jesse Woodson James.

Another famed character unfairly treated, which is to say treated with both groundless prejudice *and* historical inaccuracy, emerges in the person of Wyatt Earp, the again-legendary "Marshal of Tombstone."

The move among writers of the present has been to dirty and belittle all the great old heroes of our Western past who had otherwise survived up to now as good and honorable men and women of their dangerous and trying times. The "good guys," in other words, who had been granted by their eye-witness peers some degree of hero status. A status, by the bye, attested to by both the accepted history of their times, as well as by the folklore and legendry which so often comes closer to the living picture of the famed persona, than does the touted "real" history.

These anti-hero authorities have already killed Custer fifty or sixty times, laid to rest and/or resurrected Billy the Kid at least a couple hundred times (or so it seems, Dear Lord!) and have lately taken to zeroing in on poor old Wyatt. The Lion of Tombstone has suddenly been re-discovered to have been things as patently absurd as liar, cheat, thief, sleazy crook, backshooter, bedwetter and latent cap-and-ball homosexual.

So if, to go back to the original matter of whether or not Will Henry does consciously draw (revise) his portraits of the frontier notorious, such as Tombstone's Marshal Earp in *Who Rides With Wyatt*, the answer is, straight-out, "you damned betcha."

And the truth will be more in Will Henry's own-drawn picture than in the other fellow's widely trumpeted "true" portrait.

Would you not love to see one of these smarttail belittlers of our rightful heroes made to ride knee-by-knee with the Boy General into the Red Hell of the Little Big Horn?

Or forced to walk-down the Clantons in the dirt of the O.K. Corral, right up front and between Wyatt Earp and Doc Holliday?

I wonder what would get wet then?

Not Wyatt Earp's bed, I'll warrant.

Authors get tired of what they write. Writing is hard work. And it gets sometimes to that place in the weary road of writing one more story of the Old West, no matter how marvelous a place and time that was, where thinking up another Indian raid, or stagecoach robbery, or trail driving tale, just seems to us writers as about three jumps and a high buck short of a happy landing. So, what do we do? We take a small vacation. We don't write about gunfights and train robberies and trail drives of wild-eyed longhorn cattle, and all of that. We write about something that is fun. Something we would have done ourselves once upon a time had we ever the chance that was given to Peabody Crutchfield III when he set out with every serious determination to collect the reward money "dead or alive" on the three most dangerous outlaw killers in the history of the American frontier. If the reader will enjoy old Peabody as much as the author did, then he will reap the same rewards of the inner man. Let us ride along with our bounty hunter and see how Providence splits up the loot, and the loyalties, 'twixt Peabody Crutchfield III, and Jesse Woodson James!

— W.H.

NOT WANTED
DEAD OR ALIVE

The gang split up as was our usual dodge following a bad botched job. We made it home by roundabout and separate routes, the rendezvous being the limestone caverns above the Little Blue River. There'd been five of us rode the heist that day, and me and Dingus and Bud and Preach was the first four to make the meetup back at the Little Blue. Once there assembled, we didn't wait none for our number five man to show.

Wasn't no point in it, acherally.

He hadn't proved worth a cowflap as a horse holder on a bank job. He'd damn near let the horses get away from him when we was backing out of the bank and old Bud, startled by the new man's mistake, tripped on the boardwalk and landed out amongst the horse apples and spraddle puddles of the hitchrail, spilling the gold out of the wheatsack and all the hell over Main Street, smack square in front of the Blue City Union Bank & Trust Company. I can't even recollect the name of that new feller, but he wasn't facing no useful future in the outlaw business. Not with him taking that Single Action Army Colt slug twixt his eyes and, like I say, might nigh letting the horses get away from him as a result of it.

I want right here to add in that we wasn't no ordinary operators. Might sound to you we was, from the way things got out of hand in the Blue City job, but you couldn't be wronger. When I tell you me and Dingus and Bud and Preach made it safe and sound back to home, it was the same as me saying I and Jesse James and Cole Younger and Frank James had did it, understand? I don't mean no playnames neither.

Dingus and Bud was Jesse's and Cole's kidhood names. Frank was really called Buck in the fambly, but being such a soberass all his days, we kind of rode him a lot about his preachy ways, and how he was forever quoting the Scriptures and praying out loud for good weather, when it was raining lead slugs all about our getaway butts when we was leaving town with the wheatsacks full, so we just called him Preach now and again, and sometimes "Reverent Frank."

He never took it hard. But neither did he crack any main ribs laughing hisself silly. In all the jobs I've rode with Jesse and Frank, I don't believe Frank smiled once. He could put the damper on free sample day at the whorehouse, just by showing up in the waiting line with his Psalms Book open.

Hell, even riding by in the street.

Calling on the Lord to spare the soiled doves their tresses and their passings, Amen, Amen.

Whoa up, now. Who run me down this side-alley? Leave me get back to where we was that day on the Little Blue River after the Blue City job.

Cole — I'm going to use their history names — he was the one went forward to the river to see that there wasn't no law hanging about, and when he come back five minutes later, you could have banked his eyeballs off his cheekbones with a billiard cue. "You ain't going to believe what I just seen up yonder," he warned. "Come on along. Step light."

Well, Cole was right.

Parked yonder in the long grass of the riverbank below the limestone bluffs that was honeycombed with the James Gang's legendous hideout caverns, was something mighty peculiar, indeed — a handsome harness pony and brand-new shiny cart tethered in the bottomland brush. We all four eyed one another.

There wasn't no sign of a driver or passenger.

It was plainly a child's rig, and a rich child's, at that.

Sonofabitch. What was it doing there?

We shadowed in on it and looked it over mighty wary. We opened the baggage boot last of all, and was strick dumb with wonderment. In there, was a veritable welter of manhunters' tools of the trade. Ropes. Leg-irons. Handcuffs. Giant caps. Blasting powder. Fuse. Even a rusted old monster of a by-God bear trap of mountain man vintage and teeth enough to clamp a mastodon till he sure-enough thawed out. And last item, weirdliest of all, there was a damn yellerback paper book labeled HOW TO BE A BOUNTY HUNTER.

Well, sir, us four traded scowls, eased Colts in holsters, went on in to close at the entrance of the main cave. There, we seen something else we couldn't swaller whole: a huge spindle of towline being reeled rapidly off and disappearing into *our* cave!

We stood there stupid as storks, shifting from one leg to the other, feeling our neckhairs on the rise, just watching that ropeline ravel out, as whoever or whatever was inside kept on going deeper and deeper into our secret limestone hole-in-the-ground hideout. But suddenly old Cole, a man who plumb thunk hisself as inventful as Ben Franklin when it come to whomping up new dips and doodles of the outlaw trade, busted out a big grin.

Fingers on lips, he motioned Frank and Jesse to sneak up and take cover flanking the entrance. As they did, old Bud, I mean, Cole, he picked up the out-reeling rope, precious careful not to so much as hint at tugging on it. He just let it play out through his two hands feeling like a trolling bass fisherman for that certain giveaway "touch" of the fish noodling the bait. Of an excited sudden we seen him "get it," so to speak, and he r'ared back on his bootheels and "set the hook," and begun a'reeling in the line fast as he could hand-over-hand.

We all straightened next minute, gawking like turkeys.

Out of the cave, a-clawing and a-spitting dirt and a-cussing like a kicked mule skinner, come a towheaded and pintsized kid in a Little Lord Fontleroy suit, the rope tied 'round his middle in the manner of full-growed spelunkers to avoid getting lost underground.

Seeing Cole but not spotting Frank or Jesse hid up in the flank rocks, the kid charged the big man and fastened his teeth in his leg just above the boottop. Then, when knocked sprawling away from that exercise, he leaped up demanding to know by what right he had been hooked and hauled out of the cave. To this, Cole, who was bottomwise of a kind and sunny nature, and now beginning to warm to the kid's brashness, replied with a question of his own, wanting to know who had writ the little mole his license to dig in our private cave.

The kid looked all around as if some worried.

Then, he beckoned Cole to come closer. He wanted to make a deal. His bear-size captor frowned like he always done when trying to think, never an easy matter for the Youngers. Then he loosened it to his leery grin and tip-toed over to the kid, right square into the spirit of the game. Giving the towhead a lopsided scrinching-up of one side of his face, he cupped one ear toward him, and said, "Wink's as good as a nod to a blind mule, pard; what's up?"

The runt captive stepped back, and sized him up.

"Wink's as good as a nod to a blind mule, eh?" he said. "I like that. What is it? Shakespeare, or Omar Khayyám, the Fitzgerald Translation?"

"Naw," Cole shrugged, modestlike. "I learn't it in the Reb Calvary, from old Nathan Bedstead Forrest."

"That's Bedford," the boy said.

"One and the same," Cole agreed, not twittering a eyelid. "What you doing here, pard?"

The towhead glanced about quick one more time. He still didn't see Jesse or Frank but he didn't like me standing off behind Cole, and listening in.

"Get rid of the skinny gink," he advised Cole, jerking his head toward me. "He ain't got the sense of a pet sheep, that's plain. But I don't talk in front of witnesses."

"Beat it, D.B.," Cole ordered.

I give him my butthead look, and said, "Now wheraways in hell am I going to beat it to? This here is our hole, Thomas."

I done that to him of a time.

His Bible-writ name was Thomas Coleman Younger, and he didn't care too much to hear it spoke out loud in front of strangers.

"Back off, D.B.," he growled. "Right now."

I done it, for I was no match for Cole Younger, and when the kid thought I was sufficient withdrawed he shot his jaw and stared unblinking up at Cole's beltbuckle, and announced, right out, "I am looking for the James boys and according to my information this is their famous hideout cave and I mean to have a good gander at it."

Cole wanted immediate to know the source of his information but the tad was too foxy for that. He shook up old Cole real good, saying, "Somebody close to the Governor."

"What governor?" Cole demanded, quick with it as a weasel down a woodchuck hole.

"You know more'n one governor?" the boy asked. "We're still in Missouri, ain't we?"

"Crutchfield?" Cole paled. "Not him; not The Hangman?!"

"You know any other Governor of Missouri, Mister?"

Cole turned another shade white and came trudging over to me.

Surely the kid was roostering him, he said. He wasn't anymore cosied-up with the Governor nor was Frank and Jesse James. But what rotten luck that the wiseacre little bastard had run off from wherever his home was and stumbled square onto the legendary limestone cave hideout of the most wanted men in the State of Missouri. Looking at me, Cole raised his voice to reach the still-hidden Frank and Jesse.

"This here could get gooey as okra gumbo, happen we don't watch ourselves," he declared, playing it way overboard. "We had best advance with our pickets out."

With that, he went back to the kid.

"What else did you get from them sources, tadpole?" he boomed out. "So far you ain't showed us nothing to prove you're really after the Jameses. Why, dad bust it, you wouldn't perkonize either one of 'em, was they to jump out'n these very rocks right here this minute."

"Oh, wouldn't I, Fatso?" sniffed the kid, as Cole glared at him and pulled in his paunch. "Just take a look at this."

From inside his fancy dan coat, the boy whipped a wanted flyer on Frank and Jesse James, with pictures reputed to be of the murderous brothers, plus a screaming box-letter offer of *$10,000 DEAD OR ALIVE.*

"I aim to get me at least one of them," the kid finished. "Both if the cards fall that way. But I know you two sorrowful things ain't the Jameses, so they must be on in the cave somewheres. Out of my way, Lardo. I'm going back in."

If I knowed Jesse, he was surely blinking them well-knowed sore eyelids of his about a hunderd bats a minute to hear this, whilst brother Frank was likely praying for the poor boy's soul. Cole wasn't noted for his leadership qualities and the true Robin Hood of the Little Blue, that would be old Dingus, he was just mean enough to love watching his friend Bud sweat blood over a ten-year-old kid pushing him all over the riverbank. As far as danger or fear, I was the only honest coward there, so things promised to tighten up right sudden and with old D.B. Peecher like usual smack dab in the middle.

But Cole, if no battle general, had a flair for the theeayter and was the best actor in the entire gang when the bunch was on actual stage pulling a job. He give it a honest try, now.

Side-eying the rocks where Frank and Jesse was, he spraddled his tree-trunk legs and lit out reading his lines.

"Oh, mercy me," he announced to the boy, "all that money for them two pore little outlaws which ain't never truly did a wrong nor a sinful thing in all of their hounded lives. Dear suz, dear suz."

For a moment, he was John Wilkes Younger.

He leered. He grinned. He smacked his lips. Ogled. Strutted.

Postured. Winked wide. Scowled ferocious. Buttered-up a smile that would have melted any halfways human audience right down on the riverbank. Let the kid have it good.

"Now, you wouldn't disassemble with old Uncle Bud. would you, little pardner?" he unctioned. "Surely you ain't serious abouten that reeward money."

The kid hadn't melted a drop. "I am," he insisted promptly, "and I mean to collect every last dollar of it. I need the cash for steamship tickets. I'm running away from home." He stepped closer to old Cole and tapped him on the overlop of his belly. "Now that's your last warning. Out of my way!"

He started past Cole, then turned back.

"And another thing," he said haughty. "Don't slide no more of that Uncle Bud lard my way. I know who you are."

"The hell!" Cole said.

"The hell yes," the towhead answered. "You're the only fat outlaw worth a hoot since Friar Tuck."

Cole blinked, needing help. He appealed to the rocks on either side of the cave and, getting no response from the Jameses, wheeled about on me.

"Who the hell's Friar Tuck?" he demanded. "We ain't never see'd no flyers on him, is we?"

"Nary," I said. "Watch out for this little stoat. He'll get his teeth inter you again. He's too fast for you, Uncle Bud."

"Lay off!" Cole snapped, turning surly. He grabbed the kid by one arm, moving very fast for a feller weighed better'n two hundred and stood just at six foot. It always took a while to get old Cole ired-up, but when you had him there, you had best make tracks for the next county over. "Now, you little rat turd sonofabitch," he says to the Pony Cart Kid, "you was going to turn in pore old Jesse and Brother Frank for that there blood-money, was you?"

"We've been over this," the kid said, testylike. "Make up your mind, Fatty. Either you're in with me on this, or you ain't. Fifty-fifty. Five thousand each. Take it or leave it. I can get to South America on five thousand, even if I had figured to hit for the South Seas. Hell, if it's good enough for Butch Cassidy and the Sundance Kid and Etta Place, it is a'plenty good enough for me. At least for openers."

Cole's blink got stuck halfways. He couldn't believe it.

"What wrong has the boys ever done you?" he stalled.

"They've never done me any right," the kid said, shortlike. "You in or out?"

"Why, you — !" Cole was turning red, but the kid cut him off.

"Declare yourself, by damn!" he ordered. "And don't try no little tricks. I don't want to have to cut down on you."

Cole was not only flabbered, he was double-gasted.

Red had turnt to purple now and he r'ared up like a boar grizzly about to swat down a sowbug. I thought the kid was a goner and was getting set to run for it myownself, when of a shockful sudden the Pony Cart Kid struck.

Out from under that Fontleroy coat, the towhead whipped a tremendous old rusted horse pistol of a Civil War revolver with a muzzle hole big as a cave. He pointed this fearsome weapon at old Cole's navel cord button, took a two-handed aim and spreadleg brace as though he total intended to touch off the old blunderbuss, pointblunt. Cole give a squall that would prouden-up a first-rid heifer, and dove for the ground. The kid let fly at him with the rusted horse pistol, figuring he was being attacked. The noise and smoke was like two fast freights coming together head-on. My ears was ringing for a week after. No blood was drawed, fortunate to say, however. But old Cole's hat was reamed with a hole that must have measured about the calibre of bullprod hardrock drill, and the big feller he made it back up onto his feet, white as a coffinheld lily.

I got to hand it to him, though. He didn't fold.

"Tut, tut, sidekick," he managed shakily. "Just a little test to see iffen you was fit to trust. I'm in the outlaw trade myself, remember."

"Talk fast," was all the kid answered him.

Well, Cole, he suggested that the fifty-fifty split was fine by him, and he would join up with the kid, sure enough, helping him grab the Jameses, and so forth, like agreed.

But the damn kid wouldn't have it, now. Said the split would be twenty-five and seventy-five, with the twenty-five for Frank and the seventy-five for Jesse, and with the Pony Cart Kid taking Jesse and Cole taking Frank. All this, he plumb cool tells Cole, because he had failed the kid's test for fitness to trust.

I could see old Bud was of a mind to kill the kid, but he bluffed it out, fingering his chin and making as though to be full serious — which I figured he had best be, the way the Pony Cart Kid was still waving that horse pistol around.

But he wasn't; he was still trying to jimmy the kid.

"Well, now, lets us see here," he said. "That'll be two thousand five hundred for Frank and seven thousand five hundred for Jesse. Frank ain't going to take that as Christian, boy. He ain't going to love one Jesse being worth three Franks."

The kid drew back the hammer of the horse pistol, cocking its single action works with three bone-chill clicks familiar to all of us in the trade.

"Diddly squat on Frank," he said. "We got a deal here. Take it or leave it lay."

I couldn't believe it that Cole would still try to snooker him, but he done so. He begun talking buttergrin talk again and moving to sidle up on the kid whiles he was giving him the snakeoil come along. But that kid was born wicked in his mind. He still had the spelunker rope tied about his wrist and he noticed, how, that as Cole came in on him, he stepped square in a loop of the spelunker rope laying on the sand. Whango! The kid grabbed the loose rope and cinched up with it on Cole's off-hindleg and dumped him square on his fundement. Before he could get up off his clumsy hunkers, the kid bounced the barrel of the horse pistol off his bullet-holed hat and stretched him peaceful as a passed-out drunk on the shores of the Little Blue River.

And that was just the start of it.

Next moment, the kid was putting the howitzer-size muzzle of the pistol to Cole's woozy head, evidently meaning to blow his brains out then and there.

At this, Frank and Jesse come on the high lope out'n the rocks and kicks the kid's butt and disarms him, properlike.

Frank, a weapons collector, takes a interested look at the giant horse pistol and, casual as a dog heisting on a hickory stump, lets off one round up into the air.

Cole cried out, heart rending, grabbed his chest and plunked back to the ground. Frank bent over him and give him a tap with the still-smoking barrel of the pistol.

"You ain't been touched," he said. "Get up and introduce us to your partner."

Looking hungdog, Cole done as Frank said.

Or rather he started to.

The kid braced him midway of the move.

"Do we know these two tramps, Fatty? They going to want in on the action?"

"You might say they would; they're Frank and Jesse James."

"Just testing," the kid said. "You figure I didn't know who they was, knowing you was Cole Younger? Had to be, didn't it? Anybody else around?"

"Naw, only old D.B. Peecher, yonder. He's nobody."

The kid shot me a glance, seemed to agree with Cole, reached down and retrieved Cole's hat from the creekbank sand, dusted it off somewhat careful, returned it to the big feller sort of like as a peace offering.

"Here's your hat," he said. "Ain't hurt hardly."

Cole spit out a black curse, snatched the hat back, jammed it on his head without thinking. Naturally, he hit the goose-egg the kid had give him with the gun barrel. His eyes went to water with the pain of it, and he gasped out, "Jess, for Christ Sake, leave me skin him out alive and hang his pelt on the cornfield fence to scare off the crows. Please!"

I could see, staying back but watching, like I allus done, that the kid was finally impressed. He didn't like at all the earnestness of Thomas Coleman Younger's appeal to Jesse Woodson James. It had hit him of a sudden that these really was the James Brothers and Cole Younger. Understanding that, he had to know that the ten thousand dollars was up the chimley — and maybeso hisself with it.

Jesse and Frank, not for a minute jackassing around like Cole, set in right off to grill the kid mean and hard about his manhunt for them. Right soon, the boy begun to back water. His wiseacre ways turned to him yessirring and nosirring Frank and Jesse like they was upstanding citizens and him the no-good low-down outlaw. They finished him off with a flesh-crawler about the "Apache Anthill and Honey Smeared-On-Naked Stakeout" used by the gang to smoke out traitors and informers in their ranks, and the kid broke.

"Hold on now!" he yowled. "You dassn't harm me. I'm Peabody Crutchfield III!"

"You're who, the Third?" demanded Jesse.

"Governor Crutchfield's boy," Frank James echoed softly. "The Lord be with us. We could be in a whole heap of woe."

"Yes, by jings, you could!" the kid declared. "So you'd best give me back my weapon and my spelunker rope and my pony cart and be damned decent about it, too, understand?"

"Amen," Frank said. "The kid's right, Jess."

The two exchanged mournful headshakes.

"I suppose," Jesse sighed. "Too damned bad, though. What a chance, Buck. Damn!"

Me and Cole had sort of herded up together whilst the Jameses was confabbing, and now I seen Cole's face light up in that special way it done when the great outlaw thinker had been took with one of his stunners.

He strud over to Jesse, waving a hand the size of a antelope quarter at him. "Wait up," he advised. "Wasn't this wisenheimer kid set to turn us in for the blood money? You and Buck, anyhows. Well, whyn't we just reverse it around on him and offer to bring him in for, well, you know, ha! ha! the finder's fee?"

Frank and Jesse shared twin low whistles.

The Lord have mercy. Thank you, Lord.

It was Manna from Heaven.

Ransom manna.

"I'll make out the document," leered Cole. "I know all about drawing up such deals."

"Better leave Frank draw it up," Jesse come back quick. "He can write."

Old Cole, he scowled black as bear-sign, but stood aside.

Soon the ransom note was ready and Jesse assigned Cole to watch the kid, and me to watch Cole, whiles they crope in on Blue City and planted the demand where's it would be sure to get read — in the afternoon newspaper. There was only one hanger. What to charge for the kid. Jesse stared mean at the little turd, and said, "Peabody, how much you figure you'd ought to fetch. Be fair now. We don't want to rob nobody."

"Much as you two put together," the boy said. "Easy."

So the deal was strick on them terms — $10,000 for the safe return of Peabody Crutchfield III, to the loving bosom of his worried-sick family.

"Watch him close," Jesse said, as him and Frank swung up on their horses. "Shoot him iffen he gets away."

With Frank and Jesse vamoosed, me and Cole and Peabody Crutchfield settled down. Which means the little rattler immediate begun to try and bust loose from us. It were worser nor guarding a glob of quicksilver. Cole was supposed to keep the kid bottled, and I was supposed to keep Cole from getting kilt doing that. Sure enough, toward the last of our wait-up for the Jameses, he did give us the slip, just plain disappearing.

Leave me tell you, me and Cole was shook good.

Frank and Jesse had to be getting back right direct and we understood that if they caught us before we caught the kid, they would have our livers for dinner. We fanned out and quartered the bottomland brush frantic as birddogs with a bobwhite down in the nigh grass. We didn't find a damned thing neither. Not till we got back to the cave. There, natural and of course, was the kid waiting for us.

Know what he was doing?

Writing his mammaries, he said.

He had a flat rock on his knee and some 5¢ tablet paper from the cart and was scribbling away at a great clip.

"I'm calling it *The Adventures of the Pony Cart Kid*," he said, smugging it unbearable. "This here will be the first one."

But old Cole's fuse was lit for final.

"Yeah," he answered, like steam was coming out both his ears. "And you know something else, younker? It'll be the last one, likewise."

The kid had built a nice little fire and had on a can of coffeewater, figuring, he said, to brew up some beans he'd found mongst our cache in the cave. "Special against your return," he added, "when I knew you'd be wore down from your trailing work."

Well, of course Cole was heading for to grab him up and I reckoned strangle him once and for permanent certain. But the kid scuttled crawdad-style back from the fire and, for the second time that day, produced the rusted horse pistol.

"Hold where you are!" he yelled at Cole. "She's loaded for bear, and I can feel the trigger slipping under my thumb!" He waved the big gun and Cole skidded to a teetery halt, one foot in the fire. He give a yell to that and begun to dance around on the other, good leg, holding the burnt foot and yowling like a treed catamount. "You, Skinny," the kid included me in the arc of his cannon's wave. "Drop your gunbelt and your drawers. Same to you, Fatty," he commanded of old Cole. "You ain't much of a dancer, are you. Ain't there nothing you can do right?"

"I throttle richass kids from Jeff City with my bare-finger hands!" Cole roared at him. "How's that for something?"

"Pathetic," the kid shrugged. "Drop your drawers."

"I'll be damned iffen I do!" old Cole screeched at him.

The kid dropped to one knee and drew a two-handed dead-eye bead on Cole's parts.

"You'll be de-balled, if you don't," the kid said.

And that was how it come about that we all heard hoofbeats five minutes later, and the famous James Brothers galloped in out'n the gather of the dusk to find the notorious and deadly Cole Younger and Mrs. Peecher's weak-minded boy Dabney Bertrand sitting side-by-each on the same firelit rock slab, babybutt naked from the gunbelt down, cringed as two sheep-killing dogs, under personal guard of a ten year-old boy and a four-pound gun. "It was," as Cole later put it for the Jeff City papers, "to weep for plumb natural demortification."

He'd ought to know. Turned out he was the one got careless and had just th'owed the horse pistol back into the pony cart boot, when Jesse give it to him and told him to stache it "somewhares safe."

But all that's a turnback; right for then we was in more trouble than just the kid's humbling of me and Cole.

Jesse and Frank had got off to a nifty start in Blue City, true enough. They had met a old friend of theirs on the road into town that morning. He was U.S. Marshal Sam Bastrupp, out with a posse running down some poor fools what had derailed the 5:45 from St. Joe, blowed the express car and got $8.57 off the messenger, and that was the loot entire for the job. Since there wasn't no U.S. warrants out for the Jameses, not the present nohow, Bastrupp chatted along with Jesse and Frank till just short of town, where Jesse had said him and Buck was shunting off, and would the Marshal mind if they give him a confidential note to Governor Crutchfield?

"It's sealed," Jesse said, "and I know you wouldn't never open it, so that's why I am trusting it to you, where I surely would not the local law."

"I understand," Sam Bastrupp nodded. "Leave me have it."

Jesse and Frank went only so far on the cut-off as to where they could spy on the main road past the bend where they had parted with Bastrupp and his Federals. They had not more than settled to the watch, when the U.S. Marshal and his band came round the bend, halted, waited for Bastrupp to rip open and read Jesse's note to the Governor.

A moment later, the posse showed some agitation, and galloped off hellbent behind Sam Bastrupp, Blue City bound.

Jesse pulled out his railroad turnip and checked the time.

"Good," says he. "Time enough to catch the afternoon edition of the *Centurion*. "We'll lay up over at the Widder Gatchley's hawg farm and have her ugly daughter to fetch us out a copy from town. We'd oughter be on the way back by three o'clock."

Frank, the operating brains of the gang, give a thoughtful nod. "Best not tell the widder what happened to her boy Jubal," he advised. "That slug what hit him in the face key-holed. I only got a sideways look at him when he dropped the horses' reins, and I had to grab them. But I'd say he'll be in the icehouse all summer before anybody identifies him."

"He's lucky," Jesse said. "Had I got my hands on him, he'd of died slower."

"Hallelujah," Frank said, quietlike. "Let's go."

At this point in their story, me and Cole and the kid grabbing onto every word, Jesse said their luck had switched ends like a greenbroke bronc. They had got their copy of the paper, all right. And wished they hadn't. Because the Governor's reply to their ransom demands put the gang in a pretty tight crack. "Here," Jesse snapped, going into his coat and coming out with a tore off piece of newspaper. "Read the son of a bitch, Slats," he said to me. "It's got some words too tall for Cole." He glared at the both of us, his eyelids flicking like they done when he was fair ired. "And put your damned pants back on!"

I unrumpled the paper and squinted to the firelight:

If the outlaws insist on returning Peabody to his rightful home, they must pay over to Peabody's father, Governor Homer LeRoy Crutchfield, the sum of the same $10,000 which they sought to extort as a reasonable "reward" for the boy's safe and felicitous return. If the outlaws decide to keep his son, the Governor agrees to sign over to them the legal adoption papers, *in eturnum*, and *non corpus delicti*, and to pay the outlaws, in addition, a bonus of $5,000 earnest money, plus amnesty to leave the state, and firstclass steamship tickets to any point in Tasmania or the Tierra del Fuego, whichever is the farthest away.

> *H.L. Crutchfield*
> Governor

I give the paper back to Jesse, and shooken my head, dumbfunded. This was gritty ground to plow, sure enough. "What you aim to do, Jess?" was my next and natural question.

Now your ordinary bank and train robber would have been hard shook by this here development of the Governor refusing to buy back his kid. And why not? Wouldn't anybody in the owlhoot business know that we was in the oldest bumdodge trap a honest band of crooks could get themselves into? You know, snatching somebody there wasn't nobody wanted back? Worser even, that somebody would pay you to keep?

It didn't faze old Jess.

"We are in the grandest luck possible," he says to my out loud worrying. "Me and Buck found out from Marshal Bastrupp what this here kid
of the Governor's is doing in a pony cart half the state away from the
mansion in Jeff City." He meant the Missouri Capitol, Jefferson City,
and we all nodded, interested as hell, and he went on. "He's here with
the Governor hisself, and a whole party of nabobs, spending the week
on his Nibs' thoroughbred farm, yonder to Hickman Mills. It ain't three
hours ride from here, and only a light guard of County deputies. And
guess what else the Governor was doing earlier this very day, whilst
Cole was falling on his big butt with the gold sack; he was visiting his
money in the by-god-blessed-selfsame Blue City Union Bank and Trust
Company we was robbing! Half that gold Cole spilt in the horse apples
was his'n!"

I had to grant this was mighty stirring stuff. But I was still frowning.
I failt to see how the Governor being at Hickman Mills had anything to
do with getting our backsides out of the sling we had done slung them
in. Me, personal, I'd of been a sight happier with Peabody and his old
man snug in their covers at Jeff City.

But that was why Dingus was the leader.

"This kid is now dangerous to us as a mongoose to a clutch of prairie
chicks. He can identify us to the man. And he will do it free of charge.
With Marshal Sam Bastrupp in Blue City, what? ten, twelve mile from
Hickman Mills, we are in a fair tight, boys. Any doubts on that?"

There wasn't none, of course, and he went on, saying that we had
but the one decent chance to clear out and not leave the kid to foller us,
and that was to somehow sneak him back into the custody of his Daddy, which called for a midnight stab at the residence on the horse farm
to plant the boy, secret quiet, full square in the house, bound and
gagged and blindfolded, where he wouldn't be spotted till daybreak,
which naturally meant we had five hours to then "ride out" from there
before they found the kid and set him and Marshal Sam Bastrupp on
our trail.

Nary one of us liked the plan but we didn't have a better one and at
least it wasn't one of Cole's brainbursts.

And another thing. It ain't to be forgot that we was riding the finest
horses in Missouri. Five hours on a Jesse James Gang racer could put
you in Tim Buck Two.

All we really had to do was take the kid back.

So we brang him out of the cave, where we'd dumped him out of hearing of us, tight-wrapped in his own spelunker rope. We putten him on my horse, his feet tied under the belly, then the horse tied to the pony cart, whicht Jess made me drive because I didn't hardly weigh no more nor a well-fed dog. There wasn't no trouble on the road, and we hove in moonlight view of Crutchfield Farms, a good thirty minutes shy of twelve o'clock midnight.

"You know the plan," Dingus low-voiced. "Move on out."

Well, friends, there comes a time in the lives of all good men, even bankrobbers, when the twine begins to shorten down fearful quick on the spindle.

Things which take a lot of time explaining up to, have a poor habit of "coming off" almighty fast, once got to the nub of.

We slicked past the handful of deputies from the statehouse at Jeff City which was supposed to be guarding the place at the horse farm, and was mostly sound asleep on their pickets. Inside the house all was silent as a cemetery vault. We carried the kid through a sitting room, a pantry, and into a mighty handsome layout whicht Jess whispered had to be the Governor's library and sort of office, here at the farm. "Stick the little bastard into the big leather chair back of the Governor's desk yonder," he ordered. "Mebee he can sign a few amnesty bills for us whiles he's waiting to hear the rooster crow, ha! ha!" It were about as near a joke as Jesse James was likely to come out with, and the three on us give him a short laugh for it.

The laugh was short because it was cut off by a sudden rash of coal-oil pressure lamps flaring up from about the room and us caught flat-booted in the midst of all the glare and U.S. Marshal Sam Bastrupp standing there with a sawed-off twelve gauge cocked both hammers and little doubt crammed with No. 2 buckshot on top of about a teacup of FFg black powder. Plus, I shiver yet to add, some half a dozen hardeyed U.S. agents looking to be fifty-fifty railroad detectives and bank dicks, flanking old Sam and clicking their Colt hammers, uglylike.

"Sorry, boys," Sam says all cute and unfunny, "but all's fair in our little war, now ain't it? Cut the kid loose."

I was still tending Peabody and I had him sliced free in about two breaths and a bit of broke wind.

"Thanks, Peecher," he says, spitting out the gag. "What the hell did you rope me so tight for? I'm on your side!"

"You're all safe now, lad," the Marshal said, reaching to pat old Peabody on the head.

The kid ducked him, and give him a kick in the near-shin that would of got a buffalo's attention.

"Who the hell is *he*?" he appealed to us, some indignant.

Jesse was the one that answered him, and blinking like a lightblind bat with all fangs bared.

"Ask your Uncle Cole," he hissed. "He's the genius what thought up this whole thing."

"Never mind these fellows," Sam Bastrupp now said to Peabody. "I'm sending a man to rouse up your father and you'll be back with him any minute now. Me and my men don't require any rewards other than the happiness we've brung to your little face." He advanced again on the kid, holding out his hand for shaking purposes. "I'm Sam Ba—" he started to name hisself but never got there. Cole, beset by Jesse's distanement, and me and Frank's too, suffered a last histrionic seizure.

Stabbing an outraged finger at the Marshal, he yelled out at full-lung. "We know who you are! How dare you put a twelve-gauge scattergun on decent folks, *Sam Bass*!?! And in the Governor's very own sacred offices of this here State! Mercy sakes, it ain't hardly like you, *Sam Bass*, you foul outlaw and notrarius Texican train robber! Whatever are you doing in Missouri? And with a price on your head in five states and most of Mexico! Oh, please don't harm this innocent lamb—"

Cole put his arm about Peabody's thin-bone shoulder but the kid shucked it off with a yelp that could have been heered in Jeff City. Or leastways Hickman Mills.

"A PRICE?!" he hollered highpitch. "How much of a price?"

"Fifty thousand Dead or Alive," Cole vowed, big-eyed. "Five states, ten thousand each. Ain't you never hearn of Sam Bass, boy? He's the Texican Jesse James. Ain't you, Sam?"

Marshal Sam Bastrupp punched the twelve-gauge forward.

"This here has gone far enough," he roared out. "Back off, Peecher. Keep your hands in the air, Frank. Quit sidling left, Jess. By God, I'll cut the three of you in two. There ain't no choke left in these tubes, and the muzzles will chamber a two-bit piece, each. Want to make a quick fifty cents?"

We surely did not, and told him so, and he started one more time to move in on Peabody Crutchfield III, no hand out now.

"Boy," he growled, scowling black, "I'm Marsh—"

But again old Peabody shorted him.

"You ain't Marsh Nobody," he cried. "You're Sam, SAM BASS! You're wanted dead or alive, and since I ain't letting you take in my pals here, I guess it will have to be dead. Now stand still! I ain't that good of a shot. I wouldn't want to miss you and hit somebody decent."

With that plain spoke statement, Peabody flang wide the Fontleroy coat and, I swear to Jesus, there were the rusted old horse pistol jammed down his pants again. And, with a flourish to do proud Wild Bill Hitchcock, he shucked it forth and drew down with it, two-handed as usual, on Marshal Sam Bastrupp.

"Why, you little snotnose sonofabitch," the Marshal said, making a grab for the horse pistol, "gimme that gun!"

The Pony Cart Kid give it to him as directed.

Right square betwixt his spread legs and plowing a furrow in the hardwood floor you could have buried a cat in. Then whanging on out the front wall of the pantry and flattening Peabody's father, on his way through the parlor, and out the big plate glass winder, where it caromed off two of the Jeff City guards outside and hit a prize first-calf heifer on the next farm over.

"Drop the shotgun and heist 'em high, Sam!" the kid yells. "I got three left!"

The Marshal was impressed. He let go the twelve gauge and set up in place like Lot's wife. He might be there yet, he was that scairt. But we wasn't waiting for him to melt and run. We gathered in around Jesse for orders, but he passed the deck to Cole. He said it was him who had left the horse pistol on the kid, and that made it Cole what had saved our lives, or anyhow secured our sacred freedom.

"All a part of the plan, Jess," the big man blushed. "All a part of the plan."

"Yes," Jesse said, some guilty. "And the whole time the rest on us was thinking you had blowed-up the bridge again."

"Say Hallelujah," Frank witnessed. "Mercy, mercy."

Me, Old D.B. Peecher, I wasn't so blessed certain big Cole hadn't dynamited our retreat. "We better cut and ride, Jess," I said. "Them U.S. deputies is whispering too much 'mongst themselves yonder. They're gonna jump us, we don't get shut of Crutchfield Farms, instanter.

"Yeah," Jesse said, turning to Cole. "How's the getaway go, Bud?"

"Like goose-grease on a croupy chest, Ding," Cole grinned. "Foller me."

We done so, and it went simple as old Cole's mind. He just stopped alongside Peabody and give him a "good boy" pat on his head, and nodded, "Now, listen, pardner, don't you so much as take yore eyes off'n these here buzzards to so much as blink. Keep that horse pistol jammed into old Sam's brisket and if he twitches a nostril send him to Beulah Land."

"Remember," he wound up, "this here is the legendarious Bandit King, Sam Bass. Yore job is to keep the drop on him long enough for me and Peecher and Jess and Frank to fetch back to you, along with the Jackson County Sheriff, that five-state reeward money whicht is so rightful yourn all alone, and whicht we wouldn't tech a dime of. The Sheriff will arrest all Sam's Gang, as well. And also help you to tote all that money to the bank in Blue City, tomorrow."

The kid had his chin stuck out, and a tear in his eye.

He swore he would stand there to the death.

There was only one favor he would ask of his old owlhoot comrades and that was to let him give them enough of his gold to pay them for the gold that had been lost when Cole fell backward into the horse manure in front of the Blue City Bank.

Cole said, shucks, he didn't want to take it but we fast talked him into it. Jesse led the way in the sprint for the door, followed close as moondark shadders by me and Cole and Frank. Last we heard of the Pony Cart Kid, he was encouraging U.S. Marshal Sam Bastrupp to put any thoughts of stampeding over him to take out after us, plumb and permanent from his thickbone head.

"By God, stand still there, damn you, Sam Bass!" was the exact text. "You make one more move to get past me and I will drill you a brand-new hole for your belt buckle! How does size .44 Walker Colt fit you?"

Then, as we reached and went swift aboard our Missouri thoroughbreds, just wistful distant enough to hear it over the snorts and hoofpounds of the getaway, a final faint call come from Peabody Crutchfield III.

"Goodbye, pards, goodbye. You can trust me. I'll never flinch."

And we knowed from that that he knowed we wasn't never coming his way again.

CAPTIVE TO THE
CLANGING GATES

C hildren's games in Jackson County where I grew up during the Great Depression, had a way of being your basic shinnystick and tin can situations. As such, they got rough. Rules were needed to minimize permanent disabling, and those rules were enforced. What was required, first off, was a universal signal for calling the halt in the melee, so that the infraction might be adjudicated, and fair play restored. This "hold everything" signal was to cross index and second finger on both hands, thrust the hands urgently upward and outward, with an appropriately desperate screech of "King's X!"

This was much more than a time-out request.

King's X was an imperative.

It didn't mean that some kid was weary, winded, shin-barked or merely wanting to talk things over.

King's X meant that something was wrong; that a player was "calling the question" on the total and entire procedure.

Thus, when it was brought to my attention that in recent times Will Henry had been the subject of some heavyweight academic appraisal and criticism, and mention was made of the essay in *Twentieth Century Western Writers*, an article in *Encyclopedia of Frontier & Western Fiction*, and the full-length critical study soon to be released in the Twayne U.S. Authors Series, as well as the already-published *Will Henry/Clay Fisher* monograph from Boise State University Press, Will Henry feels compelled to leap forward, fling out the crossed fingers, and yell, "King's X!"

Modesty, alone, insists upon it.

But blushing is good for only so many humble delays.

In the end, we must face the flattery and confess that we love it. That some of our best friends are university professors, and we would do anything to continue being paid attention to by these excellent fellows of Academe. But we still dissemble. Most writers, not just Will Henry, would kill to be treated kindly on campus. There is this unreasonable benign poltergeist within all our bosoms who will not be a good spook and go away and leave us alone, but hexes us onward in our delusions that the Western can win the hearts of these lofty dons.

Well, we all know the so-far answer to that; it hasn't happened yet. When and if it ever will, remains for those who still have the time to dream.

But an honest question has been asked:

Do I welcome this academic appraisal and criticism; if not, what do I truly feel about it; how has it affected me?

Well, I would rather have it than not have it. On balance, I am left pleased. And admittedly some curious. Maybe even some bristly in the backhairs about it. Here Will Henry is, writing about the American West for 33 winters. Here they are, in the summer of the 33rd of those winters, offering, perhaps even proffering, documental evidence that the teaching academic and adjunct campus critical fraternities, alike, are stirring in Will Henry's behalf.

What kept them so long?

Will Henry has been ready since 1950 and *No Survivors.*

II

Not long ago a graduate student toiling on a Will Henry thesis wrote me to ask something I had wanted to be asked for a tooth-grinding age: Whether or not in my exchanges with academic scholars and their allied critics, I had been forced as a novelist to defend my work as "accurate" and "authentic."

Ah! the striking of the literary nerve!

Has Will Henry suffered this indignity?

Surely, you jest.

Will Henry invented the "fight-back" defense of the Western novel. And against whom, if not the academic scholars and their allied critics, would a writing man have been brought to such rude halter as has been Will Henry for his hard riding in this just cause? Of course it is the scholars and campus-oriented allies against whom we Western writers must rally. There is no comparably important enemy of our ambitions. Our dear and faithful readers off campus love us. They always have. Plainly, then, it is not they who hold the reins of Western power to win acceptance as a serious literature. Will Henry novels can sell 9,000,000 copies, and Clay Fisher novels 6,000,000 copies, and their author still not be taken seriously by the "scholars," which means automatically not so taken by their "allied critics." We are returned, perforce, to Academe as the foe to be won over, if ever the Western is to be granted its rightful place within the pantheon of American Letters.

We all know, who labor in this outcast art, that the Western, and Western writing, have been getting far more "play" on campus today than in any prior era. Let no one of us misunderstand this for acceptance. The one is as far from the other as is Neptune from the Sun. Two things must happen between "finally paying attention to" and "at least accepting" the Western, and Western writing.

(1) The Western writer must bend his every talent to plowing that straight furrow of excellence in his work. This, to the end that the scholars are given the material to challenge successfully their historic uppity sniffing at the "pennyweight pretentions" of the serious Western American literature crowd — our crowd. This redirection of effort and talent, I submit, has already taken place. There is more and better downrightly superior writing being offered in the Western and frontier area at this time, than in previous living memory. We, the Western writers, have pre-paid our dues with this remarkable creative upsurge.

(2) The academic scholars and their orbital adjunct critics must now either get their lines wet, or stick to watching the worms wiggle in the baitcan.

They can no longer have it both ways.

III

I don't know where my ongoing off-camera romance, my bluff Hail Caesar/Goodbye Brutus relationship with Academe and the academics is springing these popular leaks, but people keep wanting to know what is the single biggest problem Will Henry has with the scholar-critic's examination of his work.

Zut! Here is another of those bite-your-cheeks-while-chewing situations; it engages one's attention at the primordial level — acute pain.

Of which the author has endured his fair share from the campus *cum laddies.* Aye, and the *cum lassies,* as well.

The trouble starts with the basic fantasy that acquiring a degree in a discipline means that the acquirer knows anything about that discipline, much less everything about it. That is a rough-clipped summary, but think about it. If all that were necessary to know all about something was to take a degree in it, we could issue a doctorate in cancer and, lo, there would be no more cancer in the world. The same could be said for a Ph.D. in Bovine Excretia and the end of B.S. throughout the planet. These are rude allusions but fair. They demonstrate the folly of elevating mere opinion to the status of tenured Oracle.

In point of working reality, of course, it requires considerably more than his course-listing in the catalogue to make a useful guru for Western writing out of a simple D.Litt.

Just as Western novels of literary quality demand a born gift of talent for the art, so must be the very special judgment skills of he who would be king of the scholar-critic-examiners of Western fiction as American Literature.

The acquirable knowledge of subject gained in available study terms by the examiners should equal, or exceed, that of those whom they would examine. That is a respectful given. But to acquire the textbook background is but the lesser half of the essential problem. Our judges must be as caught up in the mystique of the Western — as consumed by its wondrous fires of the imagination — as are those of us who write them. If they do not believe it is possible for Western writing to be acceptable as American literature, where is their right to teach courses in the subject? No matter. Today's English Lit scholars seem to be *in utero* sagebrush critics. They emerge only to skin out us weak winter calves. Coming honestly to that, though, what better or more handy victim than the nearest Western novelist? Most especially that Western novelist striving to be seen also as a serious writer beyond the continued traditional prejudices against his chosen genre.

Given these modest assumptions, it is not difficult to envision the temptation of the campus critic to strike at the underbelly of the cornered Western novel. Which is to say the textbook quality of whatever hard history may be involved in the hapless author's self-evident, plainly advertised work of fiction. For there's the vulnerable rub, you see. Noble, inviolable fact versus that old devil fiction.

Obviously, it is not easy to define fiction. You cannot do it with arithmetic. Or by computer scans. Or with micro-chip word processors. Fiction is an art, not a statistic.

Ergo, our campusite who well understands that one good kick in the groin is worth a hundred pats on the popo in getting academic prose published, understands something else, too.

You can divide and conquer the facts. You can multiply or subtract the truth. And you can add up history as you never could fiction:

"Wyatt Earp was an honorable and brave officer of the frontier law."

"Who cares?"

"Wyatt Earp was a transvestite homosexual who wore a silk teddy under his horsehide vest and sprinkled sachet in his fishnet longjohns."

"Where, where? Which way did he go!?"

We writers recognize the predicament of the scholar critic captive to the clanging gates of Academe. Forever prisoner to the world of his fellow Prester Johns, he must publish harder and quicker and meaner than they, or die. It becomes simply a case of draw first blood or go under. Criticism being the fastest draw in the writing world, he turns to the terrorizing of Western writers as the easiest money around.

And it is great good fun, too.

Really.

Why, Lordy, Lordy, I would never seriously blame him for what he does to augment his fiscal tenure. I would love to put the same poignard to those dastardly felons (my fellow Western writers) who so (other than for myself, of course) ignobly deserve it.

But our campus scholar critic is, in fact, performing a vital service by keeping the reading world safe for all of us intruders into its hallowed dust. He is the clean-up man in our disordered batting order. If he weren't there to bring us in from third, we would never get across home plate. He is the man with the mule team who comes into the sanded arena to drag away the dead bulls of our continued literary embarrassments. He is the great white buzzard who pounces upon our creative carrion and bears it flappingly away before it can infect the *corpus vita* of our beloved Western story.

He doesn't need us; we need him.

Yet, oh, Dear Lord, would that he might one day understand this sole and simple truth: that, with all his classic gifts of scholarship and style, no professional critic, no matter how historically grounded, has the foggiest notion of what it is a fiction writer does.

Until that seriously critical oversight is repaired, it appears as if the East will likely remain pretty much buttheadedly Eastern, while the West will for almighty certain stay unreconstructed rawhide Western, and never the twain shall meet to sleep in the lineshack together.

Unless, of course, somebody smiles.

And moves over in the sleeping bag.

Old Warriors

A smallish sere and slate-gray bird,
Pausing on its plainly wearied way,
From wherever to what might come to pass,
Has fluttered near my lodge's door to say
It comes from Old Horse, and afar,
Bearing word that he, friend of my boyhood
And my heart, is lowly now and much afraid,
Thinking that this winter of the blowing snows
Will be his last, and he alone to face it.

The bird was rested then and would fly on
Except that I said rest a little more
Before you go, I've word for you to bear
Again to Old Horse that he may know he yet
Has us for friends, and will not go unguarded
Into this, or any other winter's cold.

The tiny creature cocked a beady, cheerful eye
At me, and fluffed itself as though in fairish
Careful study of the cause, then chirped a
Doubtful note, or three, but bobbed its head
Regardless, so to indicate, well, yes, and
Truly, it might be, but first the message
Must be heard; name it now, and quickly.

So bidden, I began; nor did I halt until the
Word was done, I, to Old Horse, old warrior
To old warrior, the small bird waiting still
As the snowflake's fall, huddled in my very
Hand for warmth against the keening wind arise
Without my lodge, and so I spoke to it,
And Old Horse, as was fit for brothers.

Attend me, T-su-kup, I ordered my old friend
As if he were at very hand, and hearing me;
This wee messenger at resting nestle here
Brings news from where you wait,
Telling of your bad-thought dreams,
Muscle's wither, mind's despair, and you,
All frail and spider-skinned and crouching
There, thinking you know the very sun
And moon wherein Kadih will call you home
And so bring ending to it all.

Pawsa! I say to that, and you,
It is a crazy thing; we no more know our
Time of tiring than does the mountain,
Or the river, or the rock,
The gods have sent no spirit bear to trail
You down; there is no panther's shade at
Demon's cry along your track,
You are not doomed, not numbered for the
Slaughter like some white man's issue beef,
You are only growing old.

Much of life is pu-kut-si, *thus not explained,*
We only know we come at last to pu-hi-ti-pinah,
The place not given, but safe to all
Who seek it unafraid, or guide another there who

Cannot find the way himself; no, T-su-kup, *my*
Brother, he has not called your name,
Kadih has others on his list ahead of you.

But do not wait for him! old warrior!
Be instead like the silver-muzzled wolf,
Lame with the trapwounds of many snows
Yet limping onward still, nose to wind and
Swinging, not lying down supine before the
Winter Giant, not tucking tail to turn,
A'whimper, thrice around,
And huddle into drift for silent mounding
Where they'll find your bones next spring.

Rather, old Nermernuh, *old comrade of*
Comanche peoples, be as the eighty-wintered
Warchief brought by the years and rigors
Of the chase to pace the confines of the
Tipi or, anon, to seek the human comfort of
The robe and smoking dung-chip fire,
There to wander back in time and mind
To better trails and grander council-fires,
Safe hidden in the sacred deeps of Cañon
Palo Duro, or open-camped beside
Broad shifting shallows of the Pecos,
Where the Crossing of the Horse's Head
Stands guardian to Quanah Parker's land,
The last Comanche pasture on this our Mother Earth.

Over there, there are no winter snows, puha!
And no wolves waiting for the laggard or
The halt, but only slant-gold sunshine ever
Warm upon the back, taking away December,
To bring again the soft-scent perfume of the

New grass, returning us to April and to May,
Saying thus that one more season
Of our time has gone, another born to also
Pass away, the very first, or last, of Kadih
Only knows how many more remain to us
At follow of the curly cows and noble-bearded bulls
Across the Grasslands of Forever.

And if, old comrade, on this final hunt
We find ourselves not first to loosen arrowed
Shaft, or hurl the bladed lance, then surely
We shall be in fair time yet to help the
Squaws, at woman's work, to peel and peg the
Taken hides upon the prairie's floor,
And heap thereon the steaming tongue and
Tenderloins, the fatted standing ribs of
Storied hump, the very prizes of what the
Gods have given us that we may prosper at
Whatever age, riding out again, and yet again
Until Kadih himself shall send to say to us
The chase is done, a'he!
And he will meet us at the river's side,
Where the grass is tall and the water sweet
And the current swifting clear,
And we shall cross together there,
Brothers of the same proud blood, warriors
All, and unafraid.

Ho, brother! Wait for me!

I have passed a poor year, also,
And fear the winter that now will come, yet
Fear it less for riding it with you who
Shared with me those summers when, fearing

No man and no future, we rode our ponies
At the charge, made immortal by our youth
And so would ride for all time safe from bark
Or blood of rifle, or angered, anguished scream
Of arrow, buried to the feathers in some friend
Of ours, or child, or woman, wagh!

Come on, old brother; ride with me.

I go not anywhere that trouble's lodge is pitched,
Do you? Of course not; let us only take this
Rounding trail through the willows here,
Where none may see us pass, and we shall go
Silently as hunted mice, or does and fawns at
Sneak, downwind of quartering pack, and so
Who might imagine two great warriors of the
People crept mutely by such rude and rutted
Path? No one, you shall see; we will get out
Of this as everything before it, alive and
Muttering mightily as to our cursed luck.

There, we're past it now, Old Horse, dear friend,
Nor will we need to come this way again,
The darkness and the cold are all behind, a'he!
There is no winter here, no howl of wind or wolf,
Only fat grass and flowing water for our ponies,
And for us, as for this little bird
Who brought us here,
Peace, brothers.
We will hunt again tomorrow.
Or tomorrow.

HENRY WILSON ALLEN

A Chronological Bibliography

No Survivors. New York: Random House, 1950; New York: Bantam Books, 1951. (WH)

Red Blizzard. New York: Simon & Schuster, 1951; New York: Pocket Books, 1953. (CF)

Wolf-Eye: The Bad One. New York: Julian Messner, 1951. (WH)

Santa Fe Passage. Boston: Houghton Mifflin, 1952; New York: Bantam Books, 1953. (CF)

To Follow a Flag. New York: Random House, 1953; New York: Bantam Books, 1956 [retitled *Pillars of the Sky*]. (WH)

Yellow Hair. Boston: Houghton Mifflin, 1953; New York: Bantam Books, 1970. (CF)

Warbonnet. Boston: Houghton Mifflin, 1953; New York: Bantam Books, 1970. (CF)

The Fourth Horseman. New York: Random House, 1954; New York: Bantam Books, 1956. (WH)

Death of a Legend. New York: Random House, 1954; New York: Bantam Books, 1956 [retitled *The Raiders*]. (WH)

The Tall Men. Boston: Houghton Mifflin, 1954; New York: Pocket Books, 1960. (CF)

Who Rides With Wyatt. New York: Random House, 1955; New York: Bantam Books, 1956. (WH)

The Big Pasture. Boston: Houghton Mifflin, 1955; New York: Bantam Books, 1972. (CF)

The North Star. New York: Random House, 1956; New York: Bantam Books, 1958. (WH)

The Blue Mustang. Boston: Houghton Mifflin, 1956; New York: Pocket Books, 1957. (CF)

The Brass Command. Boston: Houghton Mifflin, 1956; New York: Bantam Books, 1971. (CF)

Yellowstone Kelly. Boston: Houghton Mifflin, 1957; New York: Bantam Books, 1972. (CF)

The Texas Rangers. New York: Random House, 1957. (WH)

Reckoning at Yankee Flat. New York: Random House, 1958; New York: Bantam Books, 1959. (WH)

The Seven Men at Mimbres Springs. New York: Random House, 1958; New York: Bantam Books, 1960. (WH)

The Crossing. Boston: Houghton Mifflin, 1958; New York: Bantam Books, 1974. (CF)

Orphans of the North. New York: Random House, 1958. (WH)

From Where the Sun Now Stands. New York: Random House, 1960; New York: Bantam Books, 1961. (WH)

Journey to Shiloh. New York: Random House, 1960; New York: Bantam Books, 1963. (WH)

Nino. New York: William Morrow, 1961; New York: Bantam Books, 1973 [retitled *The Apache Kid*]. (CF)

Return of the Tall Man. New York: Pocket Books, 1961; New York: Bantam Books, 1965. (CF)

San Juan Hill. New York: Random House, 1962; New York: Bantam Books, 1962. (WH)

The Feleen Brand. New York: Bantam Books, 1962. (WH)

The Oldest Maiden Lady in New Mexico and Other Stories. New York: Macmillan, 1962. (CF)
CONTENTS: "The Oldest Maiden Lady in New Mexico," "King Fisher's Road," "The Redeeming of Fate Rachel," "Pretty Face," "The Chugwater Run," "Sundown Smith," "The Hunting of Tom Horn," "A Mighty Big Bandit," "Isley's Stranger," "The Deputization of Walter Mendenhall," "Ghost Town," "The Trap."

The Pitchfork Patrol. New York: Macmillan, 1962; New York: Bantam Books, 1975. (CF)

Mackenna's Gold. New York: Random House, 1963; New York: Bantam Books, 1966. (WH)

The Gates of the Mountains. New York: Random House, 1963; New York: Bantam Books, 1967. (WH)

Valley of the Bear. Boston: Houghton Mifflin, 1964. (CF)

In the Land of the Mandans. Philadelphia: Chilton Books, 1965. (WH)

The Last Warpath. New York: Random House, 1966; New York: Bantam Books, 1967. (WH)
CONTENTS: "The Pale Eyes," "Little Dried River," "Half-Blood Brother," "Red Runs the Washita," "Peace of the Pony Soldiers," "Way of the War Chief," "Maheo's Children," "The Last Warpath."

Sons of the Western Frontier. Philadelphia: Chilton Books, 1966; New York: Bantam Books, 1967 (in two volumes: *Red Brother and White; Outlaws and Legends*). (WH)
CONTENTS: "The Friendship of Red Fox," "Lapwai Winter," "Vengeance of Jesse James," "Second Chance to Santa Fe," "River of Decision," "Ghost Wolf of Thunder Mountain," "Rough Riders of Arizona," "A Bullet for Billy the Kid," "Legend of Trooper Hennepin," "The Tallest Indian in Toltepec."

Custer's Last Stand. Philadelphia: Chilton Books, 1966; New York: Grosset & Dunlap, 1968; New York: Bantam Books, 1982. (WH)

Alias Butch Cassidy. New York: Random House, 1967; New York: Bantam Books, 1969. (WH)

One More River to Cross. New York: Random House, 1967; New York: Bantam Books, 1969. (WH)

Maheo's Children. Philadelphia: Chilton Books, 1968; New York: Bantam Books, 1971 [retitled *The Squaw Killers*]. (WH)

Genesis Five. New York: William Morrow, 1968; New York: Pyramid Books, 1970. (HWA)

14 Spurs: Western Writers of America (edited by Will Henry). New York: Bantam Books, 1968. (WH)

The Day Fort Larking Fell. Philadelphia: Chilton Books, 1969. (WH)

Tayopa! New York: Pocket Books, 1970. (HWA)

See How They Run. New York: Pocket Books, 1970. (HWA)

Chiricahua. Philadelphia: J.B. Lippincott, 1972; New York: Bantam Books, 1973. (WH)

Outcasts of Canyon Creek. New York: Bantam Books, 1972. (CF)

The Bear Paw Horses. Philadelphia: J.B. Lippincott, 1973; New York: Bantam Books, 1973. (WH)

Apache Ransom. New York: Bantam Books, 1974. (CF)

I, Tom Horn. Philadelphia: J.B. Lippincott, 1978; New York: Bantam Books, 1975. (WH)

Black Apache. New York: Bantam Books, 1976. (CF)

Nine Lives West. New York: Bantam Books, 1978. (CF)
   CONTENTS: "A Mighty Big Bandit," "The Streets of Laredo," "The Skinning of Black Coyote," "For Want of a Horse," "The Redeeming of Fate Rachel," "King Fisher's Road," "The Trap," "The Hunting of Tom Horn," "Sundown Smith."

Summer of the Gun. Philadelphia: J.B. Lippincott, 1978; New York: Bantam Books, 1979. (WH)

Seven Legends West. New York: Bantam Books, 1983. (CF)
   CONTENTS: "The Deputization of Walter Mendenhall," "Pretty Face," "The Oldest Maiden Lady in New Mexico," "The Chugwater Run," "The White Man's Road," "The Rescue of Chuana," "Isley's Stranger."

Key: HWA = Henry Wilson Allen; WH = Will Henry; CF = Clay Fisher

AN ALLEN FILMOGRAPHY

The Tall Men (1954). Filmed as "The Tall Man" (1955); directed by Raoul Walsh; cast: Clark Gable, Jane Russell, Robert Ryan, Cameron Mitchell. 20th Century-Fox.

Santa Fe Passage (1955). Filmed as "Santa Fe Passage" (1955), directed by William Witney; cast: John Payne, Faith Domergue, Rod Cameron, Slim Pickens. Republic.

To Follow a Flag (1956). Filmed as "Pillars of the Sky" (1956); directed by George Marshall; cast: Jeff Chandler, Dorothy Malone, Ward Bond, Lee Marvin. Universal.

Yellowstone Kelly (1957). Filmed as "Yellowstone Kelly" (1959); directed by Gordon Douglas; cast: Clint Walker, Ray Danton, Warren Oates, Claude Akins. Warner Brothers.

Mackenna's Gold (1963). Filmed as "Mackenna's Gold (1968); directed by J. Lee Thompson; cast: Gregory Peck, Omar Sharif, Edward G. Robinson, Anthony Quayle, Camilla Sparv, Julie Newmar, Burgess Meredith, Eli Wallach, Telly Savalas. Columbia.

Journey to Shiloh (1960). Filmed as "Journey to Shiloh" (1968); directed by William Hale; Cast: James Caan, Don Stroud, Brenda Scott, Michael Sarrazin. Universal.

Who Rides With Wyatt (1955). Filmed as "Young Billy Young" (1970); directed by Burt Kennedy; cast: Robert Mitchum, Angie Dickinson, Robert Walker, David Carridine. Batjac Productions.

I, Tom Horn (1975). Filmed as "Tom Horn" (1980); directed by William Wiard; cast: Steve McQueen, Linda Evans. Warner Brothers.

NOTE: Seven other Allen novels were sold to motion pictures but never produced. They are: *Red Blizzard* (1951), *Blue Mustang* (1956), *San Juan Hill* (1962), *Pitchfork Patrol* (1962), *The Day the Sun Died* (1962; unpublished as novel); *The North Star* (1958), and *Genesis Five* (1968).

WORKS ABOUT HENRY WILSON ALLEN

Falke, Anne, "Clay Fisher or Will Henry? An Author's Choice of Pen Names," in *The Popular Western: Essays Toward a Definition*, edited by Richard W. Etulain and Michael T. Marsden. Bowling Green, Ohio: Bowling Green University Popular Press, 1974.

Gale, Robert L. *Will Henry/Clay Fisher*, Boise, Idaho: Boise State University Press [Western Writers Series], 1982.

Gale, Robert L. *Henry Wilson Allen (Will Henry/Clay Fisher)*. Boston: Twayne Publishers [U.S. Authors Series], 1984.

Walker, Dale L., "Wandering the Far Mesas: A Conversation with Henry Wilson Allen," *The Bloomsbury Review*, Vol. 3, No. 6 (November 1983), 14-15.

SEE ALSO ENTRIES ON ALLEN IN:

Etulain, Richard W. *A Bibliographical Guide to the Study of Western American Literature*. Lincoln, Nebraska: University of Nebraska Press, 1982.

Locher, Frances C., Ed., *Contemporary Authors*. Detroit, Michigan: Gale Research Co., 1980 (Vols. 89-92).

Tuska, Jon and Vicki Piekarski, Eds., *Encyclopedia of Frontier and Western Fiction*. New York: McGraw-Hill, 1983.

Vinson, James, Ed., *Twentieth-Century Western Writers*. Detroit, Michigan: Gale Research Co., 1983.

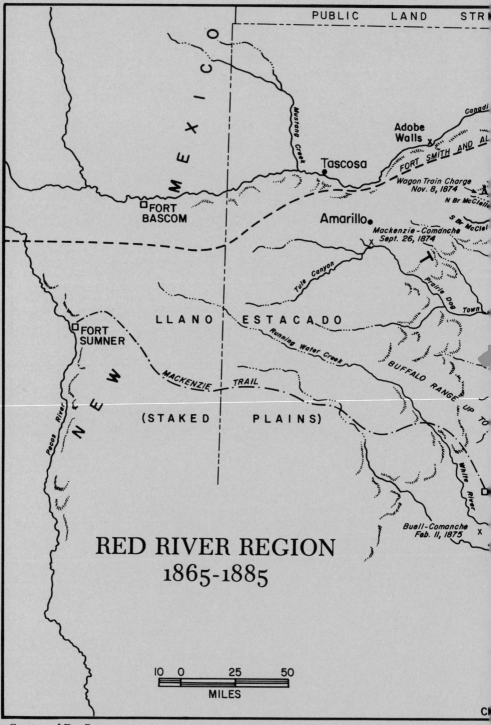

PUBLIC LAND STR

M
E
X
I
C
O

Mustang Creek

Canadi

Adobe
Walls ✗

FORT SMITH AND AL

Tascosa ●

Wagon Train Charge
Nov. 8, 1874 ✗

N Br McClella

☐ FORT
BASCOM

Amarillo ●

Mackenzie-Comanche
Sept. 26, 1874 ✗

S Br McClel

Tule Canyon

Prairie Dog Town

LLANO   ESTACADO

☐ FORT
SUMNER

N
E
W

Running Water Creek

BUFFALO RANGE UP TO

MACKENZIE   TRAIL

Pecos River

(STAKED   PLAINS)

White River

Buell-Comanche
Feb. 11, 1875 ✗

RED RIVER REGION
1865-1885

10 0   25   50
MILES

CI

Courtesy of Dee Brown